THE LIFE OF
MOSES COIT TYLER

MOSES COIT TYLER IN 1875
From a dated photograph in the University of Michigan collection.

THE LIFE OF
MOSES COIT TYLER

BY

HOWARD MUMFORD JONES

BASED UPON AN UNPUBLISHED DISSERTATION
FROM ORIGINAL SOURCES

BY

THOMAS EDGAR CASADY

THE UNIVERSITY OF MICHIGAN PRESS
ANN ARBOR, MICHIGAN
1933

TO

THE MEMORY OF

THOMAS EDGAR CASADY

PREFACE

In 1929 the late Thomas Edgar Casady submitted as his dissertation in the Department of English of the University of Michigan a critical biography of Moses Coit Tyler, based upon an examination of the Tyler MSS. deposited in the library of Cornell University and associated sources. This dissertation throws a flood of light upon Tyler's personality and upon the place which his historical labors deserve to hold in the history of the American intellect. Unfortunately Mr. Casady died before he could revise his work or add to it certain necessary chapters in Tyler's life which he would doubtless have been the first to demand. When, in 1930, it was first suggested that in view of Tyler's association with the University of Michigan it would be an appropriate thing to publish Mr. Casady's work, the task of examining his material fell upon me in my capacity of professor of English in charge of the work in American literature at the University. My first thought was that it would be sufficient to undertake a general stylistic revision of Mr. Casady's very valuable study, but it appeared upon closer examination that more was needed; and, with the kind permission of Mrs. Casady, who generously gave me *carte blanche* with the material, and who furnished me with notes that Mr. Casady had not incorporated in his pages, I have totally rewritten this manuscript life, accepting his conclusions wherever I could, but modifying them where I hoped I might improve them. Generally speaking, Mr. Casady had attempted to do little to recover the story of Tyler's early years, and here I hope I have been helpful. His excellent critical accounts of Tyler's three most important books, the two great literary histories and the life of Patrick Henry, I have retained, simply condensing them and rearranging certain portions of this material. Had Mr. Casady been alive, I venture to hope that we would have collaborated on the work in much the spirit in which I have undertaken to rewrite his admirable study.

The preface to Mr. Casady's dissertation runs as follows:

"I am indebted to Doctor Randolph G. Adams, custodian of the William L. Clements Library, for suggesting the present study to me. Through his instrumentality I was introduced to Mr. Willard Austen and Mrs. Jessica Tyler Austen who generously placed at my disposal the invaluable Tyler MSS. in the library of Cornell University. Mr. and Mrs. Austen supplied me with personal comment and reminiscence about Moses Coit Tyler. I am indebted to Professor George Lincoln Burr of Cornell University for several delightful conversations on the subject of his former colleague. I wish also to express thanks to Miss Elizabeth Steere of the William L. Clements Library, to Mr. F. L. D. Goodrich, and especially to Mrs. A. S. Ratliff of the University of Michigan Library for many services in procuring books and magazines for me from libraries outside of Ann Arbor; and to Mr. Walter M. Smith, Librarian of the University Library at Wisconsin, to Mr. H. H. B. Meyer and Miss Lottie Manross of the Library of Congress, who assisted me in bibliographical problems.

"I consider this the place also to acknowledge the scholarly monition given me through several years by James H. Hanford, Professor of English at Western Reserve University, who was not directly connected with [the writing of the dissertation] but whose influence is not absent from this thesis. Professor O. J. Campbell of the English Department of the University of Michigan criticized my manuscript and assisted me greatly in rounding it into final shape."

To these acknowledgments I am glad to add, on my own part, a word of thanks to the officials of the libraries of the University of Michigan, Yale University, Cornell University, the Hartford (Conn.) Public Library, and the Romeo (Mich.) Public Library, who have patiently answered my many questions, as also to the librarians of the Burton Historical Library in Detroit. I have also to acknowledge the help of the public officials of Calhoun County, Mich., of Detroit, and of Washtenaw County, who have assisted me to recover public records associated with the Tyler family. I should be remiss not to acknowledge gratefully the particular assistance of Miss Anne S. Pratt, the reference librarian of the Yale University Library, who has been of the greatest aid in the details of Tyler's career at Yale; of Miss Dorothy W. Bridgewater, who kindly compiled for me the record of Tyler's library borrowings at Yale, and of Mr. Alfred K. Merritt, registrar of Yale College. Mr. George H. Nelson spent a great many hours going through the books in the Moses Coit Tyler Collection at the Northern State Teachers College, Marquette, Mich., to furnish the accurate and intelligent transcriptions of Tyler's annotations upon which portions of this study are based; and Professor L. G. Vander Velde and Professor Oscar James Campbell of the University of Michigan read the manuscript of the book, giving me the benefit of their criticisms and suggestions. Finally, I must add a word of acknowledgment for the enthusiastic interest of Mr. Wilfred B. Shaw and Doctor Frank E. Robbins, both of the University of Michigan, who have given generously of their time in helping me. Professor Gregory L. Paine, of the University of

North Carolina, kindly read the entire text in proof. In general I have taken for granted the correctness of Mr. Casady's transcriptions from the Tyler MSS. No one can work with his dissertation for a year, as I have done, and not have every admiration for his assiduity and care in the collection of materials. Where I have kept his original footnotes, or merely modified the form of them, I have made no mark of change; but those portions of the footnotes which have been importantly changed or which represent additions of my own are marked by a "*J*" at the end of the passage in question.

This biography was made possible by Mr. Casady's labors, but it seems fair, since he cannot now speak for himself, for me to assume the responsibility for the interpretation of Tyler and his work here given. I should be sorry, however, if this acknowledgment of responsibility should in any way conceal the fact that Mr. Casady's manuscript furnishes the core of the book. My task was largely one of re-arrangement and rewriting.

HOWARD MUMFORD JONES.

UNIVERSITY OF MICHIGAN,
June 20, 1932.

THE LIFE OF MOSES COIT TYLER

CHAPTER I

SOME twenty years after the arrival of the *Mayflower*, three brothers named Tyler landed at Plymouth after a long voyage from their native Shropshire, seated themselves on a log, partook of their refreshments, arose, embraced and kissed each other, and then went each his way, "and it saith not that they ever again met." One settled in Virginia, one in New Haven, and one in Andover near Boston.[1]* Unconscious of destiny, the Virginia brother, by name Henry, was the ancestor of John Tyler, tenth President of the United States. Brother Job, a restless soul, was the ancestor of Moses Coit Tyler, the historian. One finds Job at Roxbury in 1665, at Mendon in 1669, then at Rowley, the later Boxford, and finally at Andover again.[2] Of half a dozen children born to Job and his wife Mary, Hopestill, or, in an early spelling, Hopstill, Tyler concerns us most. For Hopestill, who was born in 1645 and died in 1734, lived at Andover during the witchcraft delusion. In September, 1692, John Hathorne, the ancestor of Nathaniel Hawthorne, was holding court in Andover. Before him appeared Mary Osgood to answer an accusation of witchcraft, who testified that "she her-

* See end of volume for notes.

self, in company with Goody Parker, Goody Tyler, and Goody Dean, had a meeting at Moses Tyler's house, last Monday to afflict."[3] Moses, whose habitation was thus singularly used, was Hopestill's brother; Goody Tyler was Hopestill's wife, an appellation that points to the social status of the Tylers, for Hopestill was a blacksmith.[4] Frightened perhaps, or by advice of friends, Mrs. Tyler (she had been Mary Lovett, daughter of Daniel and Joanna Lovett of Braintree)[5] pleaded guilty,[6] but when the grand jury came to consider the case on January 3, 1692/93, "Mary Tyler, wife of Hopestill Tyler of Andover," Mary Osgood, Hannah Tyler, and fifteen others were declared not guilty. Samuel Sewall, of diary fame, was one of the five presiding magistrates.[7]

Perhaps attracted by the handsome offer from Preston, Connecticut, of fifty acres of free land to a blacksmith who would "ingage to supply the town with smith work five yere,"[8] Hopestill sold his Andover lands in 1697 and removed to that township. In Preston the Tylers were to remain fixtures until 1815, when the town of Griswold was formed from Preston; and in Griswold Elisha Tyler's family was to remain for twenty-two years thereafter. Successive generations played their firm, but modest, parts in national affairs. Thus Moses Tyler (1707–87), grandson of Hopestill, was a member of the committee of correspondence formed in the Revolution,[9]

and was in 1775 the largest taxpayer in Preston.[10]
His grandson, also named Moses (1761–1829), married Olive Coit (1772–1840), member of a family long associated with Preston and Griswold and equally active in public affairs: to his "kinsmen and benefactors," Samuel Coit of Hartford and George Coit of Norwich, Moses Coit Tyler was to dedicate the first of his two great histories. Colonel Moses Tyler served during the Revolution as a private in the local militia, rising afterward in rank; "long after his death his townspeople used to speak of his lofty courtesy, his military bearing, and especially of the nobility of his look as he rode on horseback"; and when in 1793 he settled in the "mansion house" on the Tyler farm, it was with the dignity of a man of affairs.

A son of this union, known as Captain Elisha Tyler (1794–1857)—the "captain" was mostly honorary—was a private in the militia called into service by the War of 1812:[11] New England Federalism saw to it that the Connecticut soldiery participated no farther in war's alarms than blamelessly to guard the coast. In 1830, his pale military honors slowly fading, Elisha Tyler married Mary Greene (1807–94), described at the time of her death, with more truth than appears in most obituaries, as "patient and uncomplaining" and of a "sunny and joyous disposition."[12] Mrs. Tyler was thirteen years younger

than her husband, whom she outlived by thirty-seven
years. She was the daughter of Doctor Rowland
Greene of Plainfield, Connecticut, described as a
"Quaker mystic," one who lived "by the inner light";
he kept a boarding school, which Mary attended
from her seventeenth year till she left it for matrimony and Griswold. To Elisha and Mary Tyler nine
children were born, of whom Moses Coit was the
fourth child and oldest son.[13]

Whatever visions Mary had of the future, it is to
be hoped that the charms of metropolitan life were
not among them, for her existence was to be spent
for some years in a succession of small communities.
The Tyler farm with its "mansion house" welcomed
her first. It was situated south of the White school-
house near Hopeville; and she must soon have discovered that she was married to a high-minded
dreamer, a man fond of books, of music, of geology,
but a man motivated by the psychology of a Colonel
Sellers. Elisha built himself an immense barn, forty
by eighty feet, three stories high, the biggest in Griswold, intending to raise silkworms on mulberry
leaves,[14] but, the silkworms not proving amenable,
he cast his eyes about for more profitable enterprise.
The town or township included in 1830 a population
of 2212. Jewett's City, "a flourishing village on the
east side of the Quinnebaug," accounted for about a
thousand of these; it was three miles from Hope-

ville, a lesser, but ambitious, community. Jewett's
City possessed one of the two Congregational
churches in the township, three "extensive cotton
factories," five stores, the Jewett City Bank (capital,
$100,000), and other splendors.[15] Connecticut was
beginning to enjoy the fruits of the industrial revolution. It made Elisha Tyler restive. He longed to go
elsewhere, just as he had longed for a college education; he longed for more fertile land, for quicker
returns, for some more profitable form of enterprise
—manufacturing, perhaps. But there was Colonel
Moses to think of, there was the farm, and there was
the Calvinistic figure of Duty, dimly ominous. Even
after the death of Moses Tyler in 1829, obstacles
seem to have intervened,[16] for it was not until a few
weeks after the birth of Moses Coit, August 2, 1835,
and six years after the death of his father, that Elisha
Tyler departed for the "more fertile region" of his
dreams.

New York beckoned him first. He took his family up the Hudson to Albany, and thence to Constantia. It was their first experience with the frontier. Oswego County had been laid out only some
twenty years before, and despite the foundry and
works of the American Iron Company, "one of the
most extensive establishments of the kind in the
state," Constantia must have been a little primitive,
containing as it did only twenty-five or thirty dwell-

ings, a grist mill, several saw mills, and an Episcopal
church. Some persons had thought it unhealthful
because of the "stagnant waters" near by (later
drained), and there was complaint of the impassable
roads.[17] Evidently the opportunity to manufacture
furnaces did not prove attractive, for Elisha left his
family with friends, and went on alone to Michigan.

He was attracted to Marshall, in Calhoun County,
which had been laid out in 1829. In 1835 Michigan
was a booming frontier commonwealth which was
applying to be admitted to the Union, and was so
admitted in 1837. The population, mostly centred
in the southern tier of counties, increased from 8000
in 1820 to about 100,000 in 1837. A "tidal wave" of
immigration was sweeping into western Michigan
and beyond, and the territorial road westward was
"literally whitened" with covered wagons.[18] The
land speculator, the immigrant, the promoter of
phantom banks, and the railroad boomer were moving over the unspeakable roads and laying out gran-
diose towns (on paper) among the oak openings.[19]
Marshall itself, having sprung up like a mushroom,
was hectic with feverish hopes. In 1833 Charles
Fenno Hoffman, the poet, had visited the town, attending a "railroad meeting" called only eighteen
months after "the first white man erected his cabin
in this section of the country." Such was the fever
of the time that the inn had not yet been plastered,

but he was impressed by the inhabitants whom he thought "much superior in character to the ordinary settlers of a new country."[20] Elisha Tyler was likewise impressed. The Calhoun County Bank (capital $100,000) was just being organized;[21] the railroad had already crept from Toledo to Adrian; and despite the existence of a flour mill in Marshall, he thought there would be room for another.[22] He hurried back to Constantia in September, 1836, sending his family home to Connecticut with the promise that in a few months he would bring them to Michigan. Then he went back to the delights of Marshall.

In May, 1837, he returned to Connecticut, and the Tyler family shortly began its westward trek.[23] For the boy Moses it was perhaps as well. Had he been brought up in Connecticut it is possible that his religious life might have been more stable, but it is also possible that the great histories of American literature with their broad national views might never have been written. A little Connecticut township, despite the glories of Jewett's City, might have kept him provincial. As late as 1840 "families were seated in the village of Griswold church with due regard to their standing in the community."[24]

A thousand immigrants were travelling into the sunset, over the Erie Canal, by primitive railroads, by stage coach, by wagon, by steamboats helped out with sails. The Tylers crawled up the Hudson valley by stage to Albany; then (exhilarating experience for Mary!) they bumped over the Mohawk and Hudson Railroad fifteen miles to Schenectady, where they transferred to the Utica and Schenectady road for Utica, a distance of seventy-six miles. In 1836 the line had not been completed, though the "greater part . . . is graded, and the work steadily progressing."[25] Let us hope that it was not too uncomfortable for the mother of a two-year-old baby. From Utica they diverged from their route to visit their friends in Constantia; thence they doubled back some twenty miles to New London on the Erie Canal, along which they proceeded at the majestic rate of two and one-half miles an hour by "line boat" to Buffalo, a distance of two hundred and thirty-two miles. The "line boat" furnished neither bedding nor food for its passengers.[26] But even line boats move; at Buffalo they boarded a steamer for Toledo, a voyage of five interminable days; and from Toledo, the rudimentary Erie and Kalamazoo Railroad, pride of the new commonwealth of Michigan, with its two small locomotives and cars "scarcely superior to a first-class stage line," carried them to Adrian.[27] The line was to be pushed on to Marshall, but the Tylers were forced to finish their journey by horse and wagon over the primitive roads.[28]

There were living in Marshall at the time John Davis Pierce, who owned a copy of Cousin's report

on the Prussian educational system, and Isaac Edwin
Crary, who borrowed the book from Pierce and
drafted the articles in the first State constitution
which created the educational system of Michigan.[29]
Elisha did not know that these two gentlemen were
profoundly to influence his son's career; he was looking for a flour-mill site. But he had been anticipated,
as a stone flour mill had just been erected at Perrin-
ville,[30] and Elisha was again disappointed. He looked
about him. Possibly Burlington, a little place even
newer than Marshall, might prove more profitable.[31]
In March he had bought two pieces of land.[32] To
Burlington accordingly the Tylers removed, where
Charles Tyler, the oldest boy, was placed in the first
school (a log cabin) kept by Miss Mary Bucking-
ham, and where two of their children were born. It
must have been difficult for Mary Tyler at first;
while they were in Marshall, Olive Coit Tyler had
come into the world; and two years later Edward
Scott was to be born and live less than a year. Whatever his mother's sorrows, Moses found Michigan
delightful; years afterwards he remembered the bucolic delights of Burlington and longed to be there
again.

But Elisha was still driven by the restlessness in his
blood, and, after a brief interval in Union City, Michigan, again moved his family. Still seeking opportunity for manufacture, he brought them to Detroit,

the vigorous economic capital of the new state, with
a population in 1845 of 13,065.[33] The Tylers went
there in 1842.[34] For a brief time, if one is to judge
from the scanty records, it seemed that Elisha's
dream was to be fulfilled. One follows the fortunes
of the family from the city directories of the day.
Thus in 1845 Elisha is listed as owner of the "Detroit Stone Ware Factory" at Woodbridge and
Third. Next year he has moved a block to Larned
and Third. Then advertisements of the "Stone Ware
Factory" disappear from the directories, and six
years later (1852) Elisha has moved to the south side
of Congress, below Brush; son Charles, who
"boards" with him, has become a partner in "Smith
& Tyler, Manufacturers and Dealers in Boots, Shoes,
Rubbers and Shoe Findings" at Woodward Avenue
opposite the First Presbyterian Church. One sus-
pects that the sonorous name conceals a shoe store.
Edward Tyler (apparently a cousin of Moses) is listed as a clerk in the establishment, but son Rowland
appears as clerk in the mercantile house of "F. F.
Parker and Bro." In 1853 Elisha has become "agent"
—of what, is not stipulated, and the family is apparently living with Charles at the corner of Franklin and Beaubien. Charles also becomes an "agent"
in 1856–7 and Elisha is living at sixty-three An-
toine,[35] but there was reason for this last change: a
fire in Smith and Tyler's shoe store destroyed the

building and half a block between Larned Street and
Jefferson Avenue, including the First Presbyterian
Church in its ravages, a combination of impiety and
disaster which led Mr. Robert Hopkins to commemorate the event in oil.[36] Moses probably enjoyed
the conflagration.

This disaster was the more heartrending because
Elisha had begun to rise in the community. When
the First Congregational Church was organized in
the winter of 1844, he had been elected a trustee—
it is true, for the short, one-year term.[37] On February
17, 1847, one finds him writing with a certain familiarity to the mighty William Woodbridge, United
States senator from the Wolverine state, to the effect
that Thomas Palmer ought to be appointed post-
master at Pewabac, that "our copper interests are
esteemed as flat as possible," and that the legislators,
though they "have done very little *in the house—
some outside,*" are likely to establish a new capital at
Lansing.[38] But the directories clearly reveal that
Elisha was not making his fortune.

The "Hon'l W. Woodbridge" probably troubled
the growing Moses not at all—unless, like Tom Saw-
yer, he imagined that a United States senator was
twenty-five feet high. If there are no extant records
of his boyhood days, we can piece together a picture
of what they were like from the reminiscences of
others. Detroit had its delights. None of the moves

recorded in the directories had taken the Tyler family more than a few blocks from the river with all its fascinations—the boats, the immigrants, the old French windmills which made the stream resemble the Scheldt. There was also Belle Isle, a superb picnic ground, chastely rechristened with appropriate ceremonies (it had been Hog Island) on the Fourth of July, 1845. And there was marshy land at the mouth of Connor's Creek, opposite the island, where bulrushes grew, furnishing fuel for autumnal conflagrations which imaginative boys compared to the burning of Moscow. Whether the elegantly uniformed volunteer firemen turned out for these Napoleonic disasters, one does not know, but there were a thrilling number of fires. One in 1842 destroyed twenty-five buildings, including the "two finest four-story brick stores then in the city," the loss being $200,000, nor was the fire subdued without the aid of the Fifth United States Regiment. What a field-day for boys![39]

Did Moses, one wonders, ever learn the "Firemen's Drinking Song"?

"Here is to Number One, drink her down;
Here is to Number One, drink her down;
Here is to Number One, for their boys are full of fun,
    Drink her down, drink her down, drink her down,"

and so on, through Number Two, whose boys "are

good and true," all the way to Number Twelve, "too far away to hear the bells."[40] There was an engine house (the "Rough and Ready" Engineer Company) on Larned, a few blocks from his home—and what boy ever failed to haunt a fire-engine? If there were no fires, and if the legislature were not in session, a lad could climb the steeple of the old capitol "by a spiral staircase, trimmed with brass candlesticks (one on either side of each step, and used by members for night sessions), and looking over the city" wonder whether other cities were as large.[41] Or, by a narrow, winding stairway, one could mount to the rough wooden platform on top of the old round-house reservoir at the foot of Orleans Street and gaze up and down the river, or across into the dominions of the British queen. In fact, a wide-eyed boy could see almost as much as Mr. W. H. Coyle saw—a local poet who struggled with blank verse to record the sights of the city:

"Dashing with speed impetuous, amid
A cloud of dust, gay-colored cabs and hacks,
The burly omnibus and rattling dray,
Whirl o'er the stone-paved, sonorous streets, as
Round the river's curving shore, a black, tall
Column of advancing smoke heralds a
Steamer from the broad blue lake. Slow creaking,
Hid beneath a ponderous pyramid
Of hay, a country wagon creeps along,
While whistling on its apex happy, sits

In homespun and straw hat the farmer boy;
A French cart next goes bouncing by, *les filles*
All seated *à la Turque* upon the soft
Warm buffaloes,[42] and bobbing up and down
With each jerk of that relic of the old
Régime, while rolling swift on flashing wheels,
Behind two snorting, shining bays, a coach
Silk-cushioned, glitters proudly by, a pet
With white-kid hand upon the panel see,—
Index of envied aristocracy."[43]

One pictures Moses envying the farmer boy on his extraordinary perch.

But perhaps Moses, a serious lad, was more interested in the conversation of his elders. One might hear them in 1845 discussing the bankruptcy of the city and telling how C. S. V. Roosevelt had grimly written from New York that " it were useless for me to express an opinion of the honesty of the majority of the committee on ways and means, who insisted upon putting off a creditor of their city, with its worthless bonds."[44] Or, if this were incomprehensible, the flags, banners, and patriotic inscriptions on the streets the previous autumn had been thrilling heralds of "an immense Clay and Frelinghuysen mass meeting." But it was even more thrilling, three years later, to watch the troops depart for Mr. Polk's Mexican War—a company of the Third U. S. Dragoons, none less than six feet high, in April; Company G of the Fifteenth U. S. Infantry, arriving out

of the "broad blue lake" from Mackinaw one day,
and departing for Mexico down the river the next.
Or, best of all, the various companies of the First
Volunteer Regiment, departing on the *Albany*
steamer at intervals for the front. And then the return of the valorous in July, 1848, with the Scotts
Guards setting off in the *Alliance* boat to meet the
warriors on Lake St. Clair (they came from Chicago), and the band, the speeches, and the parade—
and Captain Joseph Taylor running at midnight to
pound on Judge Wilkins' door and shout, "Hurrah!
my brother has licked the Mexicans at Palo Alto!"[45]
Not even the cholera scare of 1849 was so exciting.[46]

And there was always school. Where Moses'
formal education was begun, we do not know; and
the loss by fire of the older records of the Detroit public schools makes it impossible to trace his progress
through the grades. A legislative act of February 18,
1842, founded the modern school system, wiping
out or consolidating previous efforts; and, since
Elisha lived in the First Ward, it seems plausible to
suppose that Moses attended the First Ward school
which, in 1842, was in charge of Miss Diantha
Howland at eighteen dollars a month.[47] In the fall
of 1842 Moses had just passed his seventh birthday;
until his eighth he might remain in the Primary
school, whence he would pass into the Middle
school. The sessions were in two terms of three

months each, and scholars were brought up on Webster's *Spelling Book,* Sanders' series of readers, Peter Parley's *First Book of History,* Davies' *Arithmetic,* and Smith's *Geography* and *Grammar.* In the Middle school Moses would pass on to Hazen's "Definer," more Peter Parley, Olmstead's *Philosophy,* Hoskins' *Astronomy,* and other less astonishing titles. The even tenor of the new system was badly ruffled by an emotional outburst in 1844–45 over the reading of the Bible to school children; the board of education, after warning teachers not to elucidate the Scriptures on pain of dismissal, neatly sidestepped the real issue by voting that "nothing in the rules or by-laws" conflicted "with the right of any teacher . . . opening his or her school by reading, without note or comment, from any version of the Bible they may choose," and, despite the bad grammar, Catholic and Protestant were at peace. Moses was presumably interested: he entertained thoughts of the ministry. The muse of history notes that "McGuffey's Eclectic Series of Readers" was adopted that same year, and that, ten months later, Mr. Patcher addressed the board "touching his own publications." Mr. Patcher's publications (an ancient history and "Town's Intellectual Algebra") were adopted. When the legislature abandoned Detroit for the more bucolic confines of Lansing, the school board, after exorcising various legal ghosts, took

over the old capitol in May, 1848, establishing there
the first graded, or union, school of its kind in the
Northwest, William Francis, principal, with three
paid assistants and one volunteer. Moses was among
the first graduates—presumably in 1849.[48] In 1850
the precocious lad (invariably described in the city
directories as "student") was engaged at the age of
fifteen to teach school in Romeo, a village some
thirty-five miles north of Detroit.

What was the result upon him of this incessant
change, this bombardment by new experiences,
this exposure to the neurasthenia of the frontier?
His father, pathetically aware of his own failure,[49]
admonished him: "You are aware that we can do but
little, and that you will be under the necessity to rely
principally on your own efforts; therefore you will
understand that indolence you cannot afford to toler-
ate in any degree; that *dig, dig, dig* is the order of
the day for you. I should not urge you so if I did not
love you and feel such a desire for your prosperity."[50]

In addition to the paternal injunction, the ambitious young scholar[51] found another steadying influence in the First Congregational Church[52] and its
pastor, the Reverend Harvey Denison Kitchel
(1812-95). Though born in Whitehall, New York,
the minister's background was Connecticut;[53] and
when he was called to Detroit in the summer of 1848,
he was an impressive Easterner of thirty-six, "a vigor-

ous thinker, an eloquent preacher, a strong man"[54]
with a firm mouth, wide eyes, regular features
topped by a mass of hair inclined to curl and flanked
by the inevitable sideburns. A forth-putting person,
pastor of the church for sixteen years, when he was
called to Plymouth Church in Chicago, and thence,
in 1866, to the presidency of Middlebury, to which
he gave for seven years an administration marked
by "sound judgment and thorough efficiency."[55]

Middlebury made him a Doctor of Divinity, Yale
an honorary Master of Arts. Altogether an important man, one who got things done,[56] he was re-
spected, admired, and remembered by his congregation, who called him back to speak to them on important occasions.[57] And he fitted the temper of the times
with his earnest missionary zeal learned in the East,[58]
his "carefully prepared" sermons, his easy lugubrious-
ness on funerary and ceremonial occasions,[59] attractions further increased by the personality of his wife,
Ann Smith Kitchel, "a woman of great strength of
character, of rare mental abilities . . . all . . .
made increasingly effective by her education, refine-
ment . . . and virtues."[60] An irresistible combination for the earnest and wistful Moses; and, moreover, the Reverend Mr. Kitchel was interested in
literature and in the cause of temperance. Moses
promptly followed him into both fields.

Mr. J. K. Wellman thought that Michigan ought

to produce not only lumber but letters; wherefore in July, 1849, he published under the editorship of Mr. D. F. Quinby the first number of *Wellman's Literary Miscellany,* "the most pretentious and popular magazine ever printed in Detroit." Under various aliases it put up a gallant fight for existence, not succumbing until August, 1854. At one time the circulation climbed to the amazing number of 6000.[61] The pen of the Reverend Mr. Kitchel, that "student of words, their meaning, force and proper use,"[62] was called in to aid Michigan and the muses. He celebrated the dominant virtues of "The Anglo-Saxon Element in American Society" at long length; he defined the "Relations of the Family to the State" in five double-column pages; but above all he flayed the demon rum, condescending to dip a clerical pen even into fiction.[63] The cause was very much at Mr. Quinby's heart: when Mr. D. Bethune Duffield addressed the Cadets of Temperance on October 7, 1851 (incidentally ornamenting his remarks with Wordsworthian poetry), the oration appeared in the *Miscellany.*[64]

Temperance was in fact the battle cry of the times. There had been a long campaign against licensing liquor dealers in Detroit, and during the struggle John B. Gough had been imported to thunder for ten consecutive nights in June, 1850, against the saloon keepers. The young were enlisted under

the benevolent patronage of the ministers, divisions
of the "Sons" of Temperance and the "Cadets" of
Temperance being promptly formed.[65] Under the
compelling personality of Mr. Kitchel, Moses joined
not one, but both, rising rapidly in the ranks, for
in July, 1851, he took his seat as "Worthy Archon
of Chrystal Fount Section No. 5, Cadets of Temperance," and a year later became "G[rand]
W[orthy] Archon of the Sons of Temperance."[66]
As Worthy Archon of the "Chrystal Fount" section,
and with Kitchel's sermons ringing in his ears,
Moses delivered an "Address" typical of earnest ado-
lescence in the middle of the last century. He thought
that the order of the Cadets of Temperance was of
immense importance to "every true Patriot and
Philanthropist," composed though it was of mere
boys, since the "Philanthropical Politician revolving
in his mind the *present* condition of the Nation,"
asks whether the next generation shall be "— a race
of *dunces!*" The common schools, Moses hoped, "on
every bleak hill-top and in every fruitful valley"
ought to help, provided that "the tide of intemperance which has bourne (*sic*) so many of the past
generation into a drunkard's grave and a drunkard's eternity" be checked. For intemperance, it
seems, exercises a "viscious influence" on youth,
"the seed time of life." And Moses went on to picture "the number of inebriates" who would be "daily

wallowing in our gutters, and staggering through
our streets, and staggering from our docks, and *staggering into eternity,"* were it not for the Cadets. In
fact, he used words with "meaning, force and proper
use"; he drew a lurid picture of "Demon Alcohol,"
of delirium tremens with its "ten thousand clammy
serpents" and "horrid monsters" glistening from the
wall. Alas, however, for human frailty! Cadets of
Temperance, he said, are sometimes seen "standing
around the great fountains of crime, which are pouring forth their incessant stream of corruption, into
the community." Slightly confusing his figures,
Moses went on to describe the "dazzling paintings
within" which "adorn the view," the "gilded tapes-
try" that "bedecks the walls," and just as the reader
is about to wonder how so luxurious a gambling den
came to be built in simple Detroit, one learns that
"this they call the theatre." And with some ringing
temperance poetry the address concludes.[67]

But this is slightly to anticipate. Obviously such a
lad was in no danger of losing his moral equilibrium
amid the diaspora of the pioneer. Perhaps the very
uncertainty of a family life which thus stretched in
uncertain loops and curves from Connecticut
through three or four towns in Michigan and half a
dozen paternal occupations, a life so uncertain, so
unrooted and restless as Elisha's, was overcompen-
sated in Moses by this priggishness, this devotion to

puritanical ideals. For Moses was a child of the old, unreformed Connecticut; his favorite minister was a graduate of Yale theology; the friends and associates of his family were often Connecticut men. Doubtless therefore this asceticism, this prudish turning away from all but moral values was inevitable in one so young, impressionable, and precocious. He seems, across the decades, a little forlorn, a little self-righteous, but if he was forlorn, he was sturdy; otherwise, a lad of fifteen, he would not have been called upon to teach school at Romeo.

Of this first taste of pedagogy no record remains.[68] He asked that *The New York Times* be sent to him, and he seems once to have thought of becoming a dentist,[69] but neither his father nor, one supposes, the Reverend Mr. Kitchel approved. An offering to the Lord, Moses was reminded that Deacon Howard

told thy mother that from the time of your first making a profession of Religion he had selected you in his own mind for a preacher of that Religion—and wishes you to keep that position in view. To which I respond, may you become qualified, and if the Master calleth, may you be ready to say "what wilt thou have me to do?"

and to that end

"Learn to think, to speak and to write!" must ever be your motto, and that practice is the only road to perfection.[70]

A heavy responsibility for a lad in his teens, told to practice "short lectures" on his "little audience" of Romeo school children, since

Your friends here are expecting much from you and *must not* be disappointed—The little we can do for you will cost us much.[71]

The ways of father and son in the eighteen-fifties are not our ways, and it is hard to realize that these are letters from a man of fifty-seven to a lad of sixteen. But Elisha was like that.

Moses gave up his school in the spring of 1851, and, presumably to earn the money which Elisha's letter made necessary, set out courageously to the west—Battle Creek, Paw Paw, even Chicago—as a book agent. Obviously he came to no harm. The itch to write, to produce, to speak out was in him, and, again imitating Mr. Kitchel, he appeared in print, a correspondent of *The Peninsular Fountain,* a short-lived weekly temperance paper edited in Detroit by Henry C. Knight,[72] sending back the "literary" letters on men and scenes customary in such correspondence.[73] But not thus was one to become a preacher of the Word. Moses returned home to prepare for college under Mr. Kitchel. We catch some glimpse of the ambition which devoured him from a biographical essay he prepared and published in *The Literary Miscellany* in 1852 on the Reverend

Thomas Spencer, a famous infant prodigy of the
Liverpool pulpit, who died at the age of twenty-six.
The essay is quite as competent as others in the magazine, a surprising achievement when one remem-
bers that Moses was only sixteen. We have an unconscious revelation of the young author's thirst for importance and power when we read that Spencer's
sermons "are perhaps without parallel in the annals
of pulpit eloquence."[74] The temperance orator, the
correspondent of *The Peninsular Fountain,* the pro-
tégé of the Reverend Mr. Kitchel, the hope of Elisha
Tyler's old age, he too desired to be eloquent, to become a power, to speak as one having authority.
Around the frail form of the Reverend Thomas
Spencer hung the glamor of a premature demise;
no wonder that the brooding Moses was attracted
to the theme.

In the fall of 1852 seventeen-year-old Moses journeyed the forty miles to Ann Arbor, where, with ten
others, he was admitted to the "Department of
Science, Literature and the Arts" of the struggling
University of Michigan as a freshman in the classical
course. To judge by the requirements, the Reverend
Doctor Kitchel had labored to some purpose, for
Moses passed successfully the entrance examinations
"in the following studies, namely: In English
Grammar, Geography, Arithmetic and Algebra
through equations of the first degree; in the Latin

Grammar, Cæsar's Commentaries, Cicero's Select Orations, and six books of the Æneid of Virgil, or in some equivalent amount of classical Latin; in the Greek Grammar and the Greek Reader, or in some equivalent amount of classical Greek; in the writing of the Latin and Greek (with the accents); and in Grecian and Roman Geography."[75] For the age was sternly classical; Moses, contributing essays to *The Sybil*, a manuscript magazine published by the members of the Alpha Nu Literary Society, which he promptly joined, was to illustrate a paper on eloquence with many classical flourishes. We do not know where he lived; if in "North College" (Mason Hall) or "South College," having paid his admission fee, he could contemplate existence in the dormitory at "from $5 to $7.50 a year for room rent and the services of the Janitor"—George Almendinger, successor to Pat Kelly, who aroused the morning by ringing a bell borrowed from the Michigan Central Railroad.[76] He might expect a year of education to cost him from seventy to one hundred dollars, "including board, washing and books."[77] He might also look forward to family supervision, since "considering . . . the government of the students as a substitute for the regulations of home," the faculty would endeavor "to bring it as near to the character of *parental control* as the nature of the case will admit," even, one supposes, in the case of "perverse individuals," who, failing to appreciate *"the influence of persuasion and kindness"* might "forthwith . . . be returned" to parent or guardian. He was expected to retain a "strict propriety of conduct," to which end Elisha and Mary Tyler were invited by the university "to appoint a guardian in Ann Arbor" for their son, who was "required to attend prayers daily in the College Chapel" at the sound of Mr. Almendinger's railroad bell, and to be present at "public worship on the Sabbath at such one of the churches in the village of Ann Arbor" as Elisha and Mary might designate.[78]

The forty-acre campus which Moses trod with unprophetic foot scarcely dreamed of its later glories. The "truly magnificent design" of a hopeful New Haven architect hired fifteen years earlier to plan the buildings had dwindled into two edifices which served as combined dormitories and classrooms, four houses for the faculty, and a building for the medical department only two years old. Unoccupied portions of the forty acres were planted in wheat by the thrifty janitor. Strolling into the orchards which survived from the old Rumsey farm, faculty families might pluck a classical peach. There were also cows—at least, Mr. Cropsey's painting of the University in 1855 depicts them.[79] A little later Andrew D. White was to speak disrespectfully of the "unkempt and wretched" campus with "not more than a score of trees outside the building sites allotted to professors," of "unsightly plank walks" from building to building, and "meandering paths," dusty in dry weather and muddy in wet. Students, professors, and citizens were in 1854 to set out five hundred trees, most of which promptly died, but of this Moses could not know. The two gaunt dormitory-classrooms were scarcely beautiful, though Governor Barry accused the regents of "vast expenditures" for "large and commodious buildings" and the enthusiastic *Michigan State Journal* had earlier observed that "more classical models or a more beautiful finish cannot be imagined." Mason Hall (so named in 1843) contained a chapel, two recitation rooms, the library ("purchased a few years since in Europe" by Doctor Asa Gray, who, though called to Ann Arbor, obstinately preferred Harvard), and on the fourth floor, a museum ("the collections in the departments of Natural History embrace a valuable cabinet of minerals, consisting of between four and five thousand specimens"). What rooms were left were used for dormitory purposes.[80]

Despite the cows and the classical models, all was not peace on the campus. The university, small as it was,[81] was just emerging from a series of violent convulsions. Fires of resentment were still smoldering over the eternal fraternity questions, sparks from "the pile of shavings which had been thrown into an outhouse and lighted" by fraternity boys the last term-day of 1849 and noted at midnight by the weary president of the faculty after an exhausting day of "the usual public declamations."[82] For, from 1845 to 1850, Chi Psi, Beta Theta Pi, and Alpha Delta Phi had doggedly resisted the regents, the board of visitors, the legislature, the town, the rest of the student body, and the faculty, who, reinforced by obliging letters from six eastern college presidents, summarized fraternity history as "a detail of obliquities." In the spring of 1846 Professor J. Holmes Agnew (Professor Martin L. D'Ooge referred to him forty-nine years later as a better theologian than philologist)[83] had been deprived of a tutor; and since Greek and Latin occupied more than a third of the curriculum, he called upon Professor Daniel D. Whedon ("logic, rhetoric, and the philosophy of history") and Professor Andrew Ten Brook ("normal and intellectual philosophy") to take over the Latin classes. But though the faculty of arts numbered only six, professors then as now stood on their dignity; Professor Whedon rebelled and Professor Ten Brook resigned—a step he later publicly regretted.[84] In addition to these troubles, the new state constitution of 1850 totally reconstituted the board of regents, but the retiring board of "regents by appointment" did what it could: it removed Professor Whedon, who made abolitionist speeches, on the familiar ground that he "openly advocated . . . a doctrine which is . . . subversive of civil government, civil society, and the legal rights of individual citizens," constituting "a species of moral treason against the government." It also voted to end the terms of all the other members of the faculty, except Professor Louis Fasquelle (who was unflatteringly overlooked), and went out of office December 31, 1851, in a glow of moral virtue. However, it overlooked a debt of ten dollars to Professor Whedon for setting out shrubs.[85]

But Destiny intended that the institution should survive. Destiny appeared on the campus in the shape of a steam-engine in trousers. Moses did not know it; he was conceivably more gratified to learn that "the hour for morning prayers be, with the approbation of the Executive Committee of the Board of Regents, changed to a quarter before eight a. m."[86] The University had acquired a president, a six-foot giant "with a grand head set on massive shoulders," "a full suite of dark brown hair rather long and considerably disordered," a large and "somewhat Roman" nose, and a "rather long side beard."[87] Destiny intended that the new era should not be marked by drift, for "every organization requires a head—a banking company, a railroad—every corporation requires a head. An army requires a general. A ship requires a captain. . . . So a college or university requires a president."[88] The position had been variously offered to Bishop Potter, President Nott of Union College (who was later to confer a degree on Tappan's successor at Tappan's request), George Bancroft, Henry Barnard, and a Doctor Adams,[89] while, in the background, Agassiz, Professor Alexander Dallas Bache, Charles Anthon, and Elizur Deming, "a man of most estimable character,"[90] were regrettably unadventurous. But Doctor Henry P. Tappan of New York accepted at the age of forty-eight, and Michigan was in the hands of its master, for "my aim was to keep the idea of a University constantly before the public mind; to make the young men educated at the University thoroughly to comprehend it; and to engage the best efforts of the Regents and the Professors for its realization."[91] With a resident faculty of six in the literary department, he issued a catalogue like a trumpet-call. "An institution cannot deserve the name of a University which does not aim, in all the material of learning, in the professorships which it establishes, and in the whole scope of its provisions, to make it possible for every student to study what he pleases, and to any extent he pleases."[92] An ungrateful board was to drop Tappan later, but not until he had molded the University for all time.

Moses spent a blameless year. The manuscript "Examination Book" preserved in the Registrar's Office shows that he passed his nine courses with impersonal regularity—Livy, Homer, Horace, Xenophon, algebra, and geometry. The faculty, energized by the vigorous Tappan, entered subscriptions for seventeen severely academic periodicals in the second term.[93] Moses preserved a "strict propriety" of conduct; the town offered few temptations. He had come to Ann Arbor too late to view the Panorama of the Hudson River and Views of Virginia, "covering no less than 9400 feet of canvass," which an astonished village looked at for twenty-five cents a head. Let us hope that he did not have to visit Doctor E. G. Burger, who announced in *The Washtenaw Whig* that "I am every day filling many beaatiful (*sic*) DENTAL PEARLS, or in common parlance, Human Teeth, with pure Gold or Tin Foil." The *Whig* implored voters to favor Winfield Scott and Mr. Graham of North Carolina, but the state went for Pierce. Mr. Yales lectured on Temperance at the M. E. church "at 6½ o'clock P.M." on December 15, and there was a "new supply" of *Uncle Tom's Cabin* at the bookstore of a Mr. Woods. The Spencer vocalists sang at the Congregational church in February; and Moses might, but presumably did not, succumb to the lyric persuasions of a Mr. Parkhurst on Main Street who informed the town on March 9, 1853, that

"My Daguerrean gallery is now wide awake,
And I'm ready and able good pictures to take,"

with the help of "a good skylight" and "nice little cases to slip in your pocket." Moses was, however, present at the first appearance of President Tappan, and remembered the event long afterwards:

I was one of the little class of freshmen who entered the University in the fall of 1852, after an examination from which all the expected terrors were removed by the professorial philanthropy of dear old Dr. Williams. A few weeks later, I was one of that crowd of students in the literary department, then numbering as many as fifty-five or sixty men,—a mighty host we seemed to ourselves to be—who welcomed the entrance into the Chapel for the first time of President Tappan, at a glance recognizing him as a man born to command and to be obeyed.[94]

Tappan was formally inaugurated in January; the event drew from the pen of the "Hon. G. W. Peck" some bitter remarks about the "usual quantity of clerical parade" "under the regime of the Protestant Jesuits." *The Washtenaw Whig,* reprinting these observations on January 5, remarked that there were only "two clergymen distinguished as such" at the ceremony and spiritedly advised Mr. Peck to "restrain your cowardly thrusts."[95]

In his spare time Moses was writing essays which he contributed to *The Sybil,* a manuscript magazine then in its ninth volume written by members of the Alpha Nu Literary Society. He wrote on "Mental Discipline," on "No Excellence Without Labor," on

"Influence of Mountainous Scenery on Human Character," and on "Eloquence versus Tyranny"; and he contributed one ghastly attempt at a humorous letter to explain to the society that he could not write. There is nothing remarkable in the thought of these productions: he proved at great length that "Tyranny and Eloquence are antagonists," that freedom is the possession of mountain people, that the *Æneid* and Bishop Butler's *Analogy* were the products of painful thinking. But the canorous sentences are full and masculine; the young student's passionate interest in the literature of thought is evident; and, with unconscious prophecy in "Mental Discipline" he analyzed both sides of his own nature:

He who possesses an undisciplined mind finds himself unable to investigate thoroughly a subject, without numberless wanderings and digressions in the attempt. He leaves his mind upon the consideration of the desired theme, and finds it rambling far away on forbidden ground. He is ever confused and per[p]lexed by the circumstances around him, and the breathing of the winds calls of[f] his attention from his subject. His ideas are disconnected and obscure: his causes are mixed up with effects; and the whole matter is involved in mist and darkness. On the other hand, he who possesses a mind well disciplined by training, receives his subject with calmness, and pursues it with clearness, & perspicuity. For the time, he abstracts himself wholly from outward things, and shuts himself up within the well-defined limits of his mental closet: he seems to forget things passing around him, and in his plain, perceptible and cloudless advance, traces the subject of his thoughts through all its various parts. . . . The mind of the former is like a sun-glass in the hands of a nervous and excited person. . . . But the mind of the lat[t]er is, like the same instrument, held by one unagitated and cool. He brings the glass to a perfect focus, & holds it firmly upon the tinder till it burns into a blaze.

The Moses Tyler who vibrated among teaching, journalism, and the ministry as professions, never wholly satisfied with any, was ever "confused and perplexed by the circumstances around him," but the author of the great histories held the glass firmly upon the tinder till it burned into a blaze.

CHAPTER II

BUT the stars in their courses fought to send Moses
Tyler to Yale, and the struggling institution at Ann
Arbor was not, after all, to count him among its
alumni.[1] His kinsmen saw to it that this child of
Connecticut was returned for nurture to New
Haven; and had Moses desired to remain at Michigan (which apparently he did not), the combined
pressure of the Connecticut men who surrounded
him, the fact that it was impossible to study theology
at Ann Arbor, and above all, the hand of providence in the shape of an offer from Samuel Coit of
Hartford to assist the progress of his young relative
through Yale,[2] would have made it impossible for
Moses to continue there. Samuel Coit agreed with
Elisha and Mr. Kitchel that Moses was to be a minister.

Even yet, however, Moses was not wholly a dedi-
cated spirit. He had tasted the feverish wine of
journalism, and in the summer, when he was preparing to go to Connecticut, he paused at Cleveland to
report the proceedings of the seventh annual meeting of the American Association for the Advancement of Science, for *The New York Evening Post*
and *The Journal of Commerce*.[3] Presumably Elisha

and Mary saw him go with some trepidation, since the convention, which should have been held in August, 1852, "in consequence of the prevalence of cholera along the avenues of approach to Cleveland," had been postponed to Thursday, July 28, 1853, and the attendance was naturally "not so large as at the previous meeting."[4] The Second Presbyterian Church and the Rockwell Street School housed the panting scientists, who remained in session through Thursday, August 2. President Benjamin Peirce remarked in his "Opening Address," "Gentlemen, we are not convened for a light duty—our self-imposed task is not a musing child's play"; and the gentlemen who brought "freights of knowledge to distribute them to the world"[5] listened, one trusts, without "the bickerings of angry contention" or the "foul complaints of mortified vanity"[6] to "Communications" on "Strictures on the Mechanical Explanation of the Zigzag Path of the Electric Spark," "On the Fatal Effects of Chloroform," and "On the Resistance of the Vertical Plates of Tubular Bridges," with other, heavier fare. Young Tyler scribbled valiantly. Was he awed by the dignitaries —Benjamin Peirce, the Hon. William Case, Professor A. D. Bache, Professor O. M. Mitchel the astronomer, Doctor Julius Friedländer of Berlin? It was disappointing to open *The Evening Post, Weekly* for August 11, 1853, and read that: "Our

Cleveland correspondent has sent us full reports of several interesting papers read at the Scientific Convention, but they have come at so late an hour that we have only space for the following"—a paper on the reclamation of inundated lands in the Mississippi Valley by A. M. Brown of Natchez, not important enough for publication in the *Proceedings*.[7] But the report occupies almost a column, closely printed; it is clear and well organized, and Moses might well be pleased with it. He went on to New Haven and entered college September 14, 1853.[7a]

Yale in the fifties was large and important, graduating more students in that crucial decade than did Harvard, Princeton, or Dartmouth.[8] The president was Theodore Dwight Woolsey of the line of the Woolseys, the Dwights, and Jonathan Edwards, a slender, remote, imperious, active man wearing spectacles and sideburns, possessing a "clear and penetrating eye" and the bent figure of a scholar; he had edited Greek dramatists and Plato, and was now invading history and international law. His sermons in Battell Chapel, expressing his sense of "the evil—the exceeding sinfulness—of sin"[9] were thought to be impressive; and on the same day he was inducted into the presidency, he had been ordained, declaring in his inaugural address the glories of the Christian instructor who can "lead the minds of his pupils up to God."[10] He could quell rebellious underclassmen with a word,[11] and at the age of seventy he was still able to mount stairways two steps at a time.[12] But though he was a formidable person, he was not unsympathetic with youth: one of his earliest official acts was to change the hour of morning prayers, held in the dreary "Old Chapel," from five A.M. in the summer and six in the winter, to five-thirty and six-thirty, and, just as Moses was graduating, to move them down to eight o'clock.[13] The faculty over which he presided was in the fifties undergoing a new cycle of change. The eldest generation, which had grown up with the first Timothy Dwight and flourished under his successor, was rapidly passing—Taylor, who died in 1858, outmoded in a feverish and changing world;[14] President Jeremiah Day, who, after conferring degrees on thirty classes, had resigned in 1846; Kingsley, emeritus professor of Latin by 1851–52; Eleazer Fitch, the divine, who went in 1852; and the great Benjamin Silliman, moving majestically in the background, an emeritus professor in 1853. They were awful figures, relics of the antediluvian world, men who could remember Timothy Dwight's sermons and the Hartford Convention, and they looked down with olympian benevolence upon graying youngsters already meditating retirement from the faculty—John P. Norton in chemistry, Stanley in mathematics, Olmstead the astronomer, Bissell in law, a whole generation that did not survive the decade. For youth was knocking at the door, a new and vigorous group was pushing into the faculty—J. D. Dana, to whom the class of '56 addressed a formal communication certifying their "satisfaction and pleasure" in "a course so highly interesting and eminently instructive" as geology;[15] H. A. Newton, a college tutor at twenty-three, and two years later (1855) head of the mathematical department "with the privilege of a year for graduate study in Europe";[16] the astounding Hadley—"Old Hadley," who at thirty achieved Woolsey's chair, the "best and soundest philologist" of his generation, a youngster so precocious that he had skipped his freshman and sophomore years, read Hume's *History* at fourteen, and, not satisfied with the collegiate curriculum, studied German, Spanish, Hebrew, and calculus for pleasure.[17] And there was Timothy Dwight the younger, a future president of Yale, made a tutor after four months of graduate work, though he "knew just enough more of Latin . . . than they did, to enable me successfully to hear the recitations."[18]

Despite the continuing traditions of Yale, the intellectual climate during the fifties was disturbed. Experimental pedagogical ideas,[19] the intrusion of Horace Bushnell's "heretical and dangerous theological opinions" into the Connecticut mind,[20] the increasing senescence of the theological school under the

ageing Taylor[21] despite the efforts of Professor Goodrich ("Homiletics and Pastoral Charge") to keep
religion alive,[22] the coming of new scientific courses
into the curriculum,[23] which reduced the importance
of the classical literary discipline, and above and over
all, the brooding thunder-cloud of sectional strife[24]—
these fateful forces ruffled the calm of the famous
elms. But the reform of the theological school like
the Civil War lay in the troubled distance; the façade
of the old curriculum—the classics, mathematics, oratory, and then philosophy, theology, general history,
and some science[24a]—still stood imperially, a symbol
of what Dwight with unconscious irony was to call
"a certain oneness or harmony of intellectual life,"
"a good thing in itself."[25] Probably Moses was not at
first conscious of the changing mental scene.

Yale apparently refused to recognize Tyler's work
at Ann Arbor; at any rate he entered as a freshman
September 14, 1853, securing room 175 in Divinity
College.[26] He looked about him. There were a dozen
or so buildings, constituting the "Old Brick Row" set
amid their elms behind the famous Fence, Divinity
College ranking foremost "not merely because it was
youngest and newest, but because the average theo-
logue was a milder tenant than the secular col-
legian":[27] it was characteristic of Moses to house
there. Yale was not expensive: William Rey, an itin-
erant Frenchman who visited New Haven a few

years later, marvelled that students paid but $2.50 or
$5.50 per term for "ces chambres" which "m'ont
paru excellents" with their "deux pièces à coucher"
which "communiquent à une salle de travail," and
that the cost of a year at college was only from $175
to $250 "par tête." He also admired "le vaste square
appelé le *Green*," "le plus joli square rustique que
j'ai vu." Let us hope that Moses, safe in the arms
of Yale, experienced an equal delight.[28] It was not, at
first sight, strikingly different from Ann Arbor;
New Haven in 1853 had only 23,000 inhabitants,[29]
and a strolling undergraduate who walked north
up College Street (whither—to No. 6—Moses moved
as a junior), passed beyond the dip to the perilous
grade crossing and climbed up Prospect Street, saw
nothing beyond but the Hillhouse Forest and the
peaceful Connecticut landscape.[30] Indeed, Lady
Emmeline Stuart Wortley, an amiable, if gush-
ing, Englishwoman, to whom "Professor Silliman
jun." gallantly offered "elucidatory observations" on
his mineralogical collection in the late summer of
1849, complained that "the noise the katydids, tree-
frogs, and crickets make at New Haven, is incon-
ceivable—almost enough to interrupt the students
at their labours."[31] It is not probable that the katydids troubled Moses greatly; if he was not a brilliant student,[32] he was a dogged one.[33]

Whatever profound changes were at work in the

college, the outward aspects of student life were what they had been for generations of undergraduates. M. Rey marvelled at the paternalism—which, however, made the college "marcher," to the envy, he thought, of monarchical countries,[34]—albeit he noted that the perpetual religious services weighed heavily on the students, and hinted that "un esprit de sécheresse" presided over the college chapel. On Sunday walking (except to and from church) was prohibited; and for the rest, there was no theatre, no billiards, no card-playing, no dicing, no wine or beer, nor firearms allowed—at least officially, but the Frenchman, more realistic than the college officials, discovered that New Haven was "une des villes les plus dangereuses" in the point of gambling, and noted the presence of three "maisons de jeu."[35] The southerners frequented them, we may be sure, more than Moses did. That he was involved in the famous town and gown riot of the spring of 1854, when Pat O'Neil, a bar-keeper and local tough, was stabbed to the heart by a dirk in the hands of a fiery Mississippi senior, does not appear, but as the whole college turned out to resist the roughs, it is difficult to believe he remained quietly in his room, especially since a howling mob (with two loaded cannon) besieged the dormitories, and even President Woolsey counselled armed resistance.[36] Shortly thereafter there was no more football on the college green, but

Freshman Moses might have witnessed Yale's first intercollegiate regatta, if he cared to. One longs to know whether, as a sophomore, he arrayed himself in outrageous habiliments on the night of November 8, 1854, to march with his class amid torches and fireworks in that ancient piece of undergraduate grotesquerie, "The Burial of Euclid," denounced by the "Lit" in 1857 as "the annual disgrace."[37] The entire class turned out at ten in the evening for the parade, the program of which has been preserved:

ORDER OF PROCESSION

1. Band-itti.
2. Physician and Priest.
3. Undertaker.
4. Bearers [cut of coffin] Bearers.
5. Chief Mourners.
    Madame Euclid.
    Miss Anna Lytics.
      attended by
    Mr. D. A. Revised.
    Faculty and Fresh.
6. Friends of the Deceased.

The procession, attired as goblins, imps, or whatever undergraduate fancy might dictate, marched to Steinert's Hall at Orange and Court Streets, where the bier and effigy of Euclid were solemnly deposited on the platform, and the following impres-

sive ceremonial (in the hall and elsewhere) followed:

1. Overture, from Bob the Devil.
2. Introductory Ode, by Major Natur Caput.
3. Music by the Ban(d)jo.
4. Oration. (De)Cease (of) Rude Bore-us, by a member
   of the Bore(a)ed.
5. Music, Solow on the Triangle.
6. Funeral Sermon, by Moses in the Chapel Rushes.
7. Song, Time, "Skool," "Skool."
8. Procession at the funeral pyre.
9. Prayer at the Grave by the Rt. Reverend U. B.
   Damned.
10. Dirge by Asoph O. More.
11. Incantation by Hon. Sir Cumference.
12. Ad Urbem fugiamus, "Hellward he wends his weary
    way."[38]

The sixth item in this shower of puns looks suspi-
cious. Can "Moses in the Chapel Rushes" be our future theologian? And did he participate in the
annual (and rowdy) "Statement of Facts" of the
literary societies? It is cheering to know that he was
one of the managers of the junior exhibition, held
on April 2, 1856, and that, during his college career,
he managed to accumulate membership in a comfortable number of college societies—the Brothers in
Unity, the famous literary society; Kappa Sigma
Theta, a sophomore society; Alpha Delta Phi, a
junior ditto; and—greatest triumph of all—Skull
and Bones as a senior.[38a]

For it was precisely this kind of contact that he needed. Did he, one wonders, ever so far relax his austere dignity as to visit the old Pavilion Hotel, set eighty feet back from the beach among rows of weeping willows, frequented by nostalgic southern students, who soothed their homesickness by gazing at its pillars and its thick walls plastered with yellow stucco? Probably not; Moses was cautious, and the memory of Edmund Clarence Stedman, dismissed in 1851 for "having been present at a 'dance house' near the head of the wharf" not once, but often (not to speak of ending "in the hands of the police for riotous behaviour,")[39] probably reminded him that literary brilliance was unstable. But he might view discreetly Mr. Street's New Haven House in town, opened the year of Stedman's dismissal, its architectural glories not surpassed until collegiate Alumni Hall opened in 1853, designed by President Woolsey himself and erected at the princely cost of $27,000. Its lower floor was to grow gloomy with the memories of examinations, but on the upper floor the young, exuberant life of the literary societies flowed eternally. Moses promptly joined the "Brothers in Unity," and in the intervals of writing notices for *The New Haven Daily Palladium* of lectures before the Young Men's Institute,[40] he read curiously and widely in the library of the society. And he furthered his development by contact with his fellow students, many of whom rose to honor, and some of whom perhaps indoctrinated him with that dissatisfaction with the reigning curriculum which was to bear important fruits when he went to Michigan as a professor. There were, for example, David J. Brewer, '56, later a justice of the United States Supreme Court; Elisha Mulford, '55, chairman of the board of editors of the "Lit"; W. T. Harris, '58, who "affected Graham bread, gymnastics, stenography and German," and who read Humboldt's *Cosmos* and made fun of a classical education. Even more important was Andrew D. White, '57, a life-long friend, who was also thoroughly disgusted with the prevailing system.[41]

Moses faithfully attended classes, making a good scholastic record,[42] but one feels somehow that Yale had not wholly won him. His growing interest in literature found no outlet in the curriculum, since the time had not yet come for the creation of a formal department of English. Instruction in the subject was cursory, and inextricably entangled with oratory and rhetoric.[43] The consequence, it is true, was the wide diffusion of the habit of private reading among the undergraduates, but the situation did not make for enthusiastic intellectual effort. Tyler fell in easily with the custom of Dwight, Stedman, W. T. Harris, and other "intellectuals," reading a great many books, principally in literature and theology, and making notes and excerpts from them. The latter (mostly from the English classics) have been preserved in the "Commonplace Books I and II" among the Tyler papers, but luckily the list of withdrawals by Tyler from the Unity Society library permits us to see that he was reaching out in other than literary directions. In the winter of 1853–54 he read almost nothing but religious biography, but beginning in July, 1854, and extending to June, 1858, one finds him ranging from Scott's *Guy Mannering* and Cooper's *Chainbearer* to Nicholas Wiseman's *Connexion of Science and Revealed Religion* (Andover, 1837), and Edwards on the freedom of the will. Some of the entries cannot certainly be identified, but two main streams of interest appear from the "Commonplace Books" and the library withdrawals; one is that Tyler was making a wide acquaintance with the best modern English classics; and the other is that he was reading on both sides of theological fundamentalism, balancing Shelley against the "Christian library" and weighing Andover theology against Frederick Lake Williams' history of modern inventions and Emerson Davis' survey of fifty years, *The Half Century* (Boston, 1851). One may trace his dissatisfaction with orthodoxy to these Yale readings. Half unconsciously he was growing out of the world of Samuel Coit and Doctor Kitchel; the young prig who had denounced

the Demon Alcohol in Detroit was being slowly
liberalized. He could no longer agree with the obso-
lescent Hopkinsian theology of Professor Taylor.
Taking notes on one of that worthy's lectures, Tyler
copied down this statement:

the conception of the will as a freely electing power is
inconsistent with the known truth that every event must
have a necessitating cause—a cause which renders the opposite event impossible,

but against this belated echo of Jonathan Edwards,
the young student wrote that this was a "mere begging of the question."[44] He wavered. He could still
write that

If one is not accountable for his belief, he is accountable
for nothing; for all his actions spring from his belief,

a college note that he was in maturer years to label
"Rubbish."[45] But he could also dream of giving up
the ministry for teaching.[46] Whether Tyler consciously realized it or not, Hopkinsian theology, despite its official victories,[47] was doomed—outmoded
in a world of feverish political unrest. The black
shadow of the slavery question lay across all the theological schools. Abolitionism had split the protestant
faiths wide open. Almost everywhere in the North
anti-slavery sentiment went hand in hand with theological liberalism. Among the Presbyterians old-
line theology was unfortunately also the theology

of "an almost solid South."[48] In 1844 the Methodists, originally an anti-slavery body, had broken in two over the same issue; the next year the Methodist Episcopal Church South was organized. In May, 1845, the Southern Baptist Convention was formed in protest against the vote of the Baptist Foreign Missionary Board that "we can never be a party to any arrangement which would imply approbation of slavery."[49] Even among the Congregationalists the connection between radical Unitarianism and anti-slavery agitation was close. Modern thought and modern letters were revolving around the doctrine of political freedom and philosophic individualism. No wonder that the Yale theological faculty seemed moribund, or that Tyler was puzzled. He was caught between two forces: family pressure, and the pull upon him of orthodoxy as taught by the Yale professor of systematic theology, on the one hand, and on the other, the fascination of the impassioned liberalism of the anti-slavery cause. Characteristically, he tried to ride both horses at once: he enlisted enthusiastically in the cause of freedom, but he also continued on his dogged way to the ministry.

Tyler was worrying about the political situation by the opening of his sophomore year.[50] But it was toward the end of his junior term that, at the Yale meeting for the encouragement of the Free-Soil cause in Kansas, Tyler leaped unexpectedly into history. His own letter is a mirror of the event:

Yale Coll. March 23 [1856]
Sunday

My dear father,

In yesterdays N. Y. Times you may perhaps have noticed a report of a great Kansas Meeting held in this place on Thursday Evening. There is a large Colony on the point of setting out for that interesting territory from this place. Henry Ward Beecher came up on purpose to attend it and gave us a tremendous Speech. Towards the close of his remarks he made a powerful appeal to the Citizens of New Haven not to suffer their colony to go forth without a complete equipment of Sharpe's Rifles. When he had taken his seat, and amid the most intense excitement, the venerable Professor Silliman came forward to the stand and proposed that immediate action be taken in regard to Mr. Beecher's advice. He said that he would give the amount of one rifle—which would be $25, and hoped that the needed number might be at once contributed. Then gentlemen rose in different parts of the house offering one or more as they were able. When they commenced to bid, Beecher advanced from the Pulpit Sofa and stood looking down like a Monarch upon a human Sea, whose tempest of enthusiasm he had himself raised. As each man offered his gift Beecher would get off some witticism or pun, to set the audience in a roar. The number of Rifles subscribed had reached 13 and was advancing but slowly; when Beecher said that if they would raise 25 on the Spot he would raise 25 more next Sunday from his church. Then the number rose to 20, when there was a halt. At this point a Student rose in the gallery (which was crowded with men of that kind) and said, "I will pledge myself to raise the amount of $25 for 1 Sharpe's Rifle from the Junior

Class in Yale College." The move was so unusual and so
unexpected that it took the folks by storm and the way
they cheered was perfectly frightful. When the noise
which followed this remark had subsided, Capt Lines
looking toward the gallery shouted "what name?" Reply
was made "Moses Tyler." Then Beecher bellowed out
"Moses was a meek man, but he had wherewithal to stand
up!" This brought the house down again. And then Prof.
Silliman, appealing to the galleries said, "There are *4*
classes in College"; but no voice was heard from them.
The number was then quickly made up and the meeting
adjourned in tumultuous excitement.

Before I left the Church numbers of my classmates
swarmed around and expressed their gratification at my
act and their willingness to back me up. Before I went to
bed nearly the whole sum was raised. But the most ludi-
crous portion of the performance was to witness the effect
it had on the Southerners. They stormed, they swore, they
tore! That a class in Yale College should be committed to
an Abolition Emigrant Co. for a rifle seemed "infernal,"
"damnable" and a sufficient ground for dissolving the
Union. Accordingly at all the tables and in every knot
of students, for three days, the topic of debate and pro-
fanity has been your humble servant. There is one conso-
lation, however, that while my name is damned in the
most brimstone fashion by the segment of Southerners, it
is defended with equal pertinacity, tho' with less swearing
by the great body of back-bone Northerners. In view of
the whole, I am seated, quietly grinning at the tempest
which one short sentence can start up. The most grinding
part of the whole performance is that the business has got
into the N. Y. Papers, and thus it will go through the Nation that a Class in Yale College has given a Sharpe's
Rifle. Rich fun!

Truly yours,

MOSES.[51]

Scarcely the utterance of a meek and lowly Christian, this letter is important for a number of reasons. For one thing, it is the best piece of writing which Tyler had yet done. For another, underneath the charming boyish love of a row, there is a defensive note, as if Moses felt that his family would not take this as quite the best avenue to a theological degree. And finally, it is evident that he has been fascinated by Beecher's "tremendous Speech," by his ability to raise or lower the emotional temperature of a crowd, by the exhibition of personal prowess which the meeting had shown, a fascination that has its important consequences. Perhaps, after all, the pulpit *was* an avenue to power.

So for a while theology gave way to oratory. Moses, too, would sway crowds, be master of laughter and tears in a holy cause. Returning home in the summer vacation of 1856, he threw himself into the first campaign of the Republican Party. He addressed a political rally in the town hall of St. Clair, Michigan. He delivered a Fourth of July oration at Milford in the same state.[52] No report of these speeches is available, but we may conjecture their general trend from a newspaper article which Moses sent to *The Journal and Courier* (New Haven), entitled "The Great Bugbear," after his return to New Haven in the fall. The occasion was, of course, the election of 1856 which, despite all that Moses might do,

put Buchanan into the White House. When Fré-
mont argued for the non-extension of slavery, Robert Toombs announced that "the election of Fré-
mont would be the end of the Union, and *ought* to
be"; whereupon Moses set out to prove that both
Jefferson and Clay would have agreed with Fré-
mont, and, more fiery than the fiery Southrons,
concluded:

> We shall wage the war of Fremont and Liberty, un-
> moved and unappalled by the stale and ragged threats,
> which Senators of weak nerves and small souls and
> streaked livers have always raised to scare us.[53]

Out on the Illinois prairies a tall, tired, big-boned
man was gravely asking: "This *is* a sectional question—that is to say, it is a question in its nature calculated to divide the American people geograph-
ically. . . . Who is to blame for that? Who can
help it?"[54] And a thousand reckless young men were
daily increasing the difficulties which he was to
shoulder in the White House five years later. But
Moses was young and unprophetic: when he came
to be graduated, his address was entitled "Heaven
Fights on the Side of Great Principle," and (following Carlyle)[55] he declared that "the first of all Gos-
pels is this: that a *lie* cannot live forever." Against
Satan, against the shufflers of this world, the Christian needs must speak his "latent conviction," for

God is on his side. *The New Haven Daily Palladium* for July 31, 1857, thought it was the best oration on the program. The more cautious *New York Herald* said that "as regarded mere elocution Mr. Tyler excelled all other speakers and frequently 'brought down the house' by his earnest and manly defense of the right."[56] The words were out of Carlyle and Emerson, the oratory, one imagines, was that of Beecher. The beliefs were Lincoln's beliefs, too, but Lincoln was more patient with God.

Elisha did not live for that happy moment when his son received his bachelor's degree: Fate played him one more sorry trick. On Saturday, January 17, 1857, Moses received the last letter he was ever to have from his father, and "feeling assured that he was near the end of this earthly life, I instantly packed my travelling bag and started for Detroit." It was snowing heavily; Tyler and young Andrew D. White were snowbound in New York until the following Tuesday; it took thirty hours to reach Albany, and Moses did not reach Detroit until the 23d—a journey of almost a week. His father was still living, and, despite the "great journey and a great expense," it was something to have contributed a little "towards making his downward slope more happy."[57] A sad young man started back one wintry day for New Haven.

The financial problem was pressing, too, and

Moses, bewildered, scarcely knew where to turn.
Partly from necessity, partly from dissatisfaction
with theology, he taught school during his senior
year (and thereafter) in the establishment of a Mr.
A. W. Skinner of New Haven, who thought his
young helper "a very skillful, spirited, and success-
ful teacher."[58] Moses continued to assist Mr. Skinner until after he entered the theological seminary.
He also assisted Professor Mark Bailey in his classes
in elocution among the theologians.[59] But these
dashes at independence did not stop the iron march
of destiny. Following upon his graduation he felt
compelled to enter the Yale Theological Seminary
—where, fortunately, he had to pay neither tuition
nor room rent. But despite the "hopeful piety and a
liberal education" which he dutifully displayed for
admission, he was never graduated from the seminary, or from any other theological institution.

Except for a list of theological books he borrowed
from the Yale Library, we learn very little of this
year in his life. One surmises that the passage out of
undergraduate life left him lonely; that the shock
of his father's death, coupled with a deepening sense
of responsibility, made him graver. Whether he
was touched by the wave of revivalism in 1857 we
do not know. We have from this period but one forlorn letter—to his widowed mother, in which he
tries to comfort her with the thought that "we all

love you, and with six loving children upon earth, you must not feel that you are alone."[60] Did he find his studies lacking in vigor? We know only that the seminary was in its decline, that Moses remained in it for only one year. One conjectures that he would have left earlier had it not been for Jeannette Hull Gilbert—but of that, more hereafter. At any rate, at the conclusion of the year (spring of 1858), he removed to Andover "for one year only, as an independent student . . . designing to make Park's lectures my chief work."[61] Just past his majority, he could look back upon a life of perpetual change in a kaleidoscopic background. He was neither westerner nor easterner, neither theologian nor literary man. He was uncertain, lonely,[62] and restless. Perhaps Andover might hold the peace[63] he longed for. So, though "I have had many pressing invitations from western ministers to go West when I get ready to settle,"[64] Moses remained immovable in New England.

In going to Andover, despite his pretence of being an "independent student," Tyler was, in his search for faith, really marching backward. Andover Theological Seminary had been opened in 1808 at Andover, Massachusetts, as a fortress of old-time Trinitarian doctrine against the rising tide of theological liberalism, turning a frowning line of guns against both the heresies of Harvard [65] and the more pallid

liberalism of Yale.[66] Other institutions might waver;
Andover, with its "ministerial candidates trained as
they never had been in America,"[67] represented the
fascisti of the Lord. Under the statutes every professor was required to assent to the Westminster
Assembly Shorter Catechism and to declare his belief "that ADAM, the federal head and representative of the human race, was placed in a state of pro-
bation, and that, in consequence of his disobedience,
all his descendants were constituted sinners; that
by nature every man is personally depraved, desti-
tute of holiness, unlike and opposed to God . . .
morally incapable of recovering the image of his
CREATOR . . . [and] justly exposed to eternal
damnation. . . ." And "I moreover believe that
God, according to the counsel of his own will, and
for his own glory, hath foreordained whatsoever
comes to pass, and that all beings, actions, and
events, both in the natural and moral world, are
under his providential direction."[68] The shrewd
founders left no loophole through which heresy
might creep or intrude or climb into the fold. For
there was also an "Associate Foundation," the special creation of the Hopkinsian group in Newbury-
port, the regulations of which provided that every
professor "shall sustain the character of a discreet,
honest, learned, and devout Christian; an orthodox
and consistent Calvinist"; that no faculty member

might be appointed until the board of visitors had approved of his theology after an examination of it; and that the faculty should express a willingness to "inculcate the Christian faith" in opposition "not only to Atheists and Infidels, but to Jews, Papists, Mohammedans, Arians, Pelagians, Antinomians, Arminians, Socinians, Sabellians, Unitarians, and Universalists." Also every professor was required to repeat his statement of faith every five years.[69] Such was the institution founded on the eternal rock of Calvin[70] to which Tyler turned for guidance.

Repellent as this seems to us, Andover was more than Calvinism, and had its attractions. For one thing, there was the natural beauty of its surroundings,[71] and Moses was growing sensitive to nature.[72] For another, Calvin Stowe had joined the faculty in 1852 after various theological misadventures in Ohio and Maine, and if "my poor rabbi" with his long, flowing beard spent a good deal of his energy in walking to his son's grave in the cemetery, "submissive but not reconciled,"[73] it was something to one who hungered and thirsted after literature to know that (between trips to Europe) the author of *Uncle Tom's Cabin,* that "little bit of a woman —somewhat more than forty, about as thin and dry as a pinch of snuff" and "never very much to look at,"[74] lived in "The Cabin" (made over from the former gymnasium), even though in 1858–59 she was "weak and miserable" over son Henry's tragic death. She also suffered "distressing doubts as to Henry's spiritual state."[75] Still, a literary lioness is a lioness, however mournful; and one could gaze respectfully at the converted gymnasium which had given birth to the *Key to Uncle Tom's Cabin, The Minister's Wooing,* and *The Pearl of Orr's Island.* Andover had also a mild social life of a Christian and strictly conventional sort; even the lioness spoke enthusiastically of "a levee at Professor Park's last week—quite a brilliant affair," "a fishing party to go to Salem beach and have a chowder" with "these agreeable people," not to speak of singing "When I Read My Title Clear" in company on the top of Prospect Hill.[76] And "all the young men are so gentlemanly and so agreeable, as well as Christian in spirit." The class of 1859, for example, which included William H. Ward, a future editor of *The Independent,* Charles Ray Palmer, a future archæologist, John H. Shedd, later a distinguished missionary; and the class of 1860, which included Henry M. Alden, who was to guide the destinies of *Harper's Magazine,* and who had reached Andover after the most incredible struggles.[77] Moses rather liked the place; ten years later he wrote that "my one year at Andover was indeed well filled with real study and has left a taste of sweetness which delights me still."[78] Whether the sweetness resulted

from Professor Park's Calvinism is, however, doubtful; one rather feels that it sprang from a sense of
independence, from a feeling of temporary security, and from reading books that were far from
theological. Moses loved literature; theology was a
chore.[79] It was his fate never to be satisfied with the
immediate occupation in hand.

He left Andover without a degree in divinity,
and probably it was just as well. He wrote later of
the "feverish dissipations of my brief clerical career,
from the autumn of 1859 to the autumn of 1862,"[80]
and beneath the humor, one senses relief that he is
out of it. Despite its charms, there was something
unhealthy about Andover and its close, theological
brooding. One feels it in the life of the Stowes. Calvin Stowe had, or thought he had, the power to see
spirits,[81] and his wife, following the death of the beloved Henry, took up spiritualism (she later ex-
changed views with Mrs. Browning), and, just before Tyler arrived, was writing to Lady Byron that
"I think very much on the subject on which you
conversed with me once—the future state of retri-
bution," and of "the doctrine . . . of an eternal
persistence in evil necessitating eternal punishment,
since evil induces misery by an eternal nature of
things. . . ." She could only hope that "the number of the redeemed may therefore be infinitely
greater than the world's history leads us to sup-

pose."[82] So it was not a healthy place, at bottom, and it was well for Moses that he lingered only a year. As he wrote his uncle three years later, "I was not built for a parson."[83]

CHAPTER III

YOUNG Tyler was in love. The lady in the case was Jeannette Hull Gilbert, daughter of Jesse Gilbert, of New Haven. Moses had met her during his student days at Yale. The picture of her as she was in 1857, preserved in Mrs. Austen's biography, shows us a serious, sweet-faced young woman clad in a more than usually hideous costume of the period and wearing a black bonnet with ribbons down her back accentuating the long, oval outlines of the face. The smooth hair is parted in the middle above the broad, high forehead, the level brows, and the direct, heavily lidded eyes, set wide apart. The nose is full and long, the mouth level and kind, with a lingering amusement flirting in its corners; a mouth which, contradicting the level gaze of the eyes, hints at humor—a quality in her which Tyler's letters also imply. The chin is well rounded and determined, but a pair of tiny ear-rings suggests the saving weakness of a decorous vanity. The preposterous dress lets us discern little else save for the narrow, sloping shoulders. Jeannette Gilbert Tyler was devoted to her husband, and he to her, and if she figures in no dramatic episodes in Tyler's biography, she proved to be the faithful, quiet, and devoted companion of almost half a century of domestic happiness. In the midst of the manifold uncertainties of Tyler's temperament, she was always quiet, serene, and calm. He loved her with single-hearted devotion. She was the "dearest Jeannette," the "dearest old lady," the "dearest gurrl" of innumerable letters, whether these are written when Tyler was thirty or sixty, whether he was pouring out his grief over Burnside's defeat during the Civil War, or bantering her in 1895 because "your old gentleman" was getting on in years.

It was delightful to be in love, but if one were to marry, it was necessary to find a paying job. The elocution teaching and the fiery oratory of Beecher had had their effect in shaping Tyler's thirst for personal expression; for, not to speak of the "many pressing invitations" to go West which we have noted, he had already been invited to appear in some notable pulpits. While Moses was still a theological student at Yale, the impressive Noah Porter, future president of Yale, a disciple of Coleridge, professor of "Moral Philosophy and Metaphysics" and at that time also pastor of the Farmington Church, had requested the young man to supply his pulpit;[1] and the more or less radical Bushnell had that same year invited him to address his flock at

Hartford.[2] Evidently there was good stuff in the lad. Supplying pulpits, however, does not permit matrimony. Suddenly, out of the blue, came a request that Tyler become pastor of the little Congregational church at Owego, New York. Nine days after his twenty-fourth birthday, on August 11, 1859, he assumed his charge; the 24th of August he was ordained by Doctor Kitchel, who came to Owego for the ceremony; and on the 26th of October he was married.[3]

Owego, the county seat of Tioga County, lies in the heart of the rolling hills of south central New York, a few miles north of the Pennsylvania line, on the north bank of the Susquehanna River. In the fifties, "besides the court house, jail, and county clerk's office," it boasted an academy, some sawmills, and "a number of stores and manufactories"; and "such was the abundance of water for the convenience of the farmers" that a contemporary gazette gravely assures its readers that "famine is at present little dreaded in this region."[4] The village of Owego, with a population of about 3,000, originally supported four separate churches. Young Washington Gladden, laboring in 1859 to instill the rudiments of learning into seventy or eighty pupils in one room of the local public school ("not my trade"), pictures the fierce theological disputes over predestination, baptism, and the slavery question, which convulsed the village. Feeling ran so high, indeed, that when the young Presbyterian minister had prayed publicly for the souls of slaves, he had been compelled to leave the church and retreat to New England. But a protesting minority, whose thought (like Tyler's) was shaped by Beecher and *The Independent,* seceded, formed an abolitionist Congregational church, invited the young man back, and continued to labor for abolition, despite the wrath of the Presbyterians, and Episcopalian dislike. It was this young man, broken in health by the *odium theologicum,* whom Tyler was to succeed.[4a]

Ecclesiastical conditions in Owego were, it must be confessed, slightly primitive. The official "scribe" of the Susquehanna Association of Congregational Ministers was an "illiterate blunderer" who hyphenated the name of the Savior, putting "Chr" on the end of one line and "ist" at the beginning of the next. There were no hymn books with tunes, and usually no further support for the unpaid choir than the chorister's tuning-fork. The preaching had been mainly devoted to picturing hell as a lake of fire and brimstone, heaven as a place of blissful *dolce far niente* for the minority, and in Owego, as elsewhere, the Millerite belief that the world was shortly to come to an end was taken with literal seriousness.[5] Nevertheless, the countryside was beautiful;

young Gladden, fresh from his uncle's farm, had found Owego "a smart country seat" and thought it exciting to set type for the Owego *Gazette,* even printing his own compositions. The printer's apprentice, now committed to a ministerial career, welcomed the young preacher to his boardinghouse, read theology under Tyler's direction, delivered sermons in Tyler's church, and received a license to preach from the regional association of ministers at Tyler's instigation. It was the beginning of an important friendship. One may reasonably suppose that in their walks and talks the young men laid less emphasis upon doctrinal points and more upon the experience of living than the congregation might approve of. Gladden, moreover, had humor; he was sanitive; when Tyler left on his honeymoon, Gladden wrote Charles Tyler in Detroit "the funniest letter I ever read," a document in striking contrast to the awkward, anxious epistle which Tyler wrote his uncle to announce the event. Gladden's letter also gives us our first word-picture of the future historian:

He is about five feet six inches high—broad shouldered —has very light hair—walks fast, and has the appearance of being in a hurry when in the streets. He has a youthful appearance—could not be taken to be more than twenty-one years old—and a stranger would consider him remarkably honest and disingenuous. When he left he wore a suit of black clothes and a black silk hat.[6]

Gladden's humorous catalogue of the worldly pos-
sessions which Tyler left behind him need not be
taken literally,[7] but the young couple were obviously not well stocked with earthly treasure. The
wedding took place in New Haven; the wedding
journey lay up the Hudson to Albany, then across
New York for the canonical visit to Niagara; and
afterwards (by boat presumably) to Detroit, that
the admiring family might make the acquaintance
of the bride.[7a] After their return to Owego, the Tylers apparently continued to live in the boarding
house which had previously sheltered the groom.

In Owego the long winter drew slowly to a close,
the gradual spring painted the New York hills an
airy green, while, more and more ominous, a low
thunder growled in the southern sky. The Tylers
had scarce returned when John Brown went out to
execution under the Virginia heaven ("The road to
heaven," said Theodore Parker, "is as short from
the gallows, as from the throne. . . ."[8] In Concord
Thoreau agreed.) While the snow lay cold on the
Susquehanna countryside in February, an "assem-
blage of the intellect and mental culture" of New
York in Cooper Institute was hanging breathless
on the solemn words: "Let us have faith that right
makes might, and in that faith, let us, to the end,
dare to do our duty as we understand it"; and with
the April violets, the Democratic Party was com-

mitting temporary suicide at Charleston, which celebrated the event with bonfires and music. Meanwhile Washington Gladden had departed for his
first pulpit—in Le Raysville, Pennsylvania,[9]—and
the Tylers were expecting a child—Jessica, born
August 9 in the fateful year of 1860. Why linger in
Owego? The world—Tyler's world—was crumbling away, and though he did not know it, his work
as a minister was not to outlast the earthquake of
civil war. He tried to console himself by reading
Cornelius Nepos: his copy, with its annotations, is
still extant.

That summer a letter arrived from the executive
committee of the First Congregational Church of
Poughkeepsie, which had dismissed its minister, the
Reverend Chauncey D. Rice.[10] Would the Reverend
Mr. Tyler be interested in supplying their pulpit for
a year, with the possibility of permanent appointment?[11] The Reverend Mr. Tyler firmly declined
anything so indefinite, and waited hopefully to see
what the committee would do next. The committee
deliberated for six agonizing months. Tyler's record
at Owego was none too good.[12] But at length they offered him the post as their regular pastor at the salary of $1200, the duties to begin at once.[13] Twelve
hundred dollars! What could not one do with
twelve hundred dollars? And a new church?[14] And
a larger congregation?[15] The Tylers left at once for

larger fields of usefulness, and Moses was formally installed on February 7, 1861.

All in all, things seemed to be looking up. Poughkeepsie was then a city of some 15,000; its location (half way between Albany and New York) made it an important place for river and railway traffic, and one was in the stream of things. Moreover, Washington Gladden had been called to Brooklyn,[16] not so very far away, and the revered Kitchel journeyed east in the spring to carry a message of gratitude from Michigan to New England for evangelizing the West, speaking before the Congregational Library Association in Boston.[17] In comparison with Owego, Poughkeepsie, high on the river bank between its two promontories, "compactly built, spacious, and well paved," was a metropolis; "on a busy day, the throng upon Main-street would do no discredit to the principal thoroughfares of a large city."[18] A sophisticated city with educational facilities: a mile back from the river and high on a hill, the Poughkeepsie Collegiate School, "modelled after the Parthenon at Athens" and costing ("exclusive of the ground")[19] some $40,000, shed a classical air, inviting the Muses. Within a year of his arrival, Tyler was participating in a home-talent production of *Much Ado About Nothing*.[20] A place of bustle, of progress, before which the Hudson, rolling on "in its pride and beauty, dotted with the

sails of inland commerce and numerous steamboats,"[21] continually reminded the new minister
that he had moved from the little world into the
great.

Events were marching; the old United States was
crumbling away. The thunder from the South grew
ever more ominous; and Moses, who had begun
keeping a diary when he was ordained, recorded his
doubts, his anxieties, his dissatisfactions during these
tremendous days. He felt he must speak out; and
as the unheroic Buchanan administration lay dying,
Tyler summoned his forces and, not yet a month
in his new office, delivered, on March 3, 1861, the
first epochal utterance of his ministerial career—a
sermon on "Our Solace and Our Duty in This Crisis." He repeated the doctrine of his commencement
oration, the abolitionist doctrine that the duty of his
hearers was to stand immovably for the Right, and
to oppose all compromise. (In Washington, General Scott was anxiously considering his military
preparations for the morrow.) Let the Union be
dissolved if slaves can be freed no other way under
the Constitution, for "if adhering to the right will
not save the Union, then the Union is not worth
saving." (It was Garrison's doctrine.) Christians
might solace themselves, however, with the conviction that God would not suffer his beloved republic
to be divided against itself. "From 1620 to 1783,"

said Tyler, waxing wildly unhistorical, "this nation was swathed and baptized in prayer." The founding fathers had done their imperfect best; we should not blame, but improve upon, them: for

it was bad enough ever to concede this great system of wickedness. But to make such concession in 1783, in 1820, in 1850, was a very different thing from doing it in 1861. *They* sinned: but it was with a moral sense upon this subject only partially educated.

Poughkeepsie rang with his words. At the request of one group the sermon was published in pamphlet form,[22] but the columns of the Poughkeepsie *Telegraph* shook with denunciation of language thought to be too fiery for the Christian pulpit. Defenders spiritedly referred to Jesus scourging the money changers out of the temple, and then or a little later, a parishioner wrote him applauding his courage in daring to "come home to the live beating heart of the age."[23] . . . And seven days before this letter a shell had risen from the South Carolina batteries near Fort Johnson and traced its fiery curve towards Fort Sumter. And four days earlier Lincoln had called 75,000 militia into service for three months. And in Detroit, there were massmeetings where 3000 school children sang "The Star-Spangled Banner" in shrill voices, and John Tyler was enlisting in the 1st Michigan Infantry.[24]

By summer Moses was pacing the floor, or pausing to write frantic letters to Michigan:

It is about six o'clock and I am plunged in gloom over the tidings from Washington [first Bull Run]. . . . O horrors! horrors! horrors! . . . It is the attribute of a good cause that it must rise mightier even from disasters. And this infamy shall be wiped out. I have watched the position of Johnny's division throughout. We know not but the poor boy has been slain. I see it stated that Colonel Wilcox is killed. Probably John's regiment was in the thickest and deadliest of the fight.[25]

But John had not been slain, and was to fight on until a minor battle in Tennessee sent one musket ball through his left side and another through his arm.[26]

What good was it to be a minister in such times? What good to preach sermons with a world on fire? And yet, what could Moses do? Worry and responsibility had broken him in health, and on October 20, 1862, Tyler resigned the pastorate he had occupied less than two years. He had been a minister less than three. He retreated to Boston to regain his health and composure, and wrote his uncle how kind his congregation had been, and how impossible it was to go on:

. . . my whole state seemed so weak, incapable of work, and perpetually shivering on the brink of good-for-nothingness. . . . I was thoroughly disgusted and discouraged. Moreover, the doctors told me what my own consciousness confirmed, that this sort of business could not safely go on a great while longer. . . . When I brought the matter before the church, they urged me not to resign, but take an indefinite leave of absence; they would continue my salary and send me to the Mediterranean, to China, to the West Indies, and I presume to the Devil, if they believed the old gentleman could have restored me. I appreciated their kindness and most respectfully declined it. I did not wish the church to hold a mortgage on me to such an extent.[27]

What could he do next? He fancied for a time that his future lay with literature rather than with theology: his diary, during the years of his pastorates as during the years of his theological study, is filled with extracts from the literary classics,[28] and "if I had a little cottage and a few acres of land in the country," he thought, "I would take my little family and my books thither and would devote myself exclusively to literary pursuits."[29] One thing seemed sure: ". . . I shall bid good-bye to clerical life. I was not built for a parson."[30] (Twelve years later he was preaching again; twenty-one years later he became an Episcopal clergyman.) But how was he to live by literature in such times as these? Must he leave Poughkeepsie permanently?

In that enterprising city a new venture in education was taking shape, financed by a wealthy brewer who believed that "woman, having received from her Creator the same intellectual constitution as man, has the same right to intellectual culture and development."[31] Two miles east of the courthouse, a college building, modelled on the Tuileries, was nearing completion, and the first faculty of Vassar College was being gathered—of Vassar Female College, to be exact, but the adjective was removed at the suggestion of Mrs. Hale, the editor of *Godey's Lady's Book,* on the ground that "the word 'female' degrades woman, classing her merely with all animals that bear young."[32] People outside of Poughkeepsie (and a few within) thought that the college also might degrade woman,—Professor Alpheus Crosby, for example, writing in *The Massachusetts Teacher* in September, 1861, to deplore the construction of this "great boarding school or convent," involving "the multitude of cares, expenses, annoyances, restraints, vexatious regulations, and evil influences . . . incident to the amassing of so many persons in one community."[33] Professor Crosby, in fact, attacked the whole economy of the plan.

Thereupon Moses rushed to the rescue, chivalrously occupying twenty pages of *The New Englander* in October, 1862,[34] with a gallant and heated defence of Poughkeepsie, that "fair old Dutch city"; of the physical plan (including, as it did, "an appropriate bathing house"); of Matthew Vassar, who "fought his way up to the high figures from zero" (Moses paid tribute to "Home Brewed Ale," but he hurried over the brewery); of the curriculum and regulations which, taken together, would constitute "an elaborate and magnificent literary hotel." He roundly contradicted Professor Crosby ("surely wholesale is cheaper than retail"), for "the principals of the largest and best female seminaries in the United States will bear unanimous witness that, other things being equal, young ladies residing in the seminary make better scholars and nobler women, than those who can be reached only during the hours of school duty." He paid tribute to President Milo Parker Jewett, who had left the South to "breathe the free air of his native North," and, with an excited and immensely erudite survey of the status of women in all ages, he reached the triumphant conclusion that "the meanness of masculine jealousy is being shamed out of the world. The day is breaking for woman. The chivalry of the soul is to commence its golden era—never to close." The Vassar authorities were pleased; they arranged to print 600 separate copies of the article, and sent their champion a check for fifty dollars.[35] They even went further and spoke informally of a professorship, and "I may conclude to accept it."[36] But either the offer was never formally made, or, if made, never accepted, and another door was closed.

There is apparently no record of so important a family decision, but the Tylers separated, Jeannette and the baby, with the furniture, going to live with relatives in Joliet, Illinois, in the autumn of 1862, while Moses lingered in Boston.[37] The war lay heavy on his mind. What was Johnny's fate to be? Burnside crossed the Rappahannock, and by December Tyler was writing that "all these general rays converge to a searching focus in the thought of Johnny's possible fate."[37a] And yet when news of Burnside's bloody defeat reached Tyler a week before Christmas, though he found it "very discouraging," fearing that "we have neither statesmen nor warriors" ("I cannot but admire the magnificent conduct of the Southern chieftains both in council and in fight"), he was able to dismiss the loss of 15,000 men in three lines of a letter, the bulk of which is devoted to Ralph Waldo Emerson. For amid Tyler's discouragements, two interests commenced to loom larger and larger: one was the fact that he was treading the classic ground of Boston, made sacred by transcendentalist and abolitionist alike; and the other was his exercises under Doctor Dio Lewis, proprietor of the Normal Institute for Physical Education. His literary interests and his "musical gymnastics" were bringing healing to Tyler's body and soul.

It was exciting to see Emerson, Elizabeth Peabody, Garrison, Wendell Phillips, Frederick Douglass, and other great heroes of the cause, exciting to see them moving about Boston—"the brain of this continent, the great idea-builder and thought-radi-

ator"[38]—much like anybody else. One Saturday evening, when Tyler was sitting in the Public Library,
Emerson came in to read the papers—Tyler knew
it must be Emerson, it could not be anybody else.[39]
He got Elizabeth Peabody—"a remarkable woman,
although a sight of her bulky form and pulpy face
and watery eyes and a few minutes spent in hearing
her talk about kindergartens" might not impress a
stranger—to tell him about Emerson, his method of
composing, his reading, the "great blank book
which he calls his diary," his mirthfulness at home,
his rigid truthfulness. Another time he was at the
Garrisons', and Wendell Phillips came; and two
weeks later, he summoned up courage to call on
that great man and talk with him, finding him
"frank, candid, and delicate," approving of Doctor
Lewis, approving of lecturing tours if you managed
them right, approving of Moses Coit Tyler. In January there was a mass meeting because emancipation
had gone into effect, a meeting under the patronage
of Longfellow, Lowell, Emerson, Whittier, Holmes,
and others; and in February General McClellan
("a magnificent form in its proportions") affably
shook Tyler's hand. What a place was Boston!
Poughkeepsie was a mere "big Dutch village" in comparison. But Boston! In Boston, "great scholars, orators, poets, philosophers are sprinkled in the throng
of the streets; while through the mass of the people

are (*sic*) diffused an intense activity of mind, culture, thought." He poured out his enthusiasm in letters addressed to "my own dearest wife,"[40] who was expecting a child. Jeannette came to Boston during the winter, where Edward Scott Tyler (named for Moses' deceased brother) was born on January 3, 1863.[40a]

In the meantime Tyler's health was improving under the regimen of Doctor Dio Lewis, the godfather of physical education in the United States, a full-bearded, vigorous, crusading sort of man, born in 1823, a student (but not a graduate) at Harvard Medical School, a homeopathic physician in Buffalo, who, disgusted with "pill-bullets shot from the regular professional blunderbuss" and "orthodox drug decoctions" of the day,[41] had been for the last decade vigorously lecturing the country on the need of gymnastics. Now he had come to Boston, first to open a gymnasium and then to found The Normal Institute of Physical Education,[42] wherein Tyler had enrolled. Orthodox medical practitioners eyed him askance,[43] but Lewis was too full of reforming zeal to be stopped: in seven years 500 students were graduated from the Institute, to whom Lewis's *New Gymnastics* (1862), an immensely popular work, was a new gospel of health and freedom. The gymnasium at 20 Essex Street became the mecca of pedagogues; in August, 1860, the American Institute of

Instruction, then holding its annual meeting in Boston, invited Lewis to appear before it, sent a committee to investigate him, visited the gymnasium, and voted "that the members of this Institute have . . . witnessed with great pleasure and interest the exercises in gymnastics, under the direction of Doctor Lewis."[44] The public flocked in. There were exercises with dumbbells, with rings, with wands, with clubs, with "Birds' nests" ("this is a new kind of exercise, and a favorite in the gymnasium," intended to correct stooping).[45] The costumes for men were modelled after that of Garibaldi, except that "buttons should be placed on the inside of the belt, the same as on gentlemen's pants for suspenders, and the same kind of suspenders should be worn"; and the "female costume" was a triumph of ugliness.[46] And thus astonishingly arrayed, men and women (chastely separated), especially the ailing, swung dumbbells to music or threw bean bags at each other, an exercise which "cultivates a quickness of eye and coolness of nerve very desirable."[47] The Lewis exercises were an irresistible combination of fun, hygiene, æsthetics, and morality: "the exercises are arranged to music, and when performed by a class, are found to possess a charm superior to that of dancing." Their creator hoped "that his humble labors may contribute something to the beauty and vigor of his countrymen."[48]

In the pursuit, at any rate, of vigor, Tyler donned his Garibaldi costume and swung dumbbells in the "revolving mill exercise" or the "tunnel circle exercise" with the others. He forgot theology, forgot Johnny, forgot the war, he even forgot Emerson and literature. He felt himself growing stronger, felt even (volatile temperament!) that he might abandon theology, literature, journalism, and oratory, to enlist under this new crusader in the cause of health. He wrote his uncle in November:

> Thus far the experiment works well. Freedom from the exhausting care of a parish, together with the healthful exercise of Dr. Lewis's gymnastic system, are working wonders upon me. Already am I beginning to feel myself a new man. I keep myself as cheerful as I can under the circumstances. . . .
>
> Perhaps for a year or so I may devote myself to this new profession of physical culture. Doctor Lewis is anxious that I should, and assures me it will pay handsomely.[49]

But this temperate suggestion scarcely indicates Tyler's mounting enthusiasm. Once it had been Kitchel, once it had been Beecher, now it was Dio Lewis, the creator of "the musical gymnastics." Here was life, here was reality! Tyler felt his body tingling with health, his mind clearing of its fatigue. He became the disciple of Lewis; and, not satisfied with that rôle, his apostle. For Lewis, nothing loath, agreed that Tyler might carry the gospel of musical gymnastics to England; and Moses, who had dawdled over his theology, and who, despite his father, despite Kitchel, despite Samuel Coit, had failed to graduate from Andover, marched across the platform in Tremont Temple to receive his diploma from the hands of the new Æsculapius. Let us look upon his picture of the event:

In the company of an audience that thronged that vast edifice and overflowed all its outward passages, a Normal Gymnastic class of ladies and gentlemen were handed their diplomas by Dr. Dio Lewis, and were sent forth under his hearty ordination upon their beneficent mission to the world. Of that class, a considerable number had come to him a few months before in delicate and even in broken health. . . . In the exuberant energy with which they careered through their exercises on that valedictory occasion, all could see the throb and ecstasy of renovated health. We parted on our several ways; some to be in New York and Philadelphia; some to go to the valley of the Mississippi; some to remain in New England, one to be a Pioneer in the work in California, and one other— he who now writes—to introduce the new system to the public of England.[50]

This revolution is astonishing enough, but the transition from the broken clergyman of the fall of 1862 to the hearty and enthusiastic propagandist of the spring of 1863 had not been without premonitions. Gladden had observed how Tyler gave the impression of irrepressible energy, an energy too explosive for the decorous conventions of the village pulpit. Moreover, even in Owego, Tyler had been thinking about the problem of the soul and the body; he contributed, for example, an article on "Saints and their Bodies" to the *Daily Press,* in which he deplores the monastic neglect of the body too common among the religious, and advises the saints to visit a gymnasium.[51] He had been scarcely a month in Boston when, probably at the instigation of Lewis, he had addressed the Ladies Physiological Society (delightful name!) on "Christian Education,"[52] and, judging by *The Brawnville Papers,* one surmises that he preached the gospel that

since every part of our nature is the sacred gift of God, he who neglects his body, who calumniates his body, who misuses it, who allows it to grow up puny, frail, sickly, mis-shapen, homely, commits a sin against the Giver of the body.[53]

The sentiments were to be re-affirmed by Theodore Roosevelt; they were the sentiments of Hughes in *Tom Brown at Oxford,* a book that Tyler was to read after he reached London;[54] but how far Tyler was acquainted with the movement of "Muscular Christianity" in England, in the absence of any study of the vogue of Kingsley and the rest in this country, does not appear.[55]

These were but surface indications of the change;

one feels that a spiritual revolution has also taken shape. Tyler's disgust with old-line theology, with the wrong-headed asceticism of Andover, with the narrow piety of village religion, may be gauged from *The Brawnville Papers,* published before the memories of his pastoral experience had greatly faded. The village doctor who has some doubts about the Lewis gymnastics is treated with sympathy in this volume, but Deacon Snipps and his daughter Jerusha, types of New England pharisees, are caricatured with heavy-handed scorn. The deacon, who holds that a gymnasium in Brawnville "would be a most wicked concession to a carnal spirit" and who "doesn't think it becoming in a minister of the meek and lowly Jesus to skate," is unsparingly ridiculed.[56] Another portrait obviously transcribed from experience is that of the Reverend Job Fearful, pastor of the first church in Brawnville, "one of those superlatively modest and angelic dispensers of the Gospel, who, devoting their lives to the salvation of other people's souls, have never the courage to say that they have any souls of their own."[57] One feels, too, that the discussion of Henry Kirk White in that volume has been reenforced by memories of American theological seminaries. Tyler's comment is vigorous:

Success is the mother of imitation; and the unintended evil of Kirk White's radiant and rose-watery career in-

fected the colleges of Christendom. Straightway we had a
plague of Kirk Whitelings—emaciated, long-haired, big-
eyed, pious, and moony young gentlemen, who excelled in
Homer and hypochondria; cultivated prayers, poesy, and
dyspepsia; made tender reference in rhyme to their lyres,
their lutes, and their longing to be no more; sauntered
languishingly by purling brooks, when they ought to have
been kicking the football; sat up, burning an extravagant
quantity of midnight oil, when they had been much more
profitably employed snoring in their bunks; and, while
confounding the twinges of a morbid conscience with the
pangs of indigestion, and, while mistaking the depression
of abused nerves for an angelic summons to leave this Vale
of Tears, they awaited, somewhat impatiently, the time
when they also should become Martyrs to Science, be-
moaned and canonized by the principal Parish Sewing
Societies of the civilized world.

If this sort of thing had continued . . . it is probable
that . . . the word Learning would have suggested lanki-
ness, lassitude, and long hair; the chief purpose of going
to college would have been to acquire the dead languages,
an interesting cough, the tearful sympathy of old women,
and an early death. . . .[58]

The writer of this passage was a very different being
from the callow youth who had celebrated the passing of a young Liverpool minister at the age of
twenty-six. Tyler had read Hughes and Kingsley, it is
true, before he wrote this, but nonetheless, however
much *The Brawnville Papers* may owe to Dio
Lewis and British "muscular Christianity," and
however bad a book it is in many ways, the pages
of Tyler's first volume fairly sing with the joy of his

deliverance from the tyrannies of Andover and the pulpit, of Yale and Kitchel, of Uncle Samuel Coit and forced companionship with the Deacon Snipps's of this world.

And finally the change wrought in Tyler was not merely eupeptic and emotional, it was a philosophic one as well. He did not dwindle into a mere leader of calisthenic exercises; he did not accept Lewis's musical exercises until he had found a philosophic bridge out of Calvinism to the gymnasium. Nothing seems more naïve, but nothing is more significant, than the array of transcendental authority which Tyler marshals behind the outward show of dumbbell swinging and moving wands to music. The vast, miscellaneous reading poured into his notebooks is drawn upon to uphold the new evangel of health. A whole introductory page in *The Brawnville Papers* is given over to quotations from Bacon, Seneca, Salzmaun (*sic*), Emerson, Laurence Sterne, and Thomas Hughes; and the Platonic dialogues, as we have noted, are enlisted in the cause of respectability and exercise. Tyler quotes more than once from Bacon to the effect that:

For Athletique, I take the subject of it largely, for any point of ability whereunto the body of man may be brought, whether it be of activity or of patience; whereof activity hath two parts, strength and swiftness; and patience likewise two parts, hardness against wants and ex-

tremities, and endurance of torments. Of these things the
practices are known, but the philosophy that concerneth
them is not much inquired into.[59]

But it was precisely the philosophy of athletics that
Tyler inquired much into. He pillaged his reading
to prove that physical exercise, in the eyes of great
thinkers, is pleasing to God and man, the true duty
of a professing Christian, "a sacred ritual for each
day's service," the fulfillment "of a great edict of
Nature," and of "man's moral duty to have a good
digestion."[60] He was troubled lest "the sanitary re-
former" might fall "into the hideous fallacy of
ignoring God,"[61] and with the gravity of a judge
weighing precedent decisions, he balanced Milton
against Dryden, *The Arabian Nights* against St.
Paul, Horace Mann, and James Thomson.[62] When
he spoke in England, he was not content to demon-
strate the exercises with selected students before his
audience, as a simple and direct road to muscular
development, he had to do as he had done in de-
fending Vassar College, he had to go into the history of the thing from the remotest times, he had to
cite the Spartans, the Romans, Bacon, Bishop Potter, Scaliger, Milton's *Tractate,* John Locke, and
Herbert Spencer to prove that "the body is as essentially the subject of . . . educational care as the
mind, requiring for its development scientific preparation and earnest, conscientious practice."[63]

Doubtless there was much pioneering to be done, especially in the physical education for women,[64] doubtless the age required the adjectives "earnest" and "conscientious" if the thing were to be done. But it was part of Tyler's temperament that he could do nothing simply, not even the swinging of dumbbells. He must probe, must find a high moral purpose in abandoning the ministry for musical gymnastics. Now the conviction was full upon him that he had an appointed work to do, and in that faith he embarked for England on April 17, 1863.[65]
. . . And down in the Virginia Wilderness Stoneman's cavalry were annoying General Lee, and 120,000 men, having crossed the Rappahannock near a mansion known as Chancellorsville, were wondering what General Hooker had in the back of his mind. . . .

CHAPTER IV

ENGLAND! The England of John Bright and Gladstone, Lord John Russell and Benjamin Disraeli (not yet Lord Beaconsfield); England recovering from the horrors of the Indian Mutiny, now five years in the past; England grimly enduring the cotton blockade of the American Civil War. Mid-Victorian England . . . for the queen was but forty-three, and wrapped in her widow's weeds ("My *life* as a *happy* one is *ended!*")[1] and, despite national sympathy, a wave of unpopularity (remarked by Tyler in his *Glimpses of England*) was beginning to lap against the throne. Lord Palmerston was grimly enjoying his last appearance on the great stage of the world; Lord John Russell was beginning to cast anxious glances at his withering figure. Dickens was inviting the paralytic stroke which came a little later by reason of his incessant readings, and Thackeray, laboring at *Denis Duval,* was never to finish his last novel. In 1863 *East Lynne* was a relatively new book, and *Lady Audley's Secret* was even newer; Edward Lear was publishing the *Book of Nonsense,* and *Alice* was not yet even heard of (think of the Victorians without *Alice!*). *Romola* came out; and the public was anxiously

awaiting Mr. Tennyson's next volume, which
proved to be *Enoch Arden*. Some people were beginning to talk about Mr. Browning; a queer group
of fanatic painters and poets, whom Dickens had
roundly charged with immorality, were making a
fuss over a strange pamphlet by one Edward Fitz-
gerald, said to be translated from the Persian, and
an odd, red-headed boy, staying with his cousins
on the Isle of Wight, was writing an amazing thing
all about fate and death and love called *Atalanta in
Calydon*. Into the midst of this exciting, oddly different world the *Victoria* bore Moses Coit Tyler,
depositing him on English shores after a passage of
eighteen days.

The family remained in Illinois for a time, though
Jeannette, the children, and Susannah Tyler joined
him later.[2] Upon his lonely arrival (May 5, 1863)
he journeyed to London, living at No. 11 Craven
Street, Strand, with a Mrs. Henley; he "went directly" to his lodging, rang the bell, said "How do
you do?" "and went to my room, where I sit now
perfectly at home." He had no difficulties in "the
greatest city this earth ever bore upon its shaky
crust," for "I had studied the map of London so
much" that "I just walked out of the depot as familiarly as if I had been there fifty years."[3] Lewis
had apparently furnished him with proper intro-
ductions since, early in June, one finds Tyler attend-

ing a "brilliant party at Doctor Brown-Séquard's, where, in the course of the evening, I had the honor of preaching a little Muscular Christianity, and of explaining the methods of the new gymnastics." One wonders whether the demonstration was physical or theoretical. The Brown-Séquards (the wife was a niece of Daniel Webster) were apparently charmed; as they were on the point of departing for Harvard, where the husband, a distinguished physician, was to be made professor of the physiology and pathology of the nervous system, they probably gleaned some useful information from Tyler, and in return promised to help him in establishing the cause of musical gymnastics in England.[4]

Tyler lost no time. He soon founded The London School of Physical Education, in which he was chief preceptor, and started vigorously to work training pupils. He had landed in May; by July "a large and fashionable audience" in the Vestry-hall, Chelsea, was watching a class of boys from a Brompton school exercising according to the precepts of Dio Lewis. *The Weekly Record* was enthusiastic: "Their execution of these movements was in concert, and with musical accompaniment, and produced the greatest delight and enthusiasm in the spectators, who expressed their approbation by rounds of hearty applause." The audience might even be called notable, including as it did Elihu

Burritt, "the learned blacksmith," "Mrs. Bessie Inglis, the accomplished lecturer," and various school worthies; and the reporter, who thought the exercises "a rare and striking success," quoted *The New York Times* to the effect that "they are poetry in motion, and motion set to music."[5] After this triumph, inquiries came pouring in; and, by the end of the year, provincial cities like Liverpool were being told by ardent newspapers that "the system is peculiarly adapted for ladies," that "it has a great charm for all who use it in the variety and liveliness of the exercises," and that "we hope to hear of the extension of the system to many schools and institutions."[6]

Tyler became not merely the organizer of victory and the general of the campaign, but its speechmaker as well, especially in the winter of 1863–64. Always he had this hankering for public address. He had been scarce a month in London when he made it his business to hear "the famous Spurgeon" in his new tabernacle, then just two years old. Thoughtfully the American compared the orator to Beecher, who was to arrive in England that fall:

As to Spurgeon himself, he is certainly a powerful and able man, but a thousand leagues behind Henry Ward Beecher. I think his success is owing to his voice, which is rich beyond praise and modulated with great beauty; to his downright earnestness, singleness, boldness, and honesty; to his amazing fluency of speech; to his tact and knack of putting things. But he has absolutely none of Beecher's breadth of philosophic thought and ideality and spiritual creativeness.[7]

Thus wrote the former teacher of elocution, critically eyeing Spurgeon and remembering "that exquisite, wonderful, empyrean, spirituality and tenderness of filial reverence which make one of Beecher's prayers worth going around the globe to hear."[8] A more critical age was to think otherwise, but in the sixties there were many who agreed with Tyler. Seven years later, after the Tilton-Beecher scandal broke, there is a bleak line in Tyler's diary: "T.T. does not now speak to H.W. Beecher."[9] But the idol was not yet fallen; and in the autumn of 1863 Beecher came to speak before roaring audiences in Manchester, Glasgow, Edinburgh, Liverpool, and London.

Tyler spurred himself on to oratorical efforts of his own: he commenced to appear on the lecture platform in London and other cities, explaining the philosophy of musical gymnastics. His lecture was entitled "A New System of Musical Gymnastics as an Instrument in Education." After he delivered it before the College of Preceptors, March 7, 1864, the College promptly elected him to membership.[10] Besides addressing educational bodies, he spoke before health specialists, doctors, and scientists, and groups

like the Royal Polytechnic Institute, various mechanics' institutes, and literary societies.[11] This, too,
was a success. W. B. Hodgson, LL.D., F.C.P.,
thought "he had never listened to a lecture with
which he was more pleased than he had been with
Mr. Tyler's."[12] The head of the Hollywood School,
Brompton (whose pupils Tyler had trained) testified that, despite the "highly laughable consequences" following on "the awkward attempts of
beginners," the system was excellent: "the memory
especially was brought into a state of great activity,"[13] for these were mid-Victorian days when every
one was philosophical. And so the chorus increased
in volume. The Metropolitan Association of Medical Officers of Health carried a unanimous vote of
thanks to the American;[14] the London Mechanics'
Institution received the lecture "with the approbation that it well deserved."[15] *The Standard* thought
it "very striking,"[16] and *The Bethnal Green Times*
actually referred to Tyler's "genius."[17] It was all
very exciting. Once, in the autumn of 1864, when
he was lecturing on American oratory (for he commenced to broaden his scope, now that he was a success), he actually met a real, live lord in the boys'
school, not an adult, but still a lord. Fortunately the
youngster possessed "the perfect courtesy of a true
gentleman of rank," and Tyler's republican flutter
of embarrassment was not noticed.[18] And again, ap-

pearing apparently a second time before the London Mechanics' Institution, when he mentioned the name of Robert E. Lee, "a storm of cheers broke out, succeeded by hisses, and then a war of sounds tumultuous," and the mention of Lincoln provoked a similar outburst.[19] It was almost a replica in miniature of Beecher's famous Liverpool speech. Tyler commenced to taste the sweets of public power.

The original lecture continued to drape the musical gymnastics in the purple robes of philosophy, for neither Tyler nor his audiences expected to swing dumbbells for the sheer fun of the thing and without rhetoric. The speech began with a stately picture of "the mind of Lord Bacon, brooding over and methodizing all knowledge within the reach of man," and proceeded to make a majestic survey of human education, beginning with the Hebrews, to prove with supererogatory logic that "the body is as essentially the subject of its educational care as the mind, requiring for its development scientific preparation and earnest conscientious practice." He touched tactfully upon the calisthenic deficiencies of British schools, declaring that "the low tone of public appreciation upon the subject," rather than the schoolmasters, was to blame. Then he sketched briefly Lewis's theory, pointing with pride to the scientific analogy between the laws of momentum and the desirability of giving "prominence to the idea of velocity in gymnastics rather than that of weight." Lewis's scheme, he said, "adopts the plan of lively, moderate exercises, in opposition to the plan of laborious, violent, exhausting movements." And he concluded with a happy mixture of reference to tuberculosis, æsthetics, and psychology:

The great peril of our Anglo-Saxon race is from pulmonary weakness. Our gymnastics should direct their remedial enginery to that quarter. I can only hint at the peculiar benefit resulting from the habit of performing all these bodily movements in strict musical time. Whatever muscular development ensues becomes far more closely associated with the intelligence and will. The whole frame at last seems imbued with the musical principle, vitalized and permeated by some breath of harmony, grace, and accurate ease. . . . I can honestly testify, that . . . the new gymnastics rise far above the dreary level of task-work and monotonous drudgery, and are literally and permanently a pleasure. They recognize the artistic necessity of touching the play-impulse. They attempt to inaugurate, during the hour devoted to gymnastics, a sort of physical jubilee, a carnival of the emotional and vital powers.[20]

Irresistible combination! Doctor Dio Lewis gratefully remarked of Tyler: "Of all the advocates of the new system he is the most eloquent."[21]

Tyler was in fact becoming a minor person of importance; and, taking his cue from Beecher's success, he commenced to broaden the scope of his addresses to include literature and the explanation of American life, a subject on which he was always amazed to find the British both ignorant and complacent. By November he was speaking on such topics as "American Humor," "The Pilgrim Fathers," "American Oratory," and the like before a boys' school and the Greenwich Society for the Diffusion of Useful Knowledge.[22] He delivered other lectures in London and elsewhere in December, and in 1865–6, he commenced to have a considerable vogue as a public speaker.[23] Once, when he went to lecture in Newport, Wales, he was advertised as the "Great American Orator," a tribute which he recorded in his diary.[24] And he let nothing escape him that might increase his range and power.

Even before he went to hear Spurgeon, he had attended the great meeting in Finsbury Chapel, where Baptist Noel presided, and Sella Martin, the fugitive slave, and Moncure D. Conway, the Unitarian, also spoke.[25] Listening to Noel, Tyler thought him "lucid, comprehensive, and unanswerable"; and going to hear him on other occasions, came to the conclusion that this "venerable pastor" was (like himself) a believer "in the great Christ-like art of practical work."[26] Noel was clearly a success —but then, so was Spurgeon, though Spurgeon "has not said one thing which in itself greatly impressed

MOSES COIT TYLER IN ENGLAND, ABOUT 1865
From a photograph in the William L. Clements library.

me"; "his meaning was too drearily commonplace
for attention." Yet it was impossible to enter Spurgeon's tabernacle unless one came early. Thoughtfully Tyler analyzed the "grand strategy in eloquence" which this implied—Spurgeon's entrance
at the dramatically right moment, his "rich, full,
satisfying voice," his physical bigness, his fluency,
his thorough common sense and "that magnetic
overwhelming, victorious something which men
call earnestness."[27] The American pondered the
problem of power. He listened to a Madame Ver,
who told him of Gladstone and Macaulay; Gladstone he went to hear; Macaulay, he learned,
"talked just as he wrote, a stream of brilliant, epi-
grammatic, sarcastic and glowing eloquence."[28] He
lent a critical ear to a sermon by Frederick Denison
Maurice, calculated "to enrich, sweeten, humble and
strengthen the spiritual natures of those who heard
him," though the curate yawned and Tyler was not
so swept away that he could not observe how bald
Thomas Hughes was getting.[29] Or he went to hear
John Stuart Mill address a "vast public meeting"
in the summer, "the only external sign of agitation
being in the flush upon his face, and a slight nervous twitching beneath the eyes," while the speech,
interrupted by "frequent salvos of applause,"
seemed "massive, nobly simple and lucid."[30] Here,
too, was power. John Bright, whom he heard more

than once, he thought "one of the greatest exemplars of a pure, manly, and commanding eloquence that any age or any language can produce."[31] He analyzed Gladstone, Disraeli, Brougham, Lord John Russell—even the Queen. For he was becoming critical, what with his association with Conway and others, and his style, his perceptions were vastly improving.[32]

It was educative, too, to explore Great Britain—London, for instance, which "like some many-sided and opulent soul welcomes love, confidence, and even familiarity, but is unable in turn completely to reveal itself."[33] He revelled in statistics regarding its gargantuan appetites—its size, its growth, the food and drink bill of the huge metropolis. For him it was not alone a great city, but "the intellectual and moral capital of the globe."[34] Conway and he attended public meetings together, as well as private gatherings. And Tyler found it fascinating to study individuals: Clara Lucas Balfour, who had risen from cleaning doorsteps to lecturing, and Mr. Holyoake, "the most celebrated atheist now living," "a fine, intellectual, brave looking man with a woman's voice and gentle ways."[35] How Andover would have shuddered! In January, 1866, he made an excursion into western England and Wales, where men's ignorance of the United States was simply amazing: one man in Bristol told him that America had been settled by spirit-rappers about 1760 or so.[36] Cardiff utterly disgusted him, a place of "hell holes blazing and fuming," and in his diary he described in forthright terms the swinish men and beastly women he saw there. No wonder that poor people assembled in crowds before the American consulate, patiently hoping for permission to enter the United States.[37] Tyler felt his patriotism saddened and strengthened by the spectacle:

It did not nourish a boastful patriotic vanity; it was no food for national gasconade and assumption; it was a thought grander than the remembrance of our invincible citizen soldiery, of our boundless material resources; it was the simple and sacred fact that to millions in all lands who are humble and heavy-laden this word AMERICA means all that is meant by the word HOPE. These poor, sad-faced creatures, standing before the American consulate in Cardiff, seemed to symbolize the struggling masses of all the populations of Europe, their weary fight with life's hardships, their toil which returns them just enough to let them keep on toiling, their rudeness and ignorance, their unthrift, their unhappiness, and their universal looking to that star which has risen in the west, and which they think, shines not for peers, and for princes, and for taskmasters, but for men and women. And this is not a thought to build up the pyramid of national arrogance and conceit. Nay, it will rather bring tenderness to the heart and humility and tearful consecration.[38]

He was not to forget this idea when he came to write his histories.

And once he wandered into a Welsh Baptist meeting-house, an experience which he later turned into a graphic essay.[39] It was, he said, "fine; quite Druidic or Celtic"; and though he could not understand a word that was said, with his interest in oratory Tyler noted that, as the preacher approached the end of his prayer, "he reached white heat, his voice was suffused with enthusiasm; a distinct rhythm pervaded his sentences, which were delivered with a wild, strange, and rapturous chant."[40] And, in complete contrast to this experience, in the autumn he had the pleasure of piloting Louisa M. Alcott about London, "a jolly Yankee girl, full of the old Nick and thoroughly posted on English literature," as he wrote "my own darling Jennie"; when they were in Kingsgate Street, they inquired for Sairy Gamp, and "the conversation I had at the shop door with the people who thought it all earnest was killing." Miss Alcott had finally to run to the end of the street to hide her laughter.[41] In November of that year he went out to Highgate cemetery, where, for a while, nobody could tell him where Coleridge was buried, until Mr. Eagles, a seedsman, "an elderly, tall, and venerable man," directed him; Eagles told him a good deal about Coleridge, and something about Lamb. Once, when a group of the great literary men were meeting in a tavern, Mr. Eagles heard somebody give the toast, "Here's to the lasses" and then somebody else threw a large tray of glasses on the floor.[42] It was, as a matter of fact, Tyler's second visit to Highgate; he had paid his first the second Sunday he was in England, "a dreamy, sweet May day in 1863," when he had talked with Miss Howitt about Coleridge and the Gilmans, and how an ardent American admirer had once tried to buy the door of the room which Coleridge used for a study. He turned the two experiences into one of his best essays for *The Independent*.

But lecturing was not all beer and skittles; Tyler devotes a long essay in the *Glimpses* volume to picturing the peculiarities of the British attitude. Lecturing, he said, ought to be done only by first-rate men, and unfortunately in England the first-rate men either talked for no fee at all or refused to appear altogether. The "English philosophy of gentility" was the source of the difficulty. "They make a wide distinction in England between occasionally lecturing for nothing, and regularly lecturing for a fee. The one is an act of patronage; the other is an act of professional service." The audiences, too, were not broadly democratic as in the United States, but were still involved with the "ineradicable reminiscence of feudalism." "Lecturing, therefore, being the luxury of the poor, gets paid for at their price." And the lecturers, he thought, failed to deal with present reality. This was not what Lord Brougham had intended when he founded the Society for the Diffusion of Useful Knowledge; everything was now more or less second-rate.[43] It was all very annoying. But Tyler did what he could to correct British misapprehensions of the United States, a subject vastly fascinating, since some people thought that Ohio bordered on the Gulf of Mexico, others demanded why the Southern States and the Northern States did not agree on the Mississippi River as their dividing line; Stephen A. Douglas was supposed to be a capable negro, once a slave, and Henry Ward Beecher came out oddly as Mr. Beecher-Stowe.[44]

But lecturing in England was not a paying business for a man with a family to support,[45] a fact which lent poignancy to Tyler's complaints about the British attitude, nor did the musical gymnastics suffice to keep him alive. Moreover, the itch to write and to produce was still unsatisfied; he yearned to fulfill his longing for expression. Perhaps the most curious turn this eagerness took was the writing of a long, satirical poem in rhymed couplets, called *The Omnibus,* which he published anonymously in 1865. It was partly of serious intent, partly the product of high spirits, but that Tyler was desirous of retaining his anonymity, the inscription in Moncure D. Conway's copy (now in the William L. Clements Library at the University of Michigan) amply demonstrates: "To M. D. Conway with the love of The Author (qui stat nominis umbra) Mum est verbum. Dec. 14, 1865." The poem itself is vigorous, but nothing more than any clever literary man might turn out: the poet (who has read Gay and Churchill and Cowper and Crabbe) takes his seat on the top of an omnibus and surveys the great city. Unfortunately, what might have been a clever *jeu d'esprit* turns into an examination of London religion; and it is curious to see the former preacher berating High Church practices and dissenting chapels. Muscular Christianity naturally comes in for a good word, and of Tom Hughes it is observed that he shows how

"honest thought shall ever pass toll-free,"

but the forty-three pages of this little booklet add nothing to Tyler's reputation.

But verse-making, though it might satisfy his longing for expression, did not buy bread. Suppose he imitated N. P. Willis and "wrote up" his experiences. Could he not become British correspondent for some American magazine or newspaper? He had been in England long enough to make his observations valuable. And so he began his new campaign with a letter to Charles A. Dana of *The New York Tribune,* a paper which had paid him seven dollars in 1854 for an account of the Yale com-

mencement.[46] But Dana was not interested.[47] Then
he tried *The Herald of Health*,[48] a monthly magazine edited by a Doctor Trall, who held high
views of health which Dio Lewis and Tyler
shared,[49] and who, at that early date, was insisting
on the value of complete cleanliness in hospitals.
Trall, or his London agent, proved more amenable
than Dana; Tyler got one of his lectures into print
in that journal in August, 1865, and followed it
with five more articles in the following year.[50] This
was something like recognition, for the contributors
to Trall's magazine included Dio Lewis, Henry
Ward Beecher, Theodore Tilton, O. B. Frothing-
ham, and Horace Greeley. But the capacity of *The
Herald of Health* for literary articles was necessarily
limited, and Tyler next tried *The Independent,*
then edited by Theodore Tilton, and known for its
vigor and occasional coarseness of expression. His
initial article was accepted, appearing July 6, 1865,[51]
when a contract was sent him for six more at ten
dollars apiece.[52] *The Independent* liked his work,
for from 1865 to 1867 it printed not merely the
original six articles bargained for, but a total of
twenty-six articles and a sonnet on England. These
were all products of his British experiences.[53]

Tyler had found it profitable on the lecture platform to explain America to England; in his essays
he now found it profitable to explain England to

America. To appear in *The Herald of Health* was creditable, but to appear in *The Independent* was to move among the great—Louisa M. Alcott, Beecher, Garrison, Greeley, Joel Benton, Whittier, formidable as an army with banners. Ambition stirred; Tyler next tried *The Nation,* hoping to be appointed the official London correspondent. But the redoubtable Godkin had already appointed a London correspondent, and was not eager to make the newly founded[54] organ any more British in tone than necessary. Still, the idea attracted Tyler; he found the programme of the new magazine entirely to his taste,[55] and he was gratified to receive a letter from Wendell Garrison, the associate editor, advising him to send in occasional contributions.[56] Tyler's response was prompt, his first article, "American Reputations in England," appearing January 18, 1866. By 1867 he had had at least five articles accepted for that periodical.[57] He also sold six letters to *The Cincinnati Daily and Weekly Commercial,* for which he received fifty dollars.[58] But, characteristically, *The Independent,* with its mingling of liberal theology and liberal politics, became his regular organ.

There can be no doubt to the reader of Tyler's essays of 1865–7 that, after so many false starts, he had come into his own. Aside from his work as a propagandist for the ideas of Dio Lewis, Tyler's

intellectual labors in the British Isles were shaped,
it is clear, by his association with, and admiration
for, the liberal and radical thinkers of the day,
friends of the American abolitionists and oppo-
nents of secession. Tyler's enthusiasm was for John
Stuart Mill, Cobden, John Bright, Mazzini, Gladstone, Earl Russell and the like; when he wrote of
Brougham or Disraeli, though he tried to be fair, it
is evident that he has already taken his stand and
shaped his mature philosophy. The tone of his essay
on Brougham, for example, is clearly marked by
that "respectful contempt"[59] of which the essay
speaks; and in the concluding paragraph of the
Disraeli essay, one finds such sentences as: "Perhaps, after all, Mr. Disraeli may have both a conscience and a heart, accompanied, of course, by an
astonishing skill in concealing the fact—except
from his most intimate friends."[60] For radicals like
Bright and liberals like Gladstone Tyler expressed
no such dubieties. Their campaign was his campaign, the campaign of *The Nation,* of Conway, of
Beecher, of all right-thinking men, and the two nations must move shoulder to shoulder toward the
goal:

. . . when at last the armed Democracy of America, after
so many blunders and so many humiliations, proved not
only its incomparable capacity for war, but its incomparable capacity for peace—its self-control, its political

magnanimity, its new and splendid principle of loyalty and national unity,—then it was that in all civilized lands faith in government by the people awoke to a new life.[61]

So he wrote in April, 1866, proudly concluding his essay ("The New Reform Movement") by quoting from Gladstone, "the affluent, the peerless states- man," to the effect that "time is on our side. The great social forces which move on in their might and majesty, and which the tumult of our debates does not for a moment impede or disturb—those great social forces . . . are marshalled on our side . . ."[62] This was long to be Tyler's creed, deter- mining, for example, the treatment of American literature in the two great histories. Dio Lewis had rescued him from the melancholia of a minister's life; Hughes and Kingsley had shown him the dif- ference between the introspective Christianity of Andover and the possibility of living actively in the world; and the controversy in England over the American war and the second reform bill had shaped and strengthened his nascent political phi- losophy. Before the English voyage, Tyler had been an amateur fumbling after values. But in London he had won status by his own exertions; he had learned that he could write; he had learned to move easily on the plane of such men as Conway and Bright. The seal of maturity was upon him.

His writing had enormously improved. The false

and feverish rhetoric of his earlier speeches and essays was sloughed off, and the intellectual vigor of
mid-Victorian public life had passed into his blood.
His style is that of man thinking; the sentences are
lean and athletic, recalling speeches by Bright and
Cobden, and in their search for balance, their frank
acceptance of a particular point of view, the better
parts of Macaulay. And in addition these essays
have polish and suavity and grace, so that, when he
came in 1898 to collect the best of them into one
volume as *Glimpses of England,* he did not find it
necessary materially to alter what he had written
over twenty years before.

Moreover, the subject of these papers is public
life—the public life of the present as it was condi-
tioned by that public life of the past which is political history. The clash of ideas, the conflict of poli-
cies—these are his major theme; in writing of
English politics particularly, Tyler was compelled
to reckon with the sense of the past which deter-
mines British political movements. He had learned
to look backward as well as forward, had learned,
in other words, historical perspective, and something of historical method. In sounding the depths
and shallows of British opinion of the United States,
he had been compelled to mediate between two
points of view, dealing sympathetically with both,
and the lesson so learned was to stand him in good

stead when he began writing the history of earlier
American letters, particularly that of the Tory
cause. Tyler had grown to man's estate. And in
1865, while he was in London, he wrote in his commonplace book:

> It strikes me as a capital plan to write six or eight elabo-
> rate lectures on "The History of American Literature"—
> for a purely literary audience and with a view to publica-
> tion.[63]

He did not know it, but he had found his life work.

England had given him about all that England
had to give, and Tyler was determined to come
home. But how could he support himself and his
family? In March, 1866, he wrote Jeannette that he
contemplated returning to America as a professional lecturer and journalist.[64] The project was by
no means chimerical. In England he was becoming
a person so well known that travelling Americans
were sent to him with letters of introduction.[65] *The
Nation* spoke of him with respect: "Mr. M. C.
Tyler, a very creditable representative of 'Young
America' in its best sense, a graduate of one of our
colleges, and for some time a minister in this State,
has been for three years in England and Wales, for
the most part occupied in lecturing . . . we find in
the British newspapers the most favorable notices
of his performances."[66] And the London corre-

spondent of *The New York Tribune* was even more flattering:

> For the last couple of years or so there has been an American lecturing in this country, whose intended return to his own demands notice. Mr. Moses Coit Tyler came to this country [England] in 1863, partly in search of health, partly as the propagandist of the system of muscular ethics originated by Dio Lewis of Boston, to which I believe he himself was considerably indebted. In both objects he has been successful, eminently so in the latter. His popularity on a special subject probably suggested his launching out boldly into the region of history, literature, politics, wit, poetry, etc.—always as a lecturer, in which capacity he has attained such approval as, I dare be sworn, will be more than ratified on our [American] side of the Atlantic. He lectures delightfully, in a bright, easy, eloquent, thorough manner, that is half nature, half art, the two so happily blended that you can't tell where the one begins or the other ends; people come away from him quite enthusiastic in his praise. I commend Mr. Tyler to institutes and lyceums all over the country.[66a]

Finally, Oliver Johnson, associate editor of *The Independent,* wrote him that he had "made an enviable reputation among the readers" and that "of all our numerous and able writers, there is not one more popular than yourself."[67]

Should he risk it? Moses longed for his family, for America that seemed so dear and so remote. Whereupon, with remarkable practical sense, he set about creating a demand for his services. To *The*

New York Tribune and to *The Nation* he sent his press notices, and both publications obligingly called attention to him, recommending him to the lyceum circuit and to the literary societies.[68] He appointed Mr. J. H. Dudley his American representative to book lecture engagements for him from his Poughkeepsie home;[69] and he negotiated for newspaper work in the United States.[70] How many engagements Dudley secured for him is not clear—they were not many, but it was gratifying to know that one, and perhaps two, of these were for Detroit.[71] At any rate, he could not stay in England forever, and he took the plunge, sailing from Liverpool, December 5, 1866,[72] and going straight to Rockford, Illinois, to rejoin Jennie and the children for the Christmas holidays. How strange, how evanescent everything seemed! As he wrote her from Chicago: "It seems all a dream. I have not been in Rockford. I am not in America. Your next letter should be addressed" to London.[73] Home he was, however, and to stay.

But he could not remain in Rockford except for the holidays. He must work at his new-found trade. He left for Chicago early in January, where a friend scarcely recognized him, he was so changed.[74] He was discouraged to learn that it was too late in the season to hope for a regular program of lecture engagements; but he went on to Poughkeepsie to lecture, to see Dudley, to do what he could. Some engagements he made—at Worcester, New Bedford, Poughkeepsie, Gardiner, New York, Detroit. But it was not what he had pictured in England, and he wondered what he could do next. Various projects swam up towards him in his uncertainty. He had scarcely landed in America when he learned that Andrew D. White, with whom he had been snowbound in New York almost ten years before, had, after a brilliant and changeful career, just been appointed president of the new Cornell University, which was to open its doors September 7, 1868.[75] Furthermore, White wanted to do something for him. He offered to help Tyler towards the chair of history which he, White, had just vacated at the University of Michigan, or to make him a professor at Cornell.[76] Tyler hesitated. He went to Utica to reconnoitre, but the primitive condition of the campus —cows seemed to frequent every college west of the Hudson[77]—"inclined" him to think he would "not go into it."[78] Then, during July, Tyler thought of buying a newspaper in Poughkeepsie with a group of friends.[79] Before this could come to fruit, however, President Erastus O. Haven of the University of Michigan offered Tyler a visiting lectureship in elocution and history for ten weeks at $500, with the invitation to remain if he liked it.[80] The newspaper project fell through, and Tyler accepted

Haven's offer provided he might be permitted to fulfil his lecture engagements.[81] In August he went to Ann Arbor to talk with Haven, and decided to accept permanent appointment as professor of rhetoric and English literature at the University of Michigan at a salary of $1500 a year.[82]

CHAPTER V

THE University of Michigan to which Tyler thus strangely returned after fourteen years was a far different institution from the struggling frontier college he had left to enter Yale. The faculty had increased from 14 professors to 34, and the student body from 222 to 1223, including a flourishing medical college of 418.[1] Moreover, there were on the campus such notables as Edward Olney, professor of mathematics, De Volson Wood, professor of civil engineering, Thomas M. Cooley, professor of law, Charles Kendall Adams, professor of history and successor to White, and Martin L. D'Ooge, assistant professor of ancient languages. The fiery Tappan had withdrawn amid thunders and lightnings, and Professor Brünnow, the famed astronomer, had resigned in disgust at the same time, but the trend was distinctly upward. The library now contained 17,000 volumes; an observatory—probably the finest in the Middle West—had been built and was actually in use; the new law building was the wonder of the campus; a chemistry laboratory had been added; and the medical building had been expanded to accommodate the increased enrollment. New courses (the heritage of Tappan) were budding on the proliferous parent stem—law, civil engineering, physics, mining; new degrees, some of them not given anywhere else in the West, were offered; and the modern languages were rising to cast a lengthening shadow over the templed calm of Greek and Latin. The university was flooded with ex-soldiers. Successor to the redoubtable Tappan, the pacific and tactful Haven ruled until 1869, when he was called to Northwestern. By and by James B. Angell was to come—the Golden Age of Michigan.[2]

The town had grown without excitement, and regarded itself as something of an urban centre: by 1871 "there were fifteen through freight trains here each way and double tracking became imperative."[3] A new post-office was thrown open on March 24, 1865, and "drew like a circus or a star actor,"[4] and there was talk of a new courthouse, but the unterrified democracy, chiefly from Ypsilanti and Dexter, voted down this extravagance. And there were new business blocks, despite which the little city had a bucolic air. Culture, however, was certainly looking up. Doctor A. W. Chase, author of a book of medical receipts of which more than a million copies were sold, bought the *Courier* in 1869, and drifted into a squabble with Rice A. Beal.[5] The Ladies Literary Association, organized in 1866, "raised" $780.79 for books; there was a Reading Club; and in 1862 the Cosmopolitan Art Association purchased Randolph Rogers' "Nydia" and presented it to the university.[6] Nor was the faculty far behind in this exciting race; it was accustomed to meet in what were known as "Senate Sessions," when, the business being done, the wives and families and invited guests were edified with "some literary production" which formed a "leading feature" of these tremendous occasions. President Haven thought these meetings "had a tendency to promote unity and harmony," and unity and harmony, after the storm of Tappan's resignation, were very good medicine.[7] All in all, Tyler might feel pleased to come to the place, and flattered to serve in the university. The salary was not very large, but the legislature was shortly to come to the rescue of the institution.

So Tyler was happy again. He wrote his wife from New York in the summer of 1867 that he was glad she liked the move and that he "should be very happy if we could manage to go to housekeeping there. . . . We will look for a furnished house and see what can be done," and he spoke hopefully of $1500 in Ann Arbor being the equivalent of $2000 in the East.[8] Two weeks after this letter (August 9, 1867) he was to meet her in Ypsilanti; when, proceeding to Ann Arbor, they found a house at 36

East North Street (now Kingsley), overlooking the Huron hills,[9] Tyler plunged into his new duties. Much was expected of him, and he had much to expect, for he had read in *The Independent*[10] of the interest of the University of Michigan in pedagogical experiment; and undoubtedly, when he had talked with Andrew White in Albany in August, 1867, White (who showed him his library) told him of the revolution in the teaching of history which he, White, had carried out in Ann Arbor.[11] President Haven had chosen Tyler largely because of his reputation as a speaker and journalist. His main business was therefore teaching elocution and rhetoric; he had but one course in the history of literature. At first he lectured as he had been accustomed to do on the lyceum platform, but he soon found that college students needed a more informal manner. For a time he was puzzled, but he was also effective: the president, reporting to the Board of Regents after Tyler had been there a year, spoke of him as one "who by his zealous and able devotion to the English Language and Literature, and the science and art of elocution, is greatly elevating the standard of scholarship of the University in these branches of study."[12]

But Tyler, who was really a memorable teacher,[13] was not satisfied with the system. In truth, so far as English literature was concerned, conditions were ripe for reform. Michigan, to be sure, was no worse than other colleges. There as elsewhere the modern literatures, in their struggle to acquire repute, had taken over the vices of the old classical system without at the same time acquiring its virtues. The "survey" method ruled; or else, when the works of the moderns were studied directly, the classroom became a laboratory in linguistic dissection, interest being centred in grammatical structure, in punctuation, and in syntax. The beauty, the thought, the power escaped.[14] How might he, Tyler, lead his students to these healing springs? He poured out his thoughts on paper after he had been at Ann Arbor long enough to acquire experience, and his "Report to the Board of Regents" of 1872 expresses at once his dissatisfaction with the prevailing mechanisms and his glimpses of a new methodology.

His work, he said, was divided into five parts—the course in the English language which he taught to freshmen and others, his sophomore lecture course in English literature, his work in rhetoric, his labors in elocution, and the exercises in speaking and writing which he had to supervise—"the most delicate and fatiguing task that is entrusted to me." He calculated that he had commented on 182 essays and 333 speeches in one college year. Dryly dismissing the lectures on rhetoric in half a dozen lines, he spoke of the "many laborious hours" he had spent in the "private rehearsal" of student speakers, and rebelliously described the "melancholy and futile exercise of speaking in the chapel, in which the Seniors have hitherto engaged under compulsion," for which he had substituted a plan of voluntary association for extemporaneous speaking. The freshman course seemed to him (as it has seemed to how many!) a "humble task for the University to be engaged in," but he hoped he had inculcated "loyalty to our own language, and an ambition to be accurate in the use of it." But it was the course in literature which troubled him most. He had, he said, delivered ten lectures on the fourteenth century, nine on the fifteenth, and four on the sixteenth, and had held twelve recitations besides, and "the lecture room was always so crowded as to be rather uncomfortable." But "I am far from satisfied with any method yet hit upon for teaching English literature to students like ours." Scholarly inspection of all the vast bodies of literature in English being impossible, "it is my intention, next year, to take up, in a similar manner, the literature of America, and perhaps to shift the field of view with each succeeding class." It was the literature that mattered, not the textbook . . . and one student long remembered his teaching of the *Legende of Good Women*.[15] How could he bring to these eager young students the meaning of art and thought? "I have been cheered," he said, "by mani-

festations of great interest on the part of the majority
of my large class, by their polite and steady attention,
by their zeal and accuracy in taking notes . . . and in
the excellence of their preparation. . . ." He hoped
that he had given them "a good start . . . the awakening of a real love" for letters.[16]

But the "polite and steady attention" of the students was not gained without hard work on the part
of the instructor, whose zeal, knowledge, and independence of judgment held them to their tasks. It
is, of course, not possible always to know when Tyler read a book, but from the annotations which he
left in the volumes comprising his library (most of
which is now housed in the State Teachers College,
Marquette, Michigan), it is possible to watch the play
of his mind over his materials. For example, President Haven published in 1869 a textbook on rhetoric concerning which he apparently asked Tyler's
comments, and Tyler carefully read the volume,
making innumerable annotations. "Does it not,"
he writes in one place, "seem odd to call a man who
lived one hundred thirty years ago 'the late' &c?"
He says characteristically that "Dean Swift would
have been 'wrathy' at you for calling him an 'Irish-
man,'" and elsewhere implores Haven to drop
"Esquire" after proper names: "It is as shocking almost as to write S. T. Coleridge Esq, or William
Shakespeare *Esq.*" Tyler challenges Haven's defini-

tions, statements, and diction right and left.[17] Finding a reference to Hepworth Dixon's *Personal History of Lord Bacon* in a manual of English literature he was reading, he confides to the margin that Dixon's book is "a wretched book, affected, & sensational in style, disorderly in arrangement, presumptuous & inconclusive in assertion."[18] He was sometimes caustic in the case of the English classics as well. He thought that Collins's "Persian Eclogues" were no better than "tens of thousands of verses—now happily damned—of the school of Dryden & Pope." A passage in Cowper draws the scathing comment, "The contemptible cuss!"[19] He noted that Marvell's pastorals were "sickish" and that "many of his verses show deficient art, & are ludicrously quaint or mechanical." Skelton's "Elynour Rummyng" seemed "low coarse unmitigated rubbish" when he worked through that poet, concerning whom there are other uncomplimentary comments, and poor Robert Southey, whose *Poetical Works* Tyler read entire, is absolutely bombarded with objurgation; "very stupid & flimsy"; "what commonplace!"; "very school-boyish"; "vast portions of Southey seem to be prose set in metre . . . his poetry seems turned forth in a mill"; "his love poetry . . . a series of impotent spasms"; "even stupider than Wordsworth." Of Southey's ode on the death of Queen Charlotte, Tyler grimly says: "That this is poetry is proved by the fact that the lines begin with Capitals!" and he writes that "almost the only thing of Thalaba that I could read was the notes."[20]

But Tyler's notations were not, of course, merely denunciatory. A similar refreshing independence is found in his positive marginalia. He notes "a very noble passage" in one of Burns's letters to Mrs. Dunlop,[21] finds Chatterton's "Bristowe Tragedie" "infinitely superior to anything in the acknowledged poems," thought *Romola* (a copy of which he bought in 1869) "a majestic poem in prose," found Gay "as a poet . . . of the earth, earthy," remarked of Herrick's poem "To His Household Gods" that "I don't agree with him," though he found "To Musique" "most airy, dainty, graceful, musical," scribbled enough critical comment in Marvell's *Poetical Works* to furnish out an essay, and in a careful study of More's *Utopia* continually called his own attention in the margins of the book to the modern implications of his author's social theory. The adjectives "fine," "admirable," "good," continually appear; of Skelton, concerning whom his comments were frequently harsh, he could write that "there is wonderful vivacity" in "The Boke of Three Fooles," he was acute enough to admire Southey's ballads, and of "A Vision of Judgment" he wrote that "the copious eloquence of this greatly abused piece is astonishing." No marvel that this vigorous and sympathetic personality appealed to the Michigan students.

These students he tried earnestly to understand, winning their allegiance by his sympathy with their problems, his high standards of work, the merciless discipline he exacted both of them and of himself. The undergraduate *University of Michigan Magazine* viewed Tyler's dynamic personality with approval: "Our new Professor of Rhetoric takes strong ground in actual practise [in the use of English], and thus helps the literary societies, while they in turn render much assistance to his department."[22] Once when there was an interclass row between the sophomores and the juniors (1867–68), he was asked to investigate; he proposed to the guilty sophomore class that instead of baiting the juniors with mock programs of the "Junior Exhibition," they begin an oratorical exhibition of their own, and he had the satisfaction of having the class vote for his reform.[23] The following year, after this period of seasoning, he tried to analyze the campus mind. Contributing an article entitled "Enthusiasm for Alma Mater" to the student periodical, he wrote that although Michigan lacked "historical associations," the student body might yet be influenced by "some one magnetic instructor," and that "the most profound and the most intense college sentiment which a man carried away with him into the world is that which is generated by the intercourse of the students with each other."[24] The observation was, perhaps, not very original, but to the students, viewing the bearded and reverend faculty, it seemed that this young man in his thirties understood them. Nor did Tyler conclude his essay without expressing that deep glow of conviction about the significance of higher education which permeated most young professors and ardent presidents in the decades which saw the founding of Cornell and the creation of Johns Hopkins:

And, in general, the enthusiasm of a man for his Alma Mater will be great and permanent in proportion as he made a worthy use of his Alma Mater; as he had large opportunities and did not throw them away; as during his student life he was honest, generous, valiant, manly; as he did not forget, even in College, that it was one of the most sacred duties of every human being to have a good time.

But a good time under Tyler meant good hard work. "His coming," wrote a historian of the institution, "marked a change in the English department; henceforth attention was paid to the study of literature as well as to the study of its accessories."[25] A good time might imply play, but it also implied a direct approach to the material.

But it was not alone in methodology that Tyler was breaking new ground, he casually slipped into

his report to the regents a more revolutionary idea—
the teaching of American literature. No important
college or university in the country had as yet included the study of the national letters in its curriculum.[26] At Princeton, it is true, Professor John S. Hart
was writing a book on American literature, and in
1872–3 he inaugurated a course in that study,[27] so
that, in actually carrying the idea into practice, he
anticipated Tyler. But the idea is clearly set forth
in Tyler's report. Unfortunately, though he planned
his course for 1872–3,[28] he left the University for a
time, so that his plans did not immediately bear
fruit. Though he did not know it at the time, this
suggestion was the most important idea in his report.

In the meantime he was working like a dog and
liking it. He wrote his brother John that "I have
never before been so perfectly pleased with life as
at present."[29] Besides his teaching, he filled lecture engagements regularly, for he had acquired a
commendable reputation as a speaker.[30] Every
Christmas vacation he left Ann Arbor for his "annual campaign of spouting," during which he
"swung around the circle from New York to Boston to Dubuque and St. Louis."[31] He used all his
old lectures, and wrote new ones as occasion offered.[32] And he was an undoubted success. Once,
when he spoke in Grand Rapids, the newspaper re-

ported that he was a better speaker than Charles Sumner,[33] whom he adored. But that was treason, and *The New York Tribune* was more flattering because more discreet when it characterized Tyler as one who spoke "delightfully." A Rochester clipping pictures him as standing "free before the footlights," speaking without manuscript in "plain, earnest, straightforward English" in his "full, pleasant voice."[34] It was the golden afternoon of platform oratory and Tyler was gilded by its mellow glow. He was like Sumner, like Phillips, like Beecher——

But that name had lost its glamor. Poor Beecher! Poor Theodore Tilton, loyalest of friends! In May, 1870, Tyler wrote an article on "The Literary Labors of Charles Sumner" for *The Independent*,[35] and Tilton had sent him the grateful note which Sumner had written. Moses wrote his brother that Jeannette was sure Sumner would make him a consul or, at the least, minister to France, but, despite his humorous deprecation, he was pleased with Sumner's praise.[36] Then, swinging around the circle that winter, Tyler called on Tilton in New York. Tilton seemed "restless and troubled"; when Tyler took his departure, Tilton kissed him tenderly on the forehead. The next day he learned of the scandal.[37] Tyler was greatly troubled. He had thought of Sumner and Tilton and Beecher and himself as crusaders for righteousness. "My deepest nature," he wrote in 1869, "vibrates to an appeal based on the welfare of mankind, especially of America."[38] "The great politicians," he thought, "have worked for a principle & not primarily for personal promotion,"[39] and he was vastly disturbed.

In fact, Tyler had an unhappy feeling that under the consulship of Grant all was not well with the republic. Sumner was his idol ("I could have worshipped him"), and Sumner, who had broken with Grant in 1869 over the question of annexing the Dominican Republic, held that Grant " 'is curiously and subtly selfish,' " that " 'there never had been such nepotism since the Borgian popes.' "[40] The day after Christmas, 1870, Tyler, who had gone to Washington, met Vice-President Schuyler Colfax on the street, who asked him to dine, and though Tyler had an uneasy feeling that the angels were on the side of the "greatness and purity" of Charles Sumner, he accepted. He drove with Colfax in the Colfax carriage (a gift of Congressman Hooper); by and by they met Grant, and went back to the White House with him from church. Tyler recorded the conversation with Boswellian fidelity.[41] He was clearly puzzled. Grant, he thought, said things "in a manly, honest way, and as I looked at the man who uttered them with so sincere and modest a tone I could not help feeling that [manly, honest] very well described him. All the bad stories

I had lately heard of Grant seemed confuted." It was all very confusing. Back in Ann Arbor he wrote in his diary that "what is most needed in America at present is disinterested political criticism, as courageous as that of Wendell Phillips, as temperate as that of John Stuart Mill, as skilfully fitted to be listened to as that of John Bright."[42] Somehow neither Grant nor Beecher seemed quite to reach these standards. (Henry Adams, who was also in Washington in 1870, thought that "the moral law had expired—like the Constitution.")[43]

Sometimes, in addition to his usual lectures, Tyler was called upon for speeches on special occasions. In May, 1873, for example, White, who never forgot him, asked Tyler to deliver the principal address at the founding of the Sage College for Women at Cornell. (Three years before, the Michigan Regents had voted that women might be admitted to Ann Arbor, and on February 2, 1870, the first one had enrolled.)[44] Tyler's mind went back to Matthew Vassar and the absurd arguments of 1862, to Dio Lewis, to the necessities of progress, and the need for men like Henry W. Sage who would put their shoulders to the wheel. Bacon had foreseen what modern education was to be—"the true end of knowledge" was "the glory of God and the relief of man's estate." He prepared a thoughtful address on the text of progress: how from Galileo to the modern education of women humanity advanced. Ezra Cornell, Henry Sage, Matthew Vassar—they all fitted into the picture. ". . . it seems to me," he concluded, "that the best language by which to characterize the foundation, upon this spot, under all the circumstances of our time, of the Sage College for Women, would be simply to say of it in the comprehensive phrase of Lord Bacon, that it is an achievement worthy of human nature. And if it be so, who can have any doubt of the result?"[45] It was a dignified occasion, more so than when he had addressed the Woman's Suffrage Convention in Steinway Hall, New York, two years before, and *The New York Standard* had been exceedingly unkind:

> Moses Coit Tyler, a beautiful blonde [*sic*], from Michigan was the first speaker introduced to the audience. . . . After the fair speaker had recovered from a slight trepidation, and had arranged his full evening dress, he said that the seaboard states must look to their laurels, for the inland states had taken the lead in giving woman the rights she claimed. . . . After claiming the ballot the fair blonde retired amid much applause.[46]

Well, he had not been "much pleased" with that speech.[47]

A threat of assassination, and the prescription of spectacles ("the first venerable sign of senility")[48] gave a fillip of interest to the winter of 1871–72, and relieved the monotony of his incessant toil. Despite his lectures and an increase in salary,[49] it was difficult to make both ends meet in the "nice little box of a cottage" on North Street;[50] so that Tyler, in addition to his other labors, heroically tried to increase his income by authorship. For *The Herald of Health* he wrote a series of twelve articles which he called the "Minutes of the Brawnville Athletic Club,"[51] in which he pictured the struggles of an intelligent minority in a small New England village to found a gymnasium on the principles of Dio Lewis. Some of the material sprang from his experience as a lecturer in the United States; some of it from his observation of the effects of the musical gymnastics in Boston and in England; and some of it marked the influence upon him of his reading, especially in Plato, Bacon, and the books of the muscular Christianity group in England—Kingsley, Hughes, and Maurice. Tyler tried to give the sketches a popular appeal by the introduction of much dialogue, the humorous portrayal of village types, and a certain vigor of expression: if the humor was a little elementary, and the vitality a little self-conscious, one must remember that it was his only important excursion into the realm of imaginative literature. It occurred to him that the sketches, accumulated into book form, might make him some money, so, when he was in New York in 1868, he tried to find a publisher. The publishing world was much more interested in the venture than he had any right to expect; he had been unable to find any one who would bring out his letters from England in volume form. In 1869 Fields, Osgood & Company published Tyler's first real book, *The Brawnville Papers*. It was not, it must be confessed, a very good book; when Mrs. Austen published the biography of her father in 1911, she did not even discuss the volume. Tyler's later judgment was sound; presenting a copy to the Alpha Nu Literary Society at Michigan, he wrote on the book-plate: "This work is pleasant, but not deep or useful,"[52] and in later years he destroyed the plates, saying that he was ashamed of so crude a production.[53]

His industry did not flag. He poured out a stream of articles for *The Herald of Health* (in addition to the Brawnville papers), the *Western Monthly, The Nation, The Golden Age, Old and New, The Brooklyn Union,* and, above all, *The Independent.* Not counting the articles on his British experience, and excluding the twelve Brawnville essays, he published something like sixty articles from the time he came to Michigan in the fall of 1867 to his first resignation in the spring of 1873. He wrote book reviews, he discussed politics, literature, lecturing, the eclipse of the pulpit, the woman's rights movement.[54] He fought his old enemy, the tyranny of

the pulpit, particularly when this was exercised over
college education. Cornell and Michigan had both
made important steps in freeing universities from
religious control, and the orthodox were vigorous
in their denunciation. White asked him to defend
the movement,[55] and in the fall of 1869 *The Independent* carried a trenchant editorial on "Protestant
Cullenism," in which Tyler compared the demand
of Protestant churches that students be educated in
sectarian schools, to the intolerant parochialism of
the Irish Cardinal Cullen, who had lately made himself notable as the opponent of state-controlled education. Declaring that "Protestant Cullenism" was
too shrewd to attack the public-school system openly, he charged that it had selected the two universities in question as easier objects of attack, and
roundly rebuked the fault-finders:

> Meantime, we conclude with the remark that every ob-
> jection which Protestant Cullenism has made to secular
> education in the highest institutions logically applies to
> secular education in the lower institutions, and that the
> onslaught on the former means an onslaught on the lat-
> ter.[56]

Shrewd tactics, these; Tyler was learning the methods of controversy. The general level of these sixty
articles is high; unfortunately, the subject-matter
is ephemeral. Yet in the midst of them one finds im-

portant reviews and critical articles on Darwin, Emerson, and Swinburne.[57] Never had he been so alert to the movements of his time, but he judged himself with probing honesty in his diary:

I am not a poet; I have not the dreaminess, the contentment with passive sentient life, the idealism of the artist. While my powers of expression with the pen are perhaps, yes, certainly—for I will not befuddle my words by the dishonesty of sham, or of self-depreciation—superior to the average, they are not, I believe they never can be, equal to the highest, and is it worth while in literary art to be second rate?

I might be a minor poet, I think; a minor novelist, a minor dramatist. The great masterpieces of creative literature I can never, never approach.

On the other hand, when I think of the sphere of an American scholar and writer giving himself up, with pure heart, to the service of society, to the profound and conscientious study of the vast questions which now brood over our life—social and political—cultivating wisdom that his countrymen and the future may have the benefit of it; and using his powers of style both with tongue and pen to help American civilization to be a success; then I have before me a field of work which I do feel qualified to take the highest rank in.[58]

Bright and Cobden and Mill were, after all, his men; he would do in the United States what they had done in England.

Meanwhile, there were temptations. During the

fall of his third year at Michigan, he received an offer to become the editor of the *Yale College Courant,* his salary to be $3000 the first year, $4000 the second year, and $5000 the third. But he wanted time and leisure to meditate the methods by which he could make a "profound and conscientious study of the vast questions which now brood over our life," and "it did not require much exertion to decline the offer,"[59] despite the meagerness of his Michigan salary. But before the year was over he was compelled to face a more disturbing question: Bowen had bought *The Brooklyn Union,* offering him an editorial position as his "right-hand" man, and Tilton urged that he accept.[60] The salary was even better than the Yale offer—$4000 the first year, $4500 the second, and $5000 the third. Moreover, his house was mortgaged and he had other debts. And, most tempting of all, the post would introduce him into "the best of metropolitan journalism," bring him "political influence and position."[61] Was it not precisely the place for him? He was sorely tried. Tilton wrote him on January 1, 1870; Tyler meditated for a week; and on January 8 telegraphed Bowen that he could not come. He wrote in his diary that it "would have been a premature introduction to the business of the world."[62] Two years later, he was to succumb.

And then there was White, the persistent. White

was always doing kind things. In May, 1871, he offered Tyler a professorship in rhetoric and oratory at Cornell at a tentative figure of $2250; when Tyler refused (Michigan raised his salary to $2500 on July 11), White insisted that he visit Cornell. But Tyler declined because of the "insufficient pecuniary inducement" and his "impression as to the unorganized, chaotic, and uncertain state of the University."[63] The next year, when President Angell of Michigan failed to understand Tyler's hint that he was more and more interested in American history,[64] Moses opened his mind frankly to White, saying that he wanted a chair in American history and that the resources of the Michigan library were quite inadequate.[65] But this time White was noncommittal, and went no further than to invite Tyler to deliver the commencement address at Cornell on "The Study of American History."[66]

In the midst of this incessant activity, he was conscious of a slowly growing purpose, a cloudy ideal that loomed greatly on his spiritual horizons. He was undergoing a profound emotional and psychological development, which he recorded in his diary. The first year at Michigan had been too fully occupied for mental probings, but with the relaxation of the summer months he had opportunity to take stock of himself and of his mental needs. On July 17, 1868, he began to keep a fuller diary than he had hitherto done, one which might be for him "what the portfolio of sketches is to the artist,"[67] and he began by making an inventory of his development. He was thirty-three years old, "the most intelligently happy birthday I have yet had," since, after "awkward strugglings" he had, he thought, achieved "a resting place for my ideal scheme to stand upon."

The question I have daily to settle is to what immediate work shall I now put my ample health, my enthusiastic energy, my ardor of intellectual curiosity and my leisure. Shall it be mainly to production, or for a while yet mainly to acquisition? I am impelled to decide for the latter.

Wherefore he embarked upon a vast reading project, hoping to do by the time he was forty what Johnson, Coleridge, De Quincey, Lessing, Goethe, Schiller, Milton, and Lowell had accomplished at eighteen, hoping to "range over everything which I ought to have contact with in English literature," and to master foreign languages besides.[68] But the plan was too vast, too vaguely directed, and "I have several times noticed that whenever my mind has been free to move whither it would . . . it has gravitated toward the study of the law, and toward a life of practical endeavor for the good of human society." "As a literary and philosophical servant of American society," he thought, "I might be first rate."[69] And he dreamed out a program of visiting European countries to investigate their political economy and sociology, to learn their languages and literatures; perhaps he might do well to study American law. If he could but acquire the learning, the philosophical mind, the goodness and dignity, the literary taste and style of Edmund Burke! "I would follow him—even though afar off."[70]

He began bravely, for his commonplace book for 1869 shows that he read 166 books in English, Italian, and Greek literature; and, moreover, when he read an English author, he read his complete works.[71] But all this, though admirable, was unfocussed—"the problem of my life-work, though my life is probably half gone, is yet unsolved."[72] More and more he was impelled to the American theme. He thought of a novel which might depict the interrelation of politics and theology in the United States: "a character trammeled by Puritanism in early life, getting emancipated in maturity and trying to be 'hard' with a full beard. His first efforts to smoke, swear, play cards and billiards, drink, etc."

A novel to depict development in America of a Yankee "Contarini Fleming"; only poor, sensitive, conscientious, idealistic: brought up in Presbyterian Calvinism; his destination to be the ministry. Have him in childhood discuss theology. His mother tries to impress upon him gratitude for his Father in Heaven.[73]

The autobiographical element is obvious, but the wiser feeling that he was not a great literary creator prevented him from wasting time on the project. Rather, politics and history, especially American politics and history, seemed to him more and more to be his métier. After declining the offer to join *The Brooklyn Union,* he wrote:

> Here remaining in seclusion for five years longer I can steadily gain a quiet reputation and, better still, I can deepen and widen my knowledge, my mastery of principles, and my habits of thinking; and if it be my destiny to be a man of affairs, I shall enter upon such a career more coolly, with greater circumspection and certainty as to the way I want to go. . . . I have nearly completed a certain stage of literary studies; the next stage will be the study of the law, of political economy, and American history.[74]

Twelve days later he commenced reading Kent's *Commentaries,*[75] and to Kent he presently added Blackstone and various legal textbooks.[76] He also studied law systematically under Cooley.[77] But it was not law that he wanted so much as understanding of social processes. He went on to read Lord Campbell's *Lives of the Lord Chancellors,* Story, and various legal biographies.

What made the American system operate? What were its origins, its implications, its practical methodology? After his meeting with Colfax and Grant in Washington, Tyler's interest took a more and more specific turn. He wrote to Schurz, Sumner, and Colfax to congratulate them for their stand on the San Domingo question, and he tried to collect political information.[78] "The reading of books," thought Tyler, "is not an end; only a means to an end—perhaps a history of the United States, beginning with Washington's administration." Preparation, he thought, might require five years. He commenced a systematic perusal of the historians—Bancroft, Hildreth, Palfrey, and the rest, constantly referring to recent political events as he read.[79] Buckle seemed to him—at least for a time—to furnish the organic law of history.

He obsessed me for weeks together. No sentence could I shun over in reading. He shall be one of my friends for life. As a historical writer he indicates nobly, in many respects, the path to be taken by every other historical writer—the exhaustive preparation; the recognition of a spirit of the age as ruling the evolution of the events of the age, and using kings, presidents, statesmen, warriors, as the tide uses the chips that are carried upon its top; the necessity, therefore, of finding for each period and for each people the hidden law of progress.[80]

Other books were, for a time, good or bad as they approximated "the golden Buckle."[81] Could he find the law of American development? More and more the task fascinated him. "I have," he wrote in August, 1871, "at last really found my work."[82] By the close of 1871 he had read seventy-two historical works, including Rousseau and Lacretelle, seeking, like Henry Adams, for the secret of social change.[83] The seething ferment within him demanded expression, but what could he do, harnessed to elocution classes, and with only the inadequate resources of Ann Arbor at his disposal? If only he could go where the documents were, and plunge into the great project!

And then, when Tyler was East in January, 1873, on his annual lecture tour, Oliver Johnson, formerly of *The Independent,* and now managing editor of *The Christian Union,* of which Beecher was editor-in-chief, offered him the position of literary editor at a salary of $3500. Should he take it? He had refused other similar offers, but now—? He would be nearer the books, and the duties could not be very onerous. The salary was higher by a thousand dollars than what he earned at the university, and, moreover (fatal thought!), he would acquire reputation as one of the editors of "the most largely circulated religious weekly in the world."[84] But Beecher—? Andrew D. White was in New York, and in his perplexity Tyler went to consult him. White "approved of it heavily."[85] And so on January 15, 1873, Tyler signed a three-year contract as literary editor of *The Christian Union,*[86] and sent Angell his resignation.[87] He gave a farewell lecture in the Methodist Church of Ann Arbor in February just before his departure, when Angell introduced him "in most generous and touching words,"[88] and on February 16 he left Ann Arbor with his family for his mistaken adventure in Christian journalism. How much Yale and Andover were responsible for!

CHAPTER VI

The Christian Union, like *The Independent,* was a weekly journal for the American family, combining literature, religious liberalism, and a general advocacy of political reform. When it had become impossible for Henry Ward Beecher longer to remain as editor of *The Independent*[1] he had been without an organ; *The Church Union,* a minor religious journal, was to be had for little money, and, at the suggestion of John T. Howard, Beecher and his friends had formed a group to purchase the magazine that he might have an organ of his own. Because *The Independent* had not been too scrupulous about its advertising, one of Beecher's first moves was to exclude all questionable medical advertisements[2] from his new paper, rechristened *The Christian Union.* Beecher wrote in the first number: "We distinguish between oneness of Church and oneness of Christian sympathy . . . *The Christian Union* will devote no time to inveighing against sects, but will spare no pains to persuade Christians of every sect to treat one another with Christian charity, love and sympathy."[3] The de-

nominational journals joined in assailing a program which threatened their very existence,[4] but
the public was charmed, the circulation climbing
to 135,000—the largest religious weekly in the
world! Elizabeth Cady Stanton said tartly that it
was "a dull paper that represents no new thought
in morals, religion or politics,"[5] but the public
thought differently, agreeing with the editor of *The
Nation* that it was "not only the ablest and the best,
but also the most popular of American religious
journals."[6]

The periodical, whether planned by Beecher or
by George Merriam, the able associate editor, was
cannily run. Each subscriber received a copy of
Marshall's Household Engraving of Washington
(really by Stuart), or, if two new subscriptions came
in, "a new and superb steel-engraving PORTRAIT
OF HENRY WARD BEECHER."[7] There was a
superb array of carefully selected "talent," including such cloud-compelling names as Louisa M.
Alcott, Edward Eggleston, Harriet Beecher Stowe,
Rose Terry Cooke, Paul Hamilton Hayne, James
Freeman Clarke, Grace Greenwood, and "Gail
Hamilton," and a proper sprinkling of grave and
gay, of lively and severe assured the continuing interest of various classes of readers. But the great
feature of each issue was Beecher's weekly sermon.
Beecher only was named as editor. He had said,

when he went into the enterprise, that he wanted "a bishop's, not a curate's, place,"[8] and no one else was allowed to share the glory. Tyler soon discovered that he was to be his master's servant; in the eighteen months that he spent on the paper, his name did not once appear in its pages. When his first editorial appeared with a few sentences deleted, he wrote in his diary: "I don't like it."[9] For a while he buoyed himself up with the delusion that he had made "a wise and fortunate change in life,"[10] but he was presently referring to himself as Beecher's "hired man."[11]

In fact, the more Tyler learned of the situation, the less he liked it. Oliver Johnson, who stuck to Beecher through thick and thin, had great weight in determining the editorial policy, and Tyler soon learned that it was because Johnson knew the inside facts of Beecher's life, and in place of denouncing calumniators of the Great Preacher, might be trusted to treat them with gloved hands. He could be tactful where Theodore Tilton was concerned.[12] For a time Tyler used Beecher's desk,[13] and things seemed to be on the old footing,[14] but it could not last; even before *The Times* published Tilton's statement about Beecher, Tyler was thoroughly unhappy.[15] But he had only himself to blame; Beecher's manner, when Tyler first saw him in 1873, should have warned the new staff member. For

Beecher was then "a gray, haggard old man. . . . He emitted several epigrams and facetiæ, but nothing bubbled up as from a fountain of serene light and joy. . . . I thought I had seldom seen eyes and a face expressing greater wretchedness."[16] But Tyler was too conscientious to slight his job, and in the end he became a real power on the paper. Besides writing occasional editorials, he originated two regular departments, "The Outlook" (this later gave its name to the periodical which absorbed *The Christian Union*), and "Books and Authors," which he made over from a column called "Literature and Art." From these departments of the paper one is able to gauge the quality of Tyler's intellectual development.

"The Outlook," after the manner of the editorial paragraphs in *The Nation,* commented on public events of the day, especially those connected with political and moral reform. The cloudy abstractions which were the heritage of abolitionism appear occasionally; more characteristically, the column devotes itself to the American inheritance, and the deficiencies of the political scene. Typical observations are the following:

We are now pushing forward into the more generous era of the international life of the world. With this must come the higher and broader patterns of great men who are not merely national men but international men also, who compel the word patriotism to dilate to a grander meaning, and who find in every human being a fellow countryman.[17]

Evidently Moses had not forgotten his Carlyle.[18] On June 11, 1873, he analyzed the political ills of the country:

During that contest [the Civil War], while the eyes of earnest men were fixed on one great evil, another great evil—that of commercial and official profligacy—had an opportunity of creeping in unnoticed, and of poisoning the tissues of the social body. . . . Evidently the business we have now in hand is to raise the tone of commercial and official conduct.

Tyler's dominant desire to discover some law governing the growth of nations is responsible for such a paragraph as this:

Students of history have observed that the great epochs of literature have been in connection with great national convulsions, or immediately after them. The literary splendor of the ages of Pericles, Augustus, Louis XIV and Elizabeth suggests the familiar examples of this truth. America has had her great national convulsion. Is it, likewise, now to have its great literary epoch? Our national life has been developed and intensified by the agonies which have at last made us a nation. Is it too much to believe that literature, which is but the expression of the national life, will show a corresponding development of originality, vigor, raciness, and breadth? One sign of an epoch of great literary power is the presence of humor. We know that much critical fault may be found with the race of

American humorists who have risen among us of late years, but their appearance, with whatever blemishes, is really a token of good. It denotes an escape from imitation and literary conventionalism; it denotes vivacity, youthful force, hearty feeling, solid intellectual power of which these sportive freaks are only the coruscations. Humor is the drapery of the greatest intellects; it must be so of the great national epochs of intellectual action.[19]

The department of "Books and Authors" allowed him freer play, allowed him to speculate on theories of criticism and to attempt to meet the intellectual problems which Darwinism created for the devout. The passages on the function of the critic and the method of literary judgments are especially interesting as forecasting the postulates of the two histories:

The primary duty of a critic is to place himself at the stand-point of the author, and from that, and not from his own separate stand-point, to judge of the task that has been done.[20]

Sainte-Beuve, in whose enthralling pages every literary critic of this generation must search for the costliest secrets of his craft, has impressed upon the world no other lesson more important than this—that in literature the producer must be studied as well as the thing produced. "The literary result," says the great master, "is not, in my view, distinct, or at least separable, from the rest of the man and from his organization. I can relish a work; but it is difficult for me to judge it without a knowledge of the man himself. The literary study leads me naturally to the moral study."

The principle of literary judgment is fundamental. It inaugurates a method. Once adopted and acted upon in literary criticisms, it is a maxim which will sway those criticisms to a range and orbit of its own. It will give a personal coloring to discussions which may otherwise flow through a medium at once achromatic and cold. It will connect criticism with biography. It will make the study of letters a study of human nature. It will indicate that there is a law of relation between living and thinking, and that the conduct of phrase is a part of the conduct of life. It will also select authors, and not books merely, as the texts for literary discourse.[21]

The pressure to fill his column every week and the variety of books he was compelled to notice did not always permit Tyler to carry through his excellent theory, but it was a theory which was to flower in his greatest work. Meanwhile, he struggled with the flood of print, making some incisive, and some odd, judgments. His political convictions did not color his appreciation of the Confederate, Henry Timrod,[22] and he was awake to the deficiencies of Bayard Taylor,[23] but Browning he could not go: "as a poet he is a spectacle to excite lamentation and abhorrence."[24]

The Christian Union naturally attracted religious books, particularly those dealing with Darwinism, so that Tyler was brought face to face with the greatest intellectual issue of the day. That Christianity would survive the evolutionary theory he never doubted.

Reviewing Joseph Leconte's *Religion and Science,* he wrote:

> We do not find that Prof. Leconte is a Darwinist or an Evolutionist or anything else that is dreadful; but we perceive that, with his views, he might be so, and remain a devout, consistent Christian.[25]

His view is more clearly put in a notice of J. W. Dawson's *The Story of Earth and Man:*

> If, for instance, that modified doctrine of evolution which Dr. Dawson assails, and which he forcibly shows to lack several all-important links of proof, should hereafter find those links—the Divine Creator would be unimpeached by this discovery of his ways.[26]

But while his mind was tentatively hospitable, he seems not to have probed deeply into the matter, and he was capable of serious error in dealing with philosophers.[27] In truth, the atmosphere of *The Christian Union* insulated him from the realities of the issue, and he seems never to have got beyond the vague "reconciliation" of science and religion expressed in a letter written after his return to Ann Arbor, in response to an inquiry from Detroit:

> The opinions of Christian scholars and thinkers are nearly unanimous now that the Bible was not intended to be a revelation in geology, or botany, or astronomy, or any other physical science, but a revelation of spiritual truth alone; and that in all these others the writers were

permitted by the Divine Spirit to reflect the notions that prevailed in their time, without which their utterances on spiritual things would have seemed preposterous to those to whom they were addressed.[28]

His heart was not really in his work, but in the "great subject," to which he devoted every hour that he could—not as many as he wished, for he was still lecturing.[29] The Tylers (after August, 1873) were reasonably comfortable at a boarding house on West 18th Street in New York City, where the Oliver Johnsons were also living.[30] It was impossible to live in the metropolis without entering to some degree into its social life—interesting enough, since he met Bryant, John Bigelow, Stedman, and other notables[31]—but it all took time. Also, with characteristic indecision, Tyler reverted to preaching,[32] and even thought briefly of returning to the ministry.[33] Then he had to decide whether or not to become associate editor of *The New York Evening Post* at a salary of $4000, but decided that "my next move would be out of journalism altogether rather than any further into it."[34] He felt trapped, sometimes blaming himself for his "sins of hasty conclusion"[35] and sometimes blaming White for getting him into the whole wretched business.[36] But he ploughed doggedly ahead, using every moment he could for study, rejoicing in any association that pointed in the direction of American history.[37]

His mornings (when he could) he devoted to reading either in the Astor Library or in the New York Historical Society, and, in order to focus on a particular problem, he investigated the history of the early colleges in America, using the topic for an address, not merely at Syracuse, but also before the Rhode Island Historical Society[38] and the New York Historical Society, the meetings of which he attended whenever he had time. By May, 1874, he had gone through Sparks' *Writings of Washington;* lives of Washington by Marshall, Everett, and Bancroft; Jefferson's complete works; biographies of Jefferson by Tucker and Carpenter; the writings of Franklin, and Upham's *Life of Pickering,* besides much that he did not record. Through the kindness of Doctor G. H. Moon he was permitted to examine the Gates MSS. in the library of the New York Historical Society, where he also studied Rivington's *Royal Gazette* and the Lamb and Steuben papers.[39] And sometimes he was able to turn his book column to good account. Reviewing Lossing's *Life of Schuyler* he said roundly that "every fact of American history for the last century has now to be re-examined."[40] Nor did he stop with this. Examining George Lunt's *Old New England Traits,* he wrote:

If, however, early American history has seemed dry and provincial, and its social life helplessly petty, it must also be owned that a considerable part of this impression has been due, in the main, to the imperfect art of the American writers who have hitherto handled these topics. . . . American history still reserves its charms for the presence of a genius corresponding in that sphere to the greatness of Longfellow and Hawthorne in poetry and romance.[41]

Could he become that historian? If so, it would be by a new method, by following

the new school of critical historical writing. . . . characterized preeminently by simplicity both in material and form; and that means that it seeks for the whole absolute truth of history sincerely, sceptically, untiringly, and then tries to tell it plainly.[42]

His reading became increasingly critical, and he scribbled on the margins of the books he bought, observations that might go into the history. Sparks, he thought, "describes better than he narrates. His story lacks action. He fails to present the *flow* of events, to state with clearness the sequence of essential details, & to exhibit all the moving life of the story. Thus in '77 there is scarcely an allusion to the surrender of Burgoyne." "His description of a battle is vague then; you do not hear any guns or see any killing; & when he tells you it is over, you did not know that it had begun." This he wrote on a slip he left among the pages of the first volume of Sparks' *Washington;* reading that worthy's life of Gouverneur Morris, Tyler notes (with an eye to method):

"How stupidly is this History written from beginning to end [;] not a single date is given in full and we do not know whether these occurrances [*sic*] took place in the *dark ages* or yesterday from the Book, but only by hearsay & supposition." The last paragraph of the book, however, he marked "Tremendous!" Two or three times, reading Jefferson's Works, Tyler annotated "a sp[ecimen] of the favorite Southern use of unqualified superlatives. Still common," denying that George Wythe was the best classical scholar in the state because that was "another case of unqualified superlative, in Southern fashion," and declaring that Jefferson's 'Autobiography' "shows old age. It is slightly garrulous, & chronologically confusing. Of course," he adds, "it has great merit, too, particularly its delineations of great men," and he noted that Jefferson's sketch of Pendleton (*Works* of Jefferson, ed. H. A. Washington, vol. I, p. 37) was "an exquisite portrait," and exclaimed "What a portrait painter is J[efferson]!" In Jefferson Tyler found "invariable intellectual courtesy," and it is evident from the pencilled comments that Tyler's prejudice against the South was not proof against him. It is perhaps also a mark of Tyler's breadth of view that, reading Washington, he could see that a British officer in the eighteenth century could have had no other idea than "that he was quelling a rebellion" and that he reminds himself to look into "the justice of the subsequent fate of the Am. loyalists" in the same volume. He thought 1783 "the time for beginning my history," as he read, and hoped that the government would issue a complete edition of Washington's *Writings* that he might be aided thereby. Washington, he thought, "seems lifted so high above humanity as to have divine pity for it."

Perhaps even more prophetic of future achievement are Tyler's reviews of two books on the history of American letters which fell early into his hands. One of these was by John S. Hart, the Princeton professor who preceded Tyler in the actual teaching of the subject, and who had compiled a *Manual of American Literature*. Tyler wrote:

The book which furnishes the occasion for these remarks is interesting not only for what it contains, but for what it indicates. It is pleasant to have such evidence that the American people are beginning to realize that their own native writers have at least occasional claims to notice. There is something morbid and degrading in the passion with which we have worshipped exotic models in letters and have despised our own. Who shall explain the odd contradiction in our national habits of furiously boasting of American history, and steadily refusing to know anything about it? Surely, our uneasy consciousness of being provincial in literature will not be cured by remaining ignorant of what American literature is. . . . And it is not the least benefit to be hoped for from the publication of a work like this, that it may stimulate to the re-issue of early

American books now out of print, and very difficult of
access in any form. He is mistaken who thinks that there
is nothing worth reading in American literature before
Washington Irving. Our cousins in England are doing
great service to good letters by the publications of the Early
English Text Society. Why may we not emulate them
by having an Early American Text Society?[43]

The Early American Text Society still remains unborn, but Tyler returned to the importance of colonial letters three months later in a review of F. H.
Underwood's *A Handbook of English Literature,
American Authors:*

There is one feature of Mr. Underwood's plan which,
for ourselves, we regret. In beginning American literature
with Franklin, in our opinion he begins too late. Before
Franklin there were at least twenty authors who deserved
recognition, and whose writings would have furnished
some very striking specimens for this collection. . . .
To some of these writings, Mr. Underwood refers . . .
but in a way, as it seems to us, which does injustice to their
interest and their importance. . . . The result is that his
manual is made up chiefly of contemporary writings,
which in most cases are accessible in familiar editions;
while the opportunity is lost of recalling to our memory
forgotten names, and of furnishing to us some taste of
literary productions which lie beyond ordinary reach.[44]

It was a need which Tyler was to feel when he set to
work on his history of colonial letters.

How was he ever to write the work that he felt stirring within him? One thing was certain; he must at any cost, contract or no contract, get out of the trap into which he had led himself.[45] By April, 1874, he had fully made up his mind.

I shall certainly retire from journalism when a good opportunity occurs. . . . If there were a vacancy at Cornell I should undoubtedly go there; as it is, I expect to be appointed before long Non-Resident Professor of American History. That will be worth $1000 a year.[46]

This idea seems to rest upon a conversation which White and he had had at the Union League Club in the spring of 1873,[47] but nothing came of it, and in desperation, nauseated by the Beecher scandal, Tyler wrote President Angell, inquiring whether he knew of a vacant professorship anywhere. On August 5, Angell answered noncommittally,[48] but fortunately for Tyler, Charles Kendall Adams happened to be in New York City and assured him that everybody in Ann Arbor wanted him back.[49] In the mood he was in, Tyler was willing to grasp at any opportunity which would release him from slaving under his now repulsive[50] chief, so that, in August, he was corresponding with the Congregational Church at Middletown, Connecticut, and with the Plymouth Congregational Church at Philadelphia, both of which were seeking a pastor.[51] But Angell, after hearing from Adams, journeyed east to confer with Tyler, who was, at the moment, in Rhode Island. Angell assured his former colleague that he was willing and anxious to recall him to Michigan, but that there were lions in the way: the Regents had never recalled any one who had left, and Tyler must wait upon their consent. Angell returned to Ann Arbor; and on August 25 wrote that Tyler might "consider the call as fairly extended," but that the Regents objected to his lecturing and his other outside activities, and that these he must give up. Tyler was only too happy to get out of the mess, and promptly accepted on these terms. He had, it is true, a bad quarter of an hour with Oliver Johnson, who complained of the suddenness of his resignation and thought that Tyler had neglected his job for his other interests[52] (odd that the Regents and Angell and Johnson should all accuse him of divided aims!), but on September 12, 1874, he bade farewell to the office force "and marched out of *The Christian Union* office with the joy of a prisoner out of the penitentiary."[53] The Regents, on October 9, 1874, confirmed his appointment at $2500.[54] "My happiness in the solution of my destiny is calm but very sweet."[55] The trouble with Tyler was that he was always trying to improve on destiny. In his intellectual life he was still the American pioneer, restless, dissatisfied, perpetually looking into unoccupied territories for the good fortune he should have secured by minding his own garden.

President Angell's extraordinary action in breaking the general principle of the Board of Regents never to recall a professor who had once left the University of Michigan is to be explained in part by the attraction of the two men for each other, and in part by Angell's feeling that Tyler's growing prestige would make his return to Ann Arbor a good thing for the university. Tyler had been present in the parlor of the president's house that autumn day in 1869 when Acting President Frieze and the other faculty members had first laid eyes on "the youngest and liveliest college president in existence," and it had been a case of "love at first sight."[56] Twenty-seven years later it still seemed to him that, though he had served under a number of presidents, "under none of them would I more willingly live over again the years that I passed under such leadership than under that president."[57] Angell had not accepted the presidency in 1869, but in 1871 he had come to Ann Arbor in time to savor Tyler's qualities as a teacher; and at the end of his remarkable career, looking back on his associates at Michigan, his former chief wrote of Tyler:

He was already master of that attractive style which lent such a charm to everything that he wrote and inspired his classes with a love for the best in literature and for purity and vivacity in their essays and speeches. In his private study he was already showing that deep interest in American History and the early American authors which gave shape and colour to his later works. He had a fine sense of humour which enlivened his instruction and made him a most agreeable companion.[58]

And Angell, like Tyler, was in revolt against the rote-system in higher education—indeed that was one reason he had left Vermont for Michigan, an institution which "had been inspired to a considerable extent by German ideals of education and was shaped under broader and more generous views of university life than most of the eastern colleges."[59] If Tappan sketched out, Angell (in so far as any one man may be said to have done so) created the University of Michigan as a university. He carried the free election of courses to its utmost, because, though "this privilege . . . will be abused by some, the lazy and indifferent, . . . it would be folly to deny this opportunity to the industrious and aspiring for the sake of forcing a little more labor out of a few men . . ."[60] He encouraged the seminar system on foreign models;[61] he not only increased the scientific resources of the institution, but year after year he called attention to the need of a rich and comprehensive library,[62] and he continually insisted upon the organic relation of the university to the state.[63]

In the ten years from 1870 to 1880 the faculty well-nigh doubled in number, and the graduates increased by about a third[64]—in fact, with the possible exception of Wisconsin, Michigan in these ten years was the only state university in the Middle West which attained adult proportions.[65] Angell engendered a university atmosphere. There was of course some hostility towards the institution, and one or two administrative difficulties like the famous Douglas-Rose controversy occurred,[66] but in the main Angell created the security and calm which was exactly what Tyler needed.

And so on September 16, 1874, the Tylers were again in Ann Arbor—"the tranquillity of the place is like balm to my brain and nerves."[67] They took a house at 55 Ann Street,[68] and Tyler plunged once more into his real work. He was full of peace, and ready to spend the rest of his days in Ann Arbor.[69] His first task was the organization of his courses. The departmental work had been carried on by Mr. Leslie Irving, acting professor of the English language and literature during his absence, aided by Professor Hutchins, and little change had been made in the curriculum.[70] Now with Angell's approval, Tyler cut himself entirely loose from the instruction in elocution and rhetoric, and devoted his time to teaching literature. Sympathetic with Angell's ideal of university teaching, he introduced in the fall of 1875 a new course entitled "Study of Masterpieces," in which the students were brought directly into contact with literature instead of merely reading a textbook. As originally planned the first semester was devoted to Chaucer, Gower, Langland, Wyclif, Occleve and Lydgate, and the second semester to Sackville's *Induction,* More's *Utopia,* Sidney's *Apologie for Poetry,* Spenser's *Faërie Queene,* Book I, Bacon's *Essays,* Shakespeare's *Sonnets, Paradise Lost* and the *Areopagitica,* the *Dunciad,* Burke's *Reflections on the French Revolution,* Wordsworth's *Excursion,* and De Quincey's *Confessions of an Opium Eater.*[71] Tyler lectured on these works, discussed them with his class, and required the students to prepare papers on assigned topics. The next year saw some rearrangement of the course, for he experimented with it until he found what was best, but this was the general pattern of his classes. However, in his last years at Michigan, Tyler began the course in masterpieces with the *Utopia,* and ended it with *The Princess* (a new and exciting poem then, for the president of the university was still arguing the merits of coeducation), and, in addition, taught an introductory course, a course in Chaucer, a course in Shakespeare, and, immediately before he left, a course in the principal forms in prose and verse.[72] His classes all came in the afternoon, so that his mornings were free for work on his *History.* In 1875 he lectured on Ameri-

can literature, recounting for his classes the material
he was working on.[73]

As to the effectiveness of Tyler's teaching, there
can be no doubt. In his advanced work he builded on
White, and was undoubtedly influenced by Charles
Kendall Adams, professor of history, who introduced the German seminary method at Ann Arbor.[74] They were warm friends. Tyler thought
Adams "the incarnation of character and good
sense";[75] and they were both keenly interested in
the problem of university pedagogy. Both were
deeply dissatisfied with the "text-book" method;
and in Tyler's case the dissatisfaction took form after
the *History* was out of the way, when, not liking the
existing manuals, he began to revise the text he had
been using, Henry Morley's *First Sketch of English
Literature*.[76] In place of Morley's strict chronologi-
cal method, Tyler "cut it all up, rearranged the materials, recomposed the book, and struck out and put
in wherever necessary,"[77] his aim being to follow the
natural method of treating all of an author's work
together.[78] The first draft was finished in March,
1879[79]—a bigger job than he had anticipated, for
Morley was inaccurate, and it would have been easier
to write a new book.[80] But the job was done. Tyler
wrote Morley for his approval, which was promptly
given,[81] and sent the thing on to the publisher, Shel-
don and Company, of New York, the book appear-

ing in July. The Morley-Tyler *Manual* was certainly a vast improvement over most of the texts in the field. The preface contains Tyler's confession of pedagogical faith:

It is of the utmost importance, even in the use of a text-book on English literature, that students should be saved from lapsing into a passive and listless attitude toward the subject, and should be so skilfully steered in their work that they may come to know for themselves the exhilaration of original research. If I may refer to my own experience as a teacher, I would say that in my introductory course upon English literature—in which course only do I use a text-book—I have found it to great advantage . . . to parcel out among them, for direct study in the library, the most celebrated works in prose and poetry.[82]

This was relatively fresh doctrine in the seventies, and his crowded classrooms showed that it was appreciated.

One can, in fact, measure Tyler's effectiveness by the approbation given him in *The Chronicle,* a fortnightly student paper founded in 1869,[83] one of the best undergraduate publications ever to appear in the United States. The promise of a *History of American Literature* from Tyler excited an amount of interest in the undergraduate body that is a striking comment on present campus intellectualism. *The Chronicle* noted that the prospectus was on exhibition at the several book stores,[84] declared that "those who listened to the lectures will watch for it with interest,"[85] and, when the volumes appeared, urged the students, whether or not they were enrolled in Tyler's classes, to purchase copies:

The publication of a work of this kind is one of the few rare events which gives celebrity and a reputation to a university. It is one of the great achievements which add to the permanent glory of a college. We ask nothing better for our University than that it may continue to be remembered as long as "American Literature," and be held in equal estimation with it. Without presuming to cast up the odds in favor of its longevity, we think that it will stand the hundred years' test of a masterpiece. To say nothing of style, wit, or other literary merits, the book is the first of the kind containing such varied and extensive information, and must be ever consulted as a standard of reference by those making similar compilations. . . . It ranks next, and next not *longo intervallo,* to the discovery of an asteroid or the finding of a planet. We repeat again—buy. If not for the author's sake, for your own pleasure and instruction.[86]

Alumni wrote in to testify their admiration for the book,[87] saying that "we . . . who have left, with longing and regret, the halls of learning forever, owe Prof. Tyler a debt of gratitude." When controversy arose with the British publishers of Morley's book over Tyler's revision, the students defended him, for "we are deeply interested in maintaining the reputation of one of our most eminent professors."[88] When the course in Chaucer became overcrowded they offered suggestions for its improvement, though "no one can help admiring the ease and facility with which Professor Tyler manages his enormous class," and it is a tribute to Tyler's influence and to the intellectual quality of the undergraduate in the seventies that they proposed "at least one year's previous study of French and at least one year of German" as prerequisites "before one can take up the study of Chaucer."[89] It was a matter of moment when a bust of Shakespeare was put in Room L (Tyler's classroom),[90] and when pictures of great authors were hung on the walls.[91] If he endorsed a lecturer, the fact was duly chronicled;[92] if he eulogized a former student, the paper found place for his remarks;[93] if he thought that students should be interested in helping Professor Francis J. Child to collect ballads, the editor devoted the leading editorial to endorsing Tyler's idea.[94] The writing of essays in history and English, though sometimes "terribly irksome," seemed the best system "yet introduced"[95] and the young editors thought that "since the chair in English Literature was established in the University there has been a constantly increasing interest in this deservedly popular branch of education . . . due to the intrinsic merit of the study itself, but more to the masterly way in which the instruction has been imparted." It was a matter of student pride that "although room L has been supplied with many additional seats, yet they are sometimes inadequate to accommodate with sittings the constantly increasing number of visitors."[96] If a few students were bored, it was their own fault, not Tyler's: they had failed to follow his instructions.[97] His enthusiastic advocacy of a gymnasium for the university won their hearts,[98] for he had not forgotten the precepts of Dio Lewis. Once when Tyler was crossing the campus and tripped on a wire, they pictured him as thereafter following "the straight and narrow" way "without giving vent to those choice bits of emphatic English literature which were doubtless boiling up in his broad bosom."[99] When he resigned to go to Cornell, the event was noted with dismay:

> This report was received here Tuesday morning and created considerable excitement among the students. There is no member of the faculty more popular and highly esteemed by all the students and citizens, and whose loss would be more felt.[100]

Besides his courses and the two books he had written, Tyler had other interests as well. His first visit to New York after coming to Ann Arbor revealed to him what the "wrecked home" of Theodore Tilton was like,[101] and, desirous to retain his peace, "five hundred miles from the foul forces of the Brooklyn wave,"[102] he built in the spring and summer of 1875 the house on North Street (now Kingsley) near

Ingalls, with its "fire-proof brick study" "commanding the valley of the Huron"[103] which became for him
a real and permanent home. There he worked on his
lectures, his books, and his sermons. For, despite the
prohibition of the regents, he was too prominent a
figure not to be called upon for occasional speeches.
For example, in February, 1875, he gave an address
at Wooster University, which rewarded him with
"a respectable fee and the title of LL.D."[104] He also
became interested in politics, presiding over the Republican city convention on April 1, 1880, and over
the county convention on the 14th, when he was
elected a delegate to the state convention. The papers
discussed him as a possible delegate to the Chicago
national convention, but his independence in not declaring himself for Blaine, and his disgust with practical politics soon ended this excursion into "a phase
of life quite new to me."[105] But what is more distressing than these strayings is that with his characteristic hankering after fields where he was not, he
was once more considering the ministry.

The writing of sermons came to be a regular occupation with him as soon as he had settled again in Ann
Arbor, where, on November 1, 1874, he joined the
Congregational Church. Presently his Sundays were
occupied with preaching—in Ann Arbor, Pontiac,
Flint, Detroit. Once, regarding a sermon at the Jefferson Avenue Presbyterian Church in that city, he

wrote his friend White that "my preaching is altogether rationalistic, and the Presbyterians like the thing so well that they cry for it, as babies do after this new fashioned Castor Oil."[106] But his rationalism was not of a revolutionary order, if one is to judge from the manuscript sermons which have been preserved. Tyler was thoroughly safe. For example, discussing "Prayer: The Opposition of Scientific Theories," he labored to show that rain may come as the result of atmospheric conditions, but that God can also send it in answer to prayer, for God remains in control and can interpose at will—a theory which he supported by quoting pious scientists. A more able utterance is a sermon on "The Crime of Pontius Pilate," in which, employing both secular and sacred sources, he paints a picture of the grandeur of the Roman empire, portrays Pilate as "a respectable and wealthy pagan gentleman of the period— somewhat cultivated, a reader of Horace doubtless, easy-going, self-indulgent, a contemner of every sort of fanaticism or enthusiasm, liking this world and very well disposed to having a pleasant time in it." The modern application is obvious. In general the sermons were interesting, graceful, simple in style, persuasive, but never profound, though occasionally he moved his audiences deeply.[107] But the lack of depth in these discourses pointed to a lack in Tyler himself. Long ago he had sloughed off Calvinism, but he had found no satisfactory form of belief to substitute for it. It was, for him, simple enough to combat the more godless extremists among the disciples of evolution. Yet there was in him a stream of mysticism which could not be satisfied with even such rationalism as he achieved.

He took to searching his mind, to testing various forms of religion. For example, one September Sunday in 1874 he took his family to the Congregational Church in the morning, but in the evening he himself attended the Episcopal service.[108] The Anglican ritual attracted him by its beauty, and, moreover, the church itself was new.[109] Moses found himself more and more attracted by the poetry, the mysticism of the Episcopal form of worship. It had dignity, power, "a most impressive and beautiful service,"[110] a fortress of the soul against the bleakness of Calvinism, the aridity of scientific rationalism.[111] Like Browning's bishop, he came to feel (but for a higher reason) that St. Andrew's ever was the church for peace. He pondered for months. Finally, in the spring of 1877, he took his resolve, was confirmed in the Episcopal Church by the bishop of the diocese of Michigan, subscribed sixty-five dollars to the building fund, and in 1879, 1880, and 1881 was elected a vestryman.[112] Jessica Tyler followed her father into the Episcopal fold.[113]

But his struggle was still for unity of spirit. Sometimes he felt the presence of the dead close at hand. On December 7, 1878, he recorded in his "Commonplace Book" that he "felt impressed by the presence of Susy," and he asked his wife to try to write for Susan. Mrs. Tyler took pencil and paper, when "her hand was moved to write these lines—I being out on the piazza during the process." And there followed a message from Susy, encouraging Moses to write books, and saying that she, Susy, was happy.[114] Next year, being forty-four, he wrote that:

Upon the whole, though I have made some mistakes, I am not dissatisfied with the outcome of the past ten years. My life to-day is peaceful, healthy, busy, and independent. I have beloved ones near me, a delightful home, and every prospect for further usefulness in my vocation as a writer. . . . I don't feel older, though I am conscious of wider and deeper experiences than ten years ago. . . .[115]

But it was an effort to keep this mood. He tried Arnold as a medicine—"I must not get beyond the reach of Matthew Arnold's cool Socratic influence . . . ," and he set Macaulay before him as an example of undivided aim.[116] It was good to be recognized as the eminent author of a history of American letters, but within, there was ever a feeling of the dreamlike evanescence of the world. He wrestled deeply with himself, with God:

My spiritual struggle at present is to keep a vivid faith in the idea of a real and considerate personal God, in whose all-wise and all-loving mind my life has been minutely planned—so minutely that even all my mistakes are taken into account, and have been permitted, as a part of the manifold process of discipline and victory in my life. Only in this way can I keep from repining at the past.[117]

But could he believe in this far-off form of Calvinism? Had he known the will of God? Sometimes, especially when he was struggling to decide whether or not to go to Cornell, he was "depressed horribly." And late in December, 1880, he talked with the bishop about taking orders—"at least deacon's orders," for he did not want to make another profound mistake.[118]

CHAPTER VII

In tracing the genesis and development of the first of Tyler's two great histories of American literature, it will be necessary to turn backward in this chronicle and gather together several loose ends. The incentive to write the book had been long in forming, and represented the crystallization of various interests all the way from the period of his British activities through his first years as a teacher in the University of Michigan, his activities as a commentator on books and politics in *The Christian Union,* and his participation in the modernizing of literary instruction at Ann Arbor. The *History* was produced from a fusion of interests: his desire to write a worthy scholarly book, his sense of the need for intelligent participation in American public life, his search for a fundamental principle of social development which would explain the characteristics of nations and of peoples, his yearning to use literature as an instrument whereby students might be led to an understanding of the national culture. Above all, as Tyler's notebooks and diaries show, he needed an enduring focus for his tremendous energies, his wide curiosity, his emotional disturbances, his vague spiritual unrest. His life, until he began work on this, his main achievement at Mich-

igan, represented motion without progress in a
sense, and though all he had done and all he had
been proved useful to him in his work, had it not
been for his labors as a historian, Tyler would not
now be remembered as a pioneer investigator. Before the composition of the first *History* his career
had been active but, in the deepest sense, aimless;
after the appearance of *The History of American
Literature, 1607–1765,* though he might waver,
its author possessed a hard-won status, he was Moses
Coit Tyler, the first great historian of the national
mind expressed in literature.

Thus in 1875, though Tyler was forty years old,
and though he had planned and executed a great
mass of literary work, he had really accomplished
nothing of importance. An inferior book—*The
Brawnville Papers,* an anonymous satiric poem, a
group of magazine contributions, a series of lectures
and sermons, a few reports,[1]—such was the sum of
his accomplishments. It is possible that he would
never have got beyond these had there not come an
external incentive which served as a precipitate for
his vague and vast ideas. George H. Putnam, the
publisher, aware of Tyler's promise, and feeling that
a manual of American literature would be a paying
venture, wrote Tyler asking him to compile one.[2]
At first, Tyler saw nothing further in the idea than
such a manual as he was to make out of Morley's

book; he replied therefore to the effect that he would undertake the work, and suggested that he suffix a review of American literature to a revision of Arnold's *Manual of English Literature*—a mere classroom job. Putnam, however, wanted something original,[3] and Tyler withdrew from the scheme on the ground that he did not wish to waste his time on a mere text-book.[4] On July 31, 1875, Putnam wrote again, repeating his offer for a book on American literature only. In the meantime, Tyler had awakened to the possibilities, and in strong excitement (evident in the letter) he wrote Putnam as follows:

Ann Arbor, Mich.
9 Aug. 1875.

Geo. H. Putnam, Esq.

My dear Sir:

Since receiving your letter of the 31 July, I have been taken from my desk by out-door engagements and have really been unable to write sooner. Besides I wanted to let our business soak awhile in unconscious mental fermentation, that there might be no mistake about the final decision. Upon the whole I am inclined to go on with the thing after all, provided the suggestions I am about to make do not present to you any insuperable objections.

(1) With God's help I mean to do in this life no more hack-work, and no more second-hand work of any sort. Alas, I have done eno' already. If I do this work, I must do it thoroughly and artistically, from knowledge of my own in every case, from a direct study of the *quellen*. I am a special student of American history, and have paid particular attention to what we dignify as literature in

America in the 17 and 18 centuries. Still, if I make a critical "Survey" of the field, I shall need to run over it again. So of the greater and more fruitful period of our own century. Therefore.

(2) I must have time enough to satisfy both my scholarly and my literary conscience. Probably I could not have the book ready for your hands before May 1, 1876.[5] I have the materials well in hand, and I can set apart a good deal of time for the work: but I should not dare to hope for an earlier achievement of the thing.

(3) My salary here supports me snugly: but if I want extra money for books I need to do extra work for it. Should I set about this business, I should need some books that are not to be had here. Would you like to furnish them to me at the usual discount, charging them to me, and letting the payments for them wait till we see whether my book brings in anything?

If you can manage these things, I authorise you to announce the book as in preparation. With reference to the possible use of Arnold's book on English literature, of course it would be best to say nothing about it at present.

Faithfully yours,
MOSES COIT TYLER.[6]

Much credit is due to Putnam for immediately endorsing the greater scheme latent in Tyler's letter, for he answered at once, agreeing to Tyler's proposals. Tyler replied with kindling enthusiasm on August 27, 1875, saying that he had already begun a task "which grows more and more attractive as I think of it," and adding:

With reference to the time of completion, I can see the great importance of having the book ready for taking the

Centennial enthusiasm at its flood. All that I can say is that I will do my best. If I had my whole time and the necessary books within my reach I could do it. As it is, I have my university work to occupy and fatigue me; and shall have to borrow and buy and bring here works which in New York or Boston would be accessible to me in public libraries. However, my habits of application are pretty good, and I may pull through to the goal sooner than I have supposed. If I can get down to the Revolutionary war by Christmas I shall quite expect to be ready with the rest by April 1.

He was, of course, not ready; books are seldom prepared on schedule. Moreover, as the correspondence shows, he did not in the beginning plan the thorough and definitive work which he completed, but had rather in mind a general survey of American letters to his own time, for the letter continues:

As to title, if it were not for the arrogance of it, I should prefer *History of American Literature*. Suppose we begin with the modest one which you seem to have fallen upon, and call it *A survey of American literature*. If when the thing is done it seems worthy of being called a *history,* I suppose that nobody would be hurt by our changing it to that. I shall be in New York at Christmas and shall save up a bundle of topics to consult you about.

Because of his fire-proof study, "the most complete literary workshop in the West," as, with pardonable pride, he described it,

I can ask with some grace of such friends as George H. Moore[7] and Benson J. Lossing[8] the loan of some books difficult to get in the market at short notice.

Have you among your friends any one of whom I could borrow rarities in early American literature? In a week or two, when I shall have ascertained what I can lay my hands on here and in Detroit, I will send you the names of some of the books I may need.[9]

Tyler may be said to have inaugurated the heroic age of scholarship in American literary history, a judgment the more certain when one watches his ceaseless efforts to secure books. The University of Michigan library had then no special collection of early American material, nor was there a great deal of it in the state or in the Middle West. In the case of the more esoteric documents, everything had to be borrowed or bought; and presently Tyler was battling on two fronts, on one against the library deficiencies of Michigan, and on the other against the ceaseless demands on his time by reason of his variety of interests. Thus, on August 27, 1875, he wrote to Detroit inquiring about the files of the Collections of the Massachusetts Historical Society and of the New York Historical Society, which were apparently not in the Michigan library.[10] Three days later he wrote George H. Moore, the librarian of the New York Historical Society, on the same question.[11] On September 2 he asked Putnam to secure Sabin's *Reprints* for him. On September 21 he wrote for twenty-one more early American items, including the William Byrd MSS., Morton's *New*

England's Memorial, Johnson's *Wonder-Working Providence,* and the works of Anne Bradstreet, adding:

> Books I *must* have; and if I exceed the amount you care to have me take on copy-right account, let me know it freely; and I will make some special arrangement with you.[12]

During the summer of 1876 the ceaseless quest went on, for President Angell, at that time in Rhode Island, was trying to obtain certain books for him at the John Carter Brown Library in Providence,[13] and the librarian of Yale University had procured a few of the books which Tyler had requested him to find.[14] In view of the deficiencies which he faced and overcame, Tyler's success is a miracle of perseverance and painstaking care.

And he had to fight himself and the university to preserve his working time. During October, November, and the first part of December, 1875, he was busy working up a new course in English literature, and studying German and Anglo-Saxon.[15] On December 15 he left (apparently ignoring the original injunction of the regents) for his annual lecture tour, from which he returned on the 31st,[16] but he was unable to resume serious work until the ninth, when he resolved to "warn [ward?] off the morning hours all work not connected with American History and Literature."[17] He then began the composi-

tion of the first chapter of his book—on Anne Bradstreet, after which he turned to Nathaniel Ward.[18]
But interruptions continued; by February 29, despite incessant labor, he had written no more than
these two studies. Why had he ever promised the
book by April 1? And yet he felt that his method
was right, that his work would not be thorough unless he studied all of the available sources. But the
book, on this scale, would be elephantine; what
should he do? He would not do shoddy work—that
he had resolved; and so, in March, he wrote Putnam once more to acquaint him with the altered
scale of the projected study. He would be fair to
Putnam and gave him a chance to withdraw from
the bargain, although he hoped that Putnam would
see the possibility of a thorough treatment on the
scale he was working. Tyler's letter is so important
that it must be given in full:

Ann Arbor, March 28, 1876.

Messrs. G. P. Putnam's Sons.
    Gentlemen:
    I have been feeling for some time past that I must write
you at some length a letter which should report to you the
progress of my labors on the book I have promised to write
for you; and especially because in grappling with the subject I find the work if done in a scholarly way far slower
and far more extensive and difficult than I expected.
Moreover, in actually dealing with it I discover the possibility of making a far more interesting and important
book than I expected; and while I stand ready to com-

plete for you the *Outlines* or *Survey* of American literature (if on reading my statement you still desire it) I
have also determined to make a book to be published by
some one and constituting an elaborate *History of American Literature* in at least two and perhaps in three volumes.

To go back a little, let me say that ever since I under-
took the writing of the *Survey* for you I have worked at
it very industriously, never stopping except for university
duties, sickness, rest, and other inevitable interruptions.
The subject has constantly grown upon my interest; and
I have no greater satisfaction in life than to be engaged
upon it. And I have made good progress; but I find it
utterly impossible to get it done within the limits of the
time that we have set for ourselves. You will remember
that I told you from the outset that I should take no conclusions at second-hand, but should express my opinion
of every author from my own original study of him. Observe that even if I were willing to compile a book (as
Swinton or Quackenbos[19] does) out of other people's labors, I could not do this in American literature; for other
people have not wrought in this field sufficiently to make
their labors available in that way. In English literature it
is very different; there every period has been traversed by
great and sure scholars like Warton, Marsh,[20] Hallam,
Morley, Masson, Macaulay, and so on; and by simply
reading a few of these authors a clever book fabricator
like Swinton could knock together a *Survey of English
literature* without the need of studying directly one soli-
tary author whom he includes in his *Survey*. But not so
in American literature—especially for the period prior
to the present century, which may be described as the interior of Africa is on the maps—"unexplored territory."
I find almost no help from previous investigators of
American literature in the seventeenth and eighteenth

centuries; so that even if I were willing to compile my book for you, I could not do it.

But as I told you from the beginning, this is a sort of work for which I have no respect, and I will not do it; and the only way in which I can write a *Survey of American literature* is actually to make a survey of it. That I am doing day by day and night by night, with honesty, perseverance, and great joy; and when I get the work done it will be real work and will stand. I take every document into my own hands and read it through critically, and write out in extenso my opinion of it; and when in that way I shall have gone over all the important documents in American literature, it will be easy for me to go back over my own work, and either elaborate it into a full history or compact it into a survey—or both. In fact, both ought to be done, and the latter may as well as not be done first. Now for the upshot:

1. If on this presentation of the case you would rather have me work up for you the more extended treatise to be called a *History*—leaving the *Survey* for after consideration—that I am willing to do.

2. But if—as I suppose—you prefer the *Survey* first and anyhow—leaving the *History* out of view—then I will keep at the *Survey;* and will labor faithfully with might and main, to get it ready for you just as soon as it can be got ready by honest work. But it cannot be finished within the period already named; and, in fact, I cannot fix upon any precise date by which it shall be done. The element of time is unspeakably inferior to the element of thoroughness. It vexes me as I trudge along, to think of a day by which I am bound to reach my journey's end. All that I can say now, after this my first experience in trying to write a book on a stipulation involving time, is that it is impossible for me to be bound by that stipulation.

3. If, however, you are going to be seriously inconvenienced by this fact, then I offer to·dissolve our agreement altogether, and return to you in cash the amount of the books which you have advanced to me on copyright account. I am myself captivated by my task; and though I have felt reluctant to ask you to furnish me with any more books on so distant a prospect, I am compelled to buy a great many more. In fact, at whatever expense, I am bringing to Ann Arbor quite a rare library of originals in American literature.

Think the matter over; try to understand the condition of my task; and let me know your decision in your own good time.

Faithfully yours,

MOSES COIT TYLER.[21]

This is an admirable letter, illustrating at once Tyler's fundamental honesty of mind, his ethical delicacy, and the absorbed delight he experienced in this full use of his powers. If Putnam did not yet quite glimpse the whole import of Tyler's ideal, it is eternally to the publisher's credit that he chose not to hold his author to the original bargain. Trusting in Tyler's good judgment, he wrote in reply that

we are sorry of course to learn of the delay that you find will be necessary in the preparation of the "Outline" or "Survey," but we recognize fully that in a work of this kind, conscientiously and thoroughly prepared, the standard and methods of the author can not fairly or safely be interfered with, and as we want the work, desire it to be thorough and satisfactory, and prefer to have it from your pen, we can only accept your decision as to the time that you will require for its preparation. . . . We should suppose the "Outline" or "Survey" would naturally come first.[22]

There was rejoicing in the brick study on Ingalls street, and Tyler bent once more to his task. The months went by, the ceaseless search for original material went on, the notes accumulated, for it was, indeed, real work, and would stand. The summer of 1877 he spent in the East, reading in libraries at New York, Boston, Cambridge, Worcester, Providence, and Philadelphia; apparently he had an important interview with Putnam while he was in New York, for we hear no more of the "Outline" or "Survey," but instead, of the "History of Colonial American Literature."[23] What work it was, but how absorbing, too!

When, overcome by heat and fatigue, and having got in New York all that it could give me, I went to the seaside for a week and made good use of the privilege of doing nothing but eat, sleep, swim, and sit by the beach gulping down that delicious ocean air. I rallied like a wild ass's colt, and at the end of my week, with fresh vigor, started for this place [Boston]. I am luxuriating in the incomparable literary treasures of the Boston libraries. At this time I am engaged in the Public library, the largest in America.[24]

A full-length history of American literature on this scale would never be done. So, lest he be overwhelmed by his materials, Tyler commenced shaping his book after his return to Ann Arbor. Ceaselessly he checked and verified what he had written. Nothing was to escape him if he could avoid it; no detail was too unimportant in a work that was to indicate what scholarship in the modern field might be.[25] There were various business details to settle, too,[26] but where both parties were eager in the cause of excellence, no shadow of difference arose between them. Finally, on October 18, 1878, the work was done; Putnam had in hand the manuscript of the last chapter.[27] Already Tyler had received specimen pages— "I make a fool of myself over it for twenty-four or forty-eight hours," for, as he whimsically observed, "it giveth me huge satisfaction."[28] He was pleased with himself,[29] pleased with Putnam's cordial and unfailing interest.[30] The long labor of the proofs was exhausting, for he was resolved that in rising to the height of his great argument, he would leave little for carping critics to find fault with.[31] Another vexation was the question of the number of volumes— Putnam standing out for publication in one volume for a while, but at length wisely acquiescing in Tyler's demand that the work appear in two.[32] On November 5, 1878 (he noted, for some strange reason, that it was Guy Fawkes day), the weary author sent off the final batch of proofs ("my last act for the book that is about to be born") and was "diverting his impatience" by compiling a list of recipients of review copies.[33] Haven Putnam told him the work would be out the following Saturday. There was a solemn excitement in the thought.

In November, 1878, there was published *The History of American Literature, 1607–1765,* by Moses Coit Tyler, in two handsomely bound octavo volumes, comprising 622 pages in all, and Tyler had carved his name unforgettably on the temple of renown. By way of relieving his nervous tension, Tyler plunged into the revision of the Morley *Manual.*[34]

The *History* was impressively received, for the Centennial exposition of 1876 had quickened interest in the national past, albeit a magazine like *The Atlantic Monthly* expressed a point of view still extant when it wrote that

the incredulous reader, especially after noting the dates on the back and seeing that the two volumes bring the history . . . only as far as 1765, is half disposed to leave the volumes unopened, lest they should prove to be backgammon boards or lunch-boxes. To take an interest in American literature previous to 1765, seems to him very like the marchioness's delectation over orange-peel and water, requiring a very hard make-believe.[35]

And there were not lacking those who seemed to take the position that Tyler had either discovered or created colonial literature by a kind of *élan vital.* But the historian, though, as he told Putnam, he found "almost no help from previous investigators," exhibited little desire to pose as a discoverer, and had gratefully employed the labors of his predecessors where he could; the difference between them and Tyler lies in the point of view, and in the laborious, first-hand acquaintance with over one hundred and fifty years of intellectual history which forms the basis of his volumes.

Previous treatments of the colonial letters had been either superficial or condescending. A nervous patriotism had led many to begin the story of American literature with the Revolution on the theory that almost everything before that time had been British.[36] Patriotism, in fact, had perverted judgment: Rufus W. Griswold, that characteristic representative of the fabulous forties, had put together his endless anthologies for the purpose of furthering republican virtues. For example, his *Readings in American Poetry* (1843), "designed principally for the use of schools," is introduced with a blast against the effete foreigner:

The books hitherto published for this purpose have been mainly or entirely compiled from the writings of foreigners. It is believed that even in a literary point of view this is inferior to none before the public, and that in some respects it is superior to all others. The poems which it contains are essentially American, in spirit as well as by origin.[37]

Aside from Kettell's *Specimens of American Poetry* (1829), which Tyler found extremely valuable,[38] the most useful of his predecessors had been the *Cyclopædia of American Literature,* edited by G. L. and E. A. Duyckinck as revised by M. L. Simons in 1875,[39] which, in its revised form, included some 900 authors. Tyler found the Duyckinck *Cyclopædia* important as a guide,[40] but, aside from the fact that an encyclopædia is not a history, the Duyckincks had confined themselves to authors already "reasonably well introduced," and the colonial field had not especially interested them.[41] The truth is that, although Tyler read manuals by Tuckerman, Nichol, Underwood, and Hart,[42] he found little in the way of a purely literary or intellectual history of the country to guide him, and was compelled to blast a Roman road through the wilderness with such aid as the historians and bibliographers might furnish.[43] In view of his difficulties the wonder is not that he made occasional slips, but that, amid a thousand difficulties, his work remains monumental still.

The time and the man had come together. In a world removed from the superficial handbooks which satisfied the pedagogical needs of the age, there was a mass of material collected by faithful antiquarians and known to the professional historian, but utterly unread by the literary—or even the academic—public: the collections and libraries of historical societies, forgotten anthologies, pamphlets and sermons piously preserved, a thousand dusty pieces to be worked into the mosaic of Tyler's volumes. What was needed was, first of all, sympathetic and intelligent exploration, and then a binding thread to hold the narrative together. Tyler wrote what in another would have been arrogance: "I have studied, as I believe, every American writer of the colonial time, in his extant writings,"[44] and it was literally true—he had not only read them, he had studied them. But he did not seek to out-do the Duyckincks or Peter Force: "I have not undertaken," he said, "to give an indiscriminate dictionary of all Americans who ever wrote anything, or a complete bibliographical account of all American books that were ever written."[45] He sought to combine scholarship of the profoundest sort with historical art: he included only those books that have "some real significance in the literary unfolding of the American mind" and that have "some noteworthy value as literature."[46]

But literature was not for him mere *belles lettres,* and in truth his two tests are well-nigh synonymous. He was writing a study in culture history; his interest was political in the grand sense; and if he lacked our recent economic prepossessions, his work remains nonetheless broadly based, firm, and solid.

There is but one thing more interesting than the intellectual history of a man, and that is the intellectual history of a nation. The American people, starting into life in the early part of the seventeenth century, have been busy ever since in recording their intellectual history in laws, manners, institutions, in battles with man and beast and nature, in highways, excavations, edifices, in pictures, in statues, in written words. It is in written words that this people, from the very beginning, have made the most confidential and explicit record of their minds. It is in these written words, therefore, that we shall now search for that record.[47]

When this passage was published Arnold's *Essays in Criticism* were thirteen years old, Whistler was winning a farthing's damages from John Ruskin for a pot of paint, flung in the public's face, the *Studies in the History of the Renaissance* was five years old ("to maintain this ecstasy, is success in life"), Oscar Wilde was at Oxford, and *The New Republic* had just passed into another edition. But Tyler had taken his stand with the old order:

Literature as a fine art, literature as the voice and ministress of æsthetic delight, they had perhaps little skill in and little regard for; but literature as an instrument of humane and immediate utility, they honored. . . . They wrote books not because they cared to write books, but because by writing books they could accomplish certain other things which they did care for.[48]

Not for him the æsthetic approach; he was primarily the historian, and a reviewer in *Scribner's Monthly* wrote precisely:

It is the history, as all true literary history should be, of the life of the people. . . . Nothing we have read gives us so clear a vision of the conditions and forces of colonial life as do these two volumes."[49]

Tyler scarcely groups his writers into schools, is not interested in source or influence, but instead, opens almost every chapter with an exposition of the historical milieu in which his subjects are to be seen.[50] He was fundamentally a historian.

If he was thus a far-off disciple of Macaulay, he was also a follower of Sainte-Beuve in whom "every literary critic of this generation must search for the costliest secrets of his craft."[51] Sainte-Beuve had made criticism a branch of biography; Tyler likewise was not happy until he had "seen" the man who produced the work. His *History* is therefore full of happy portraiture, the more charming for a certain old-fashioned, rhetorical fulness. Of this trait his picture of Edward Johnson, the author of *The Wonder-Working Providence of Zion's Saviour in New England,* is a characteristic example:

He was a very devout and explicit Puritan; his square, stalwart common-sense made itself felt in public and private affairs; and it is significant of his soundness of brain that, amid the general frenzy of the early witchcraft excitement, he was one of the few that kept their heads cool and opposed all judicial prosecution of those uncomely hags that were suspected of unlawful intimacy with the devil.

Had a man like this—a ship-carpenter and farmer, unlettered, unversed in affairs, a sort of rural alderman and militia-hero—lived anywhere else than in New England in the seventeenth century, we should by no means have suspected him of any inclinations toward authorship. . . . It was no ambition of authorship that prompted Edward Johnson to write his book, but an important tangible result which could be achieved in no other way. He handled the pen as he did the sword and the broadaxe—to accomplish something with it. . . . To him it seemed plain that the planting of God's church and state in New England was a thing that God himself had taken a very active part in, in fact was directly responsible for; that instead of being calumniated, it ought to be celebrated, and that the straightforward way of doing this would be merely to give a history of the wonder-working providence of God in the country spoken of [New England]. This single object, held steadily before him as he wrote, gave an epic unity to his work, and makes it strong and interesting yet, notwithstanding the literary clumsiness of the author.[52]

How naturally the work seems to rise up out of the man thus painted! But it is Tyler who has deduced the man from the work, and drawn this animated picture.

The trick of dramatizing the writers of the colonial past gives animation and interest to pages that might otherwise be dull. Richard Mather is presented first at the moment when the Archbishop of York was excommunicating him; the discussion of Increase Mather shows President Chauncey stopping him in his Latin oration at Commencement; judicious extracts enliven the discussion of the al-

manacs of Nathaniel Ames; Mather Byles is first
glimpsed as he ascends his Boston pulpit to receive
the denunciations of his parishioners for having remained through the siege to pray for the oppres-
sors.[53] Sometimes, it is true, Tyler's search for the
faculté maîtresse betrays him; his predisposition for
finding conceit and egotism in Cotton Mather has
led him to be ungrateful to the *Magnalia* for the
help he has had from it,[54] forgetting that Mather
confessed to leaving many "untractable" facts out
of his "history."[55] Moral judgments occasionally got
in the way of Tyler's literary acumen,[56] but on the
whole it is wonderful how evenly the balance is
held: the ribald George Alsop receives tribute for
his "jovial, vivacious, and most amusing production," despite its Rabelaisian tinge,[57] but the "wonderful memoranda" of young Jonathan Edwards
are given equally sympathetic treatment;[58] the
Southerners and the writers of the middle colonies
are discussed with the same discernment that distin-
guishes the treatment of the New Englanders.
Among Tyler's triumphs are his resuscitation of
Daniel Gookin and his discovery of John Wise.

Yet on the whole, despite the general absence of
bias, there is a warmth and richness in the New
England sections of the book, lacking in the discussion of writers living outside of that enchanted
ground. The New-Englanders were his people, their

problems were his problems, and their inheritance was, at long last, his own. He sought, indeed, to trace the unfolding of the American mind, to present feelings and attitudes that were "characteristically American," but for him, as for so many historians of his generation, the characteristically American was rooted in the characteristically New England. For example, Tyler found in volume four of the Force *Historical Tracts* works by Thomas Morton, Samuel Gorton, and John Child—writers unfavorable to the Puritan régime—but he did not discuss them in his book. In volume three of the same collection there is a well-written narrative by a cavalier, Colonel Henry Norwood, entitled *A Voyage to Virginia*; Tyler, however, omitted it, and such is the power of his *History* that Norwood does not to this day figure among the monuments of our early literary history. His positive hatred of Andros and Laud led him into sad overstatements;[59] he sometimes praised what was unworthy his praising because it seemed "genuine American talk";[60] and in the case of the literature of Bacon's Rebellion his bias led him into positive error.[61] But when all is said by the devil's advocate that can be said, Tyler had written a truly great historical work, generous in its sympathy, revolutionary in its scope and range, brilliant in style—an enduring study, the first great work of scholarship in the field of American literary history. He touched the dry bones of colonial letters and they sprang to life.

But could he continue at this high level? He had planned to write the literary history of his country in three or four volumes; the first two were done; and he had stepped into the company of scholars of the first rank, a major figure. Recognition swiftly followed—election to corresponding membership of the New England Historical and Genealogical Society,[62] to membership in the Massachusetts Historical Society in February, 1879, to the American Antiquarian Society in April, to the Rhode Island Historical Society in 1880.[63] He was made free of the commonwealth of scholars, and corresponded with his kind on equal terms. Western Reserve University invited him in May, 1879, to deliver the Phi Beta Kappa address. Henry Morley had heard of his "high fame," and was glad to have him revise the *Manual*.[64] Finally (but this is to anticipate) White, who had been non-committal before, wrote him that, should he, White, resign as president of Cornell, Tyler might expect to go on to "greater triumphs" as his successor.[65] White did not resign, despite Tyler's sleepless nights,[66] but the Lowell Institute in Boston actually invited him, westerner that he was, to deliver a series of lectures on his favorite topic, and to the preparation of these lectures he devoted the months of January and February, 1881. The first address he gave on March 16, using the material he later incorporated in chapter one of *The Literary History of the American Revolution;* the sixth and last, on April 1. His month in the East was a revelation of the standing he had achieved: Rowland Hazard thought of him as a possible candidate for a professorship of history at Brown;[67] he conversed familiarly with Longfellow, Howells, Lathrop, Thomas B. Aldrich, and President Eliot of Harvard; Justin Winsor "expressed a deep interest" in his coming to Cambridge as a professor;[68] he lectured before various eastern historical societies;[69] he contracted to write a biography of Patrick Henry for the American Statesmen Series which J. T. Morse was editing—he was, in short, a great man. It was hard to continue with the slavery of exacting scholarship amid this adulation, this excitement.

Even before the book was off the press he was writing E. D. Neill concerning the Rev. Mr. Duché, chaplain of the Continental Congress, whom he was to discuss in the next volume,[70] but the *Manual* distracted him, and though on August 7 he began in earnest (as he believed) to study the revolutionary period,[71] he was, in truth, tired. Vainly he put before him a watchword from Trevelyan on single-mindedness, urging himself

to pursue it without remissness and without misgiving; to withstand resolutely all counter-attractions, whether they come in the shape of distracting pleasures or of competing desires.[72]

But he was famous now, and he might treat himself to a little rest. The next day he read Macaulay and Dickens; the next, Macaulay, Goethe, and a little French, for "I have been alarmed at my loss of facility in reading French and am trying to recover it."[73] A week later he persuaded himself that he was just "doing a lot of miscellaneous reading . . . to freshen my mind before settling down to close work on my next volume."[74] Thus the weeks drifted pleasantly by. He joined the Episcopal Church. He could afford to be angry with *The Nation* and condescending towards *Faust*.[75] The summer went past; it was pleasant to sit in his study (christened Hillcroft) and loaf as the warm autumn breathed on the hills by the Huron River and hung the pleasant streets with shimmering gold. And then suddenly it was October—he had done nothing; he commenced excusing himself to his diary, and resolved to plunge into work once more:

Ann Arbor, 13 October, 1879. It is almost a year since I left off work on American literature. Since then I have given six months to the dreary labor of revising and publishing my Morley book, and during the past three and a half months I have given myself up to intellectual recreation. I think it is now time to settle down to steady work on my next volume. My plan for the present is to give the time between breakfast and 9 A.M. to French, from 9 to 1 to American literature. This latter will include not only books on American literature, but books relating directly to my handling of American literature—*e.g.,* English literature from Pope to Carlyle inclusive; French literature for some space; together with general European and American history for the eighteenth and nineteenth centuries.[76]

He was in his middle forties now, and felt time slipping underneath his feet. So he returned to Drake—at the letter "D" where he had left off in August, and spiritedly finished the job by the 24th —and then thought of something else to do, puttering around his study at miscellaneous tasks. And there were lectures to compose, and the first thing he knew it was December, and nothing done yet. So, on the shortest day of the year he took a new resolve: "I really begin; and I begin with Thomas Paine,"[77] and then on December 26, he resolved to begin serious work with the new year.[78]

Which he really did, for January 1 was a day "of great splendor; just cool enough; the air vibrant with inspiration,"[79] and he labored away regularly (I "despair of making the entire field of American history attractive, yet I think the fault is in the historian"),[80] reading Paine, Freneau, Trumbull, Dickinson, Carver, Robert T. Paine, Stephen Johnson, Rush, and Fisher Ames, besides much else, by May. One morning in March he had his "first glimpse of a plan for organizing my last volume, 1765–1815," a scheme which he worked out like a historian rather than like a literary critic;[81] and then, somehow or other, he got interested in politics,[82] and it was summer again. He persuaded himself he would work better if he went to the eastern libraries and studied there. Now he was forty-five, but "still, whatever is, is right! Let me try to stick to that."[83] He returned to Ann Arbor in the autumn; on September 20, 1880, he received his disturbing letter from Andrew D. White, and was totally upset; even by November he could not sleep because of it.[84] The year, despite his triumphs, closed "more sadly than it began"; he worked for a while partly on a sermon on "Manliness" and partly on Jonathan Odell, the Tory; he went to talk with the bishop about taking orders;[85] and then, as we have seen, he went east to lecture. And on March 1, 1881, he received another disturbing letter from White, who had not resigned, but who wanted to make him a professor at Cornell.

CHAPTER VIII

TYLER had received his letter from White just four days before he left Ann Arbor for his Lowell Lectures in Boston. He waited for a few days before answering it, for he had been "awfully pressed by work and by social distractions, and am nearly ready to drop with fatigue."[1] He thought the problem over and over. White had written from the American Legation in Berlin on March 7:

Suppose that our Trustees established a Professorship of American History and Literature at the coming Commencement at a salary of say $2250 to $2500 would you be inclined to accept it? Your answer shall be seen by me alone. There is much reason to hope that our increased means will enable us to do this very soon. Give me your views fully on the whole subject.

The situation would be in many respects attractive. The collection of American books in the University Library, including as it does Sparks' private library as well as those which I have myself brought together, give you much material. Then you would be near the Historical Societies of New York and Brooklyn to say nothing of New England. With our present railway communication a new and broader lecture field would be easily open to you. But, best of all, your college work would thus be brought entirely into a line with your literary work.[2]

How kind, and yet how disturbing! When White had written him confidentially about the Cornell presidency, Tyler had told him that administrative work would "hinder too much my work as a student and writer of American history," and now this had been offered. Well, he could not come for the salary mentioned, and besides Harvard might want him.[3] And could he leave Michigan? He returned from his lecturing to receive a second letter from White saying that "$2750 in Ithaca is very nearly, if not quite, as good as $4000 in Cambridge," and that he would not recommend Tyler to his trustees without Tyler's consent.[4] Why could he not, he wondered, decide these things simply and easily? He wrote White again on the fourth of May, and the next day entered in his diary a note on the vanity of history writing and "these nineteen years of secular life: the bewilderment of them, the small result, the sin, the frivolity!"[5] For he was getting older now, and the curling hair and luxuriant beard which the Ann Arbor campus knew in 1875 was changing. In 1884 a writer on *The Detroit Times* said he looked like a Scotchman with "his sandy beard, slightly sprinkled with gray, hair of somewhat lighter shade, prominent cheek bones and keen, restless eyes. . . . His forehead is high and prominent, the hair receding to the verge of baldness, and nose of a decided type." And his voice was "inclined to unsteadiness," and the innocently pitiless reporter further observed that he talked like a scholar rather than an orator, more like a thinker than like an elocutionist,—he who once dreamed of rivalling Beecher.[6] Yes, he was growing old. It was harder to make changes, and when he did make them, he could not be sure they were right. Perhaps it was better to stay where God had called him, for "I cannot lead in the tumultuous, oratorical, public life of a preacher, without breaking down."[6a] The dream of being a great orator was over.

But in the meantime White had written another letter, one such as only White could compose, full of enthusiasm and affection, and touching, with conscious or unconscious shrewdness, every argument that could move the hesitating man in Ann Arbor, telling him that "the country is longing for" a great American historian who would work from original sources, and suggesting that he write Henry W. Sage, the second father of Cornell University.[7] Tyler knew Sage, he knew Cornell, he knew and loved White, and it was hard to refuse. On the 12th of May he poured out his troubles to Sage, and two days later, he had a walk with Professor Frieze, the acting president at Michigan, for Angell was off on one of his diplomatic ventures. Frieze did not want him to go and "thinks sufficient money can be raised here to buy a library of Americana." Moses passed wakeful hours, but he prayed God for light and "my mind became irradiated, and for the first time I seemed to see my way to Cornell made luminous."[8] Then Sage wrote, offering $3000 and telling him to come and look the situation over. So he went to Cornell and talked with everybody, and returned, and on May 23, hoping it was "the will of God," he telegraphed Sage he would come.[9] Things seemed to clear up suddenly; in addition to the coming increase in salary, he received that same month the last installment of a $5000 legacy left him by his uncle, Samuel Coit, so that, when he had lifted the mortgage on his home, he had $1500 in free cash. For the first time in forty-six years he was financially independent.[10]

But it was hard to leave Michigan and Hillcroft and Ann Arbor, and with a full heart Moses wrote out his letter of resignation, saying that he went to Cornell only because it could give him larger facilities and ampler private means. "I had," he said a little sadly, "no desire to leave the University of Michigan. . . . I have found multitudes of young men and women who were to me as willing workfellows in noble tasks; and in this happy sphere of robust and inspiring work, I had hoped to spend the remainder of my life." He ended his letter to Frieze on the graceful cadence that he was leaving the university at "the full height of its great prosperity."[11] (On January 13, 1881, he and Professor Adams had been appointed to present a plea for a new library to the legislature.[12] But that was so uncertain!) And then, when Sage had his acceptance, "comes an intimation from President Barnard that there is a vacancy at Columbia." He "read the letter at Moore's book store. The cold sweat came out on my body, and I almost reeled in my chair." Seven thousand dollars—and New York! What a trial of his faith![13] He did not know what to do—he could not tell his wife, though he wrote to his brother John, and he telegraphed and wrote to New York.[14] Sadly he packed and shipped his books, thinking that probably God wanted him to go to Cornell anyway, but when the time came to leave the study where he had written his great book, it was very hard: "I should not have had the courage to resolve to go away" from the "dear old sacred home of my soul," he thought, "had I known" what it was to cost.[15] Even after he reached Cornell, despite his belief that God was guiding him, he continued to flirt with Barnard at Columbia, writing him October 8 that he was still a candidate, telegraphing that he would accept, if elected, and finally, on January 28, 1882, withdrawing from the ghastly competition.[16] He had had to struggle to resign himself to the mysterious ways of God.

As the train paused on the brow of the hill before descending to Ithaca, Tyler, poised

"Far above Cayuga's water
With its waves of blue,"

might look down on the lake, on Ithaca with its population of 12,000 "framed in by hills covered with a wealth of foliage," and eventually gaze at East Hill, crowned by Sage Chapel and the university buildings. The level space below the hills was "dotted with handsome residences, with sloping lawns and pretty shrubbery." It *was* a pretty place, with its old colonial houses set among the innumerable trees, the rolling hills, the sheen of the lake, the seven streams, "concerning which [Ithaca] challenges the world."[17] Even Ann Arbor was not so lovely.

Moses did not have to stop with his family at the pillared "Clinton House," "the finest hotel between New York and Buffalo,"[18] for Henry W. Sage, bearded, shrewd, and genial, invited the Tylers to stay with him,[19] a pleasant ending to a hot trip in July. The new professor presently engaged a suite of rooms at the Cascadilla Building above Cascadilla Creek, where the family lived until November, 1882.[20] By and by he built a house—"Hillcroft," named for the Ann Arbor home.[21]

That Tyler had bettered his professional situation by coming to Cornell in the summer of 1881 was not immediately obvious. For Cornell had been born in controversy, and antagonism had been its spiritual food for the thirteen years of its existence —the hostility of small colleges, the denunciation of

various religious denominations, the attacks of pedagogical conservatives, the assaults of lawyers, the
fault-finding of politicians. The chapter in the *Autobiography* of its first president which sketches its history from 1868 to 1874 is significantly entitled
"Rocks, Storms, and Peril."[22] White, backed by Ezra
Cornell and Henry Sage, had done wonders in as-
sembling a faculty of distinction, but as he had been
three times appointed to diplomatic posts which
took him away from Ithaca, he had not been able to
give his whole time to the university. From 1879 to
1881, he had been in Berlin, and the vice-president,
Professor Channing Russel, had been at the helm.
Russel was an excellent lecturer, but as an adminis-
trator, White said, he was one who "had a dre'dful
winnin' way to make folks hate him."[23] Conditions
finally grew so desperate that in June, 1880, the
alumni demanded that White return.[24]

In the fall of 1881 White accordingly came home
to repair the damage if he could.[25] He found the income less than it had been since 1872; student fees
were at their lowest ebb; and there had been no important bequest to the university since 1868–9.[26]
Moreover, the expenditures for the year exceeded
the income of the institution. Finally, the student
body showed an alarming decline; the year that
White returned there were fewer students at Cornell than there had been in any previous year, and

the decline had unfortunately been steady. The year
after his return found only 312 students in attendance (1880).[27] The faculty numbered forty-four,
but of these only sixteen were in the humanities.
The library, the condition of which White had
held out to Tyler as a particular inducement to
come, was in truth not good. Despite an appropriation of $20,000 for books in 1880, Tyler wrote that
White had certainly "misrepresented the state of
the library to me; and has not kept his promise to
me about the purchase of books."[28] To increase Tyler's disappointment, Mrs. Jennie McGraw-Fiske,
who had recently died, had left a fund of a million
dollars to the Cornell library, but the will was con-
tested, bitterness developed between the Fiske heirs
and certain of the trustees, and after nine years of
negotiation and litigation, the Supreme Court of
the United States denied the validity of the bequest.[29] It was all very discouraging. No wonder
that the alumni requested a survey of Cornell University to be made, a report which is one of the most
interesting documents in the history of higher education in the country.[30] It was a good fighting document, the first pages of which were devoted to "the
correction of erroneous impressions concerning the
university." Perhaps the most cheerful statement in
it, so far as the faculty was concerned, was that,
though trustees had appointed "too many profes-

sors for the funds available," hereafter "every member of the instructing body should receive a salary on which he can support himself and his family with *ease and comfort*."[31] Moses was no doubt gratified to learn that the work in American History was "in most able hands."[32]

But for the present he was working hard, finding an "incredible stimulus in the fact of having my professorship in the line of my literary studies."[33] White had written him in May of his desire to strengthen the new department of history, political and social science, and general jurisprudence, and the strengthening had taken the form of Tyler's appointment to the first professorship of American history in the country, for the other instructors in the department—Herbert Tuttle, Goldwin Smith, Henry C. Adams, Charles K. Adams, and Edward A. Freeman—were non-resident lecturers.[34] To have such a chair had been long a dream of White's, who protested in his report of 1871-2 that "it is a curious fact, and one not very creditable to our nation, that at present if any person wishes to hear a full and thorough course of lectures on the history of this country, he must go to Paris or Berlin for it."[35] Now Moses Tyler, the first important historian of the national letters, was to create the first chair of American history.

He took only a sober joy in the situation, however, for he was vastly troubled; that fall he offered his "unworthy life" to God and Bishop Harris made him a deacon in the Episcopal Church.[36] And now he had a new set of lectures to prepare; characteristically going back to the beginning of things, and remembering Buckle, he investigated prehistoric America, and the physical geography and anthropology of the continent with a view to picturing the primitive state of the land.[37] He worked steadily until September 20, when he delivered his first lecture, but, in view of Garfield's death, he spent a large part of the period in talking about the assassinated president.[38] The rest of the first term he lectured on prehistoric America, for he was in no hurry to get on; at Cornell one was expected to do things with German thoroughness. The second term he lectured on the development of civil government in America, discussing each colony in turn, speaking slowly so that the students might take down what he said. The students were disappointed at first, for it was deadening, but by and by, as he mastered his materials, Tyler spoke with his old-time vehemence, and became once more the delight of a campus.[39] He went to hear E. A. Freeman in November, finding him "dull and tedious to an almost deadly degree,"[40] and returned to his own work better satisfied. Once he brought an ax-head to class and proposed founding a museum of American archæology at Cornell.[41]

MOSES COIT TYLER AS A CORNELL PROFESSOR
From a photograph owned by Mr. William L. Clements.

But the year closed sadly—"a pathetic year, indeed"; he was very serious-minded, talking with bishops and finding fault with them—in his diary—worrying about his soul, worrying about the Columbia business, though, once he had made up his mind to withdraw, "my spirit sings like a lark, under the joy which this resolution gives me."[42]

In March, 1881, he had agreed to write a life of Patrick Henry for the American Statesmen Series, but he found it impossible to do so many things; he wrote Morse in December, asking permission to lay the project aside until he had more leisure.[43] Leisure, however, refused to come; in February he lectured before the Peabody Institute;[44] and at intervals he wondered when he would go on with the history of American literature. The news of great men passing away saddened him; he chronicled with regret the news of Darwin's death and then that of Emerson. By and by it was May and "one year ago, by the day of the week, Jeannette and I were received here by the Sages and inspected the university, and I was conquered."[45] He did not seem cheered by the thought. The truth was that he was working too hard, and would have to pay for it. At the close of the college year his physician ordered him away from Cornell for three months.

He went to Europe with Hiram Corson ("I never travelled with a more delightful companion"), and on the way over, Tyler conducted the ship-board religious services, and was superior to actors and actresses. "I remember the emotion with which I first caught sight of Europe sixteen years ago. I can't enjoy that sentiment now, or call it back." And he solemnly told the "youngsters" to be young.[46] But, once landed, all his eagerness came back and he ran hither and yon in England investigating churches and historic spots, drinking it all in again, forgetting Cornell and its troubles, writing everything down in the graphic fragment of a travel diary which his daughter has printed.[47] Lowell called on him—a great honor, for the ambassador was not supposed to make the first advance—and awe-struck Mr. Bowker told Moses that it was "the leader of American literature calling on its historian." Lowell assured him that "men like you . . . have not the least influence" on American civilization, and invited him to breakfast, where he met Froude, Leslie Stephen, and Matthew Arnold, who wanted to come to America. He was sleeping better now, and liking England very much, but "I am cured of all lingering desire to live here."

And then Paris, where he jumped off an omnibus (sacrificing fifteen centimes) to stare at Victor Hugo reading in a window, watching him "with respectful admiration and venerating scrutiny," until Hugo finally turned his back. And then Switzerland . . .

and Germany, and finally Liverpool, and so home, "as eager now to go home as I was three months ago to come to Europe." He was completely cured of his melancholy.

For the year 1882–3 Tyler offered two courses of three terms each in American history, the first covering the field from his lectures on prehistoric America to 1765 (this for juniors), and the second, from 1765 to 1865, for seniors. He was "greatly enjoying my work this year . . . getting it well in hand, and have a grip on my classes that I never had before." They gave him a new classroom which was "a great comfort and help"; it reminded him of Michigan.[48] Presently he was offering two seminaries besides, in which "he was occasionally persuaded to draw upon his reminiscence of public men."[49] But this was a weakness which he more often sternly conquered. By and by, when the President White School of History and Political Science was organized, he was offering graduate seminars in the long room in the Library Building, with its shuttered windows, the plaster cast of Augustus Cæsar, the files of Hansard, *The Congressional Record* and other impressive works marshalled along the shelves, and the primitive electric lights dangling from the ceiling.[50] There, once a week, "difficulties and discoveries are presented and dealt with, and regular accounts are given of new publications and of other notable events relating to the progress of research elsewhere in American history."[51] For he was a famous professor, and reasonably well contented. White also was pleased: "In no part of the world today is there so complete a course in American History, either in extent or equipment, as can be found here, and I congratulate you that we have in charge of it a Professor whose high reputation in this field is acknowledged both in the old world and in the new."[52] Honors were offered him—the presidency of Trinity College (Hartford, Connecticut), which he declined; the degree of Doctor of Humane Letters from the Regents of the State of New York.[53] He was included in a list of forty immortals chosen by ballot among the readers of *The Critic and Good Literature,* outranking Dana, Whipple, Lathrop, Story, and Parkman.[54]

But these baubles, which might have pleased him once, had lost their fascination:

My heart has almost wholly deserted literary work— the inspiration for which was love of fame. This has now lost its power over me. Fame is an illusion in the universe. The only motive worthy of a man is love. Under that motive, I am impelled straight to the work of the ministry. I await God's orders.[55]

But God had not yet spoken clearly, and in the meantime Moses was ordained a priest at St. John's Church in Ithaca, conducting the services from May to July, 1883, in the rector's absence, and organizing a guild for the Episcopalian students.[56] The day of his ordination was "the most solemn day in my life,"[57] yet he did not forsake his profession, working occasionally at his biography of Patrick Henry, puttering at American literature, listening critically to Goldwin Smith's lectures ("he talks such English as one rejoices to hear") and finding him pessimistic.[58] Life was not joy, but duty; perhaps he was wrong in teaching (it was the old, old conflict), but perhaps also it was "a question of health,"[59]—he could not afford another breakdown. He kept drearily at his chores: "the literary attractions of my period (1765–89) do not yet excite my interest. The whole task is a—task to me."[60] Did he remember the far-off *Christian Union* days when he had written that every fact concerning American history needed to be re-examined? By the end of his second year he had begun to "feel adjusted to my new home,"[61] but the fact did not keep him from attending a diocesan convention in Rome, New York, or from spending the summer in England and France with White, who wanted Max Müller to come to Cornell.[62] Tyler noted that Barnum had once sent Müller proposals for exhibiting him, but "he is of a fine English family and of course declined."

The next year things went on placidly; Tyler was working regularly at the material for the next part of his *History,* and mildly enjoying it, save for occasional lapses into religious melancholy. Somehow he felt that he must continue at his post until he had finished that task; then his "secular life will be paid off, and I shall be free in honor to give my time, voice, pen, soul, body, to direct work for the souls of men."[63] He liked his study (which he called a den); he took a mild interest in politics; he convinced himself for the hundredth time that the "academic relation to the world" was the one for which he was called and chosen.[64] And that summer he bought a lot in the cemetery near the campus, though he did not mention the fact to any member of his family at the time.[65]

Amidst these cross-currents the movement of his life was nevertheless forward, though he might not know it, and the register of his professional engagements testifies to the grasp and solidity of his mind. In 1883 he delivered the commencement address at Cornell, choosing for his subject "The Historic Beginning of our Present American College System." Even earlier that year he described for the New York Historical Society "Bishop Berkeley's Visit to America, 1729–31, and its effect on Higher Education"—an early form of the essay which he subsequently included in *Three Men of Letters.* On September 9, 1884, he delivered before the newly organized American Historical Association a paper on "The Influence of Thomas Paine on the Popular Resolution for Independence," in which he tried to solve the problem why, when up to July, 1775, there had been no feeling for independence in the country, when, as late as December, the New Hampshire legislature totally disavowed aiming at independence, independence was six months later the avowed aim of the Revolution. The causes of this "rapid transition" were, he thought, complex, but the admirably named *Common Sense* of Paine, that "ill-taught, heady, and slashing English castaway," had had its profound influence.[66] Tyler was a little unfair to Paine, but it was a good paper, one that pointed toward his second *History*. On May 7, 1885, he again addressed the New York Historical Society on "Francis Hopkinson, Revolutionary Statesman and Satirist,"[67] and a year later (April 27, 1886) he made a strong plea before the American Historical Association for the preservation of family papers and other historical materials:

American society is composed of more movable elements than was the case even in the colonial time. We have few examples of families maintained through several generations in the same homes; our houses are of combustible material; and our habits are those of recklessness as to fires. The result of our present social conditions is that the kinds of historical documents now referred to, if retained in private custody, are peculiarly liable to neglect, and even to destruction.[68]

On such occasions he spoke as one having authority.[69]

In truth, Tyler was among the active forces in the furthering of historical study during the eighties, and one of the founders of the American Historical Association. The leading spirit in this enterprise was Charles Kendall Adams, still professor of history at the University of Michigan, who wrote Tyler on May 10, 1884, asking if "the time hasn't come to unite our forces in the formation of some sort of an Association."[70] Tyler, Herbert Baxter Adams of The Johns Hopkins University, and Frank B. Sanborn, secretary of the American Social Science Association, all of whom C. K. Adams addressed, agreed that the time was ripe for such a project. Among themselves (after adding John Eaton, president of the American Social Science Association, to their group) they agreed on a proposal, drew up a circular of information, and distributed copies among persons likely to be interested. Tyler had especially in charge New York and the middle states. A call was issued for an organization meeting to be held at Saratoga, September 9, 1884; the American Social Science Association was to meet there September 8–12, and offered the "advantage of its name and existing organization, the use of its hall for historical sessions, and [last but not least among the inducements] special rates at the United States Hotel." Notices were also sent to the leading newspapers and magazines, which found space for them and for comment on the idea. *The Springfield Republican* thought that the association was "one of the felt wants of this country"; *The Independent* and *The Nation* printed editorials; and *The Boston Herald* remarked (with some acuteness) that the call for this meeting "registers the rise of a new generation of Americans and the growth of a better method in the study of history." Among the "younger school" of historical writers it enumerated C. K. Adams, Tyler, Judge Chamberlain, Andrew D. White, and Frank Austin Scott.[71] If a new school existed, Tyler, whose disgust with the old-fashioned, rhetorical historians was growing,[72] had been a powerful force for change.

Interest in the new association was gratifying, and the prime movers of the enterprise planned "a private gathering of the friends" of the association to discuss the problem of organization. Tyler called the meeting to order, and nominated Justin Winsor for permanent chairman, and the twenty-five "friends" present unanimously voted Winsor into the chair. Then Tyler took the floor to move that the association be formed on a basis independent of the American Social Science Association, and had the deep delight of seeing his motion prevail over the opposition of "Hon. John Eaton," president of

the Social Science Association. Then they created a
constitutional committee, and Tyler was put on
that; and when, by and by, they had the first formal
public session, everything was as neatly ordered as
if it had been a political convention. The next day
the constitution was adopted, "General John Eaton"
(the various secretaries do not seem to have followed
the same style book) magnanimously moving that
it be so, and by unanimous vote it was so ordered.
White was elected president, and Moses Coit Tyler
was put on the executive committee. His place
among the dignified sobrieties of history was secure.
A pardonable complacency shines through a diary
entry made after he returned home from these excitements:

> The most satisfying privileges in life have come to me
> here. I can imagine how I might be happier even than I
> now am; but never before have I been so happy—so deep-
> ly, soundly, solidly happy. The great fermentations of
> existence are done. I have found my niche, my sphere,
> my vocation, my horizon, even my burial place.[73]

Alas! As long as he lived he was going to assure
himself that he had found his sphere, and at the
same time gaze longingly at other horizons!

But there were still some things that could annoy
him, and one of them was the Plumed Knight.
Always Tyler had voted the Republican ticket, but
he had been a charter member of a Civil Service

Reform Club, organized at Cornell in 1882,[74] and he did not like Blaine. So he became a conscientious mugwump and voted for Cleveland; the closeness of the election made him write excitedly in his diary about "the verge of a great national peril" and "awful possibilities," which did not eventuate.[75] The more he saw of Cleveland, the better he liked him; and when it was finally conceded that Cleveland had won, Tyler wrote to congratulate him and included a word for reform. Cleveland's reply pleased him, "showing a clear and firm intelligence respecting the Civil Service as reformed from the spoils system."[76] When Cleveland puzzled him, Tyler wrote to Edgar Apgar, the man who had "made" Cleveland; Apgar wrote back to explain things, and Tyler had made another interesting contact. For Apgar died the next year; his friends, wishing to commemorate his many endearing qualities, resolved on a memorial volume, and asked Tyler to edit it. This he consented to do, composing for it a small life, and gathering a collection of anecdotes.[77] The writing seemed to come easily enough; after returning from a lecture tour to New York ("the horrible Beecher business. Ten years ago!"),[78] his mind seemed to crystallize; he recurred to his half-forgotten contract with Morse, and on January 22, 1886, wrote that gentleman "to ask whether my promise to write 'Patrick Henry' for his series, is outlawed."

He was depressed about his *History,* but perhaps
"an excursion into another field will restore my
spirits."[79] . . . And on August 2, 1885, he was fifty
years old.

Perhaps he had expected too much of his new
situation; perhaps his religious life was still troubling him, though the outer world found him as
genial as ever; perhaps it was his health. Certain it
is that the impression one receives from the records
of these first years at Cornell is of a spirit subdued,
seeking a basis for life, and perhaps finding only a
doubtful one. The entry in his diary for January 1,
1884, is the keynote of this time in its sobriety, its note
of muffled doubt: "I enter the New Year in high
health, and with spirits clear and confident, though
chastened. The one grief of my life is that I fell
away from the noble cause that I began. Yet—what
lessons I have had! Could I have learned them in
any other way?"[80]

CHAPTER IX

TYLER's agreement to write a life of Patrick Henry
had been made in the spring of 1881. Now, five
years later, Morse wrote him in response to his inquiry that, although the publishers had put the contract aside, he would be glad to have the book, adding that there should be few quotations.[1] Hitherto
Tyler had been dawdling at the task, but working
at the Apgar volume had re-kindled his creative
enthusiasm. One Sunday, when he was too brain-
weary to go to church, he lay on his back, and
thought, and prayed, and meditated on plans for
the book.[2] He went to work with an unusual rush
of energy, reading Wirt's life and Everett's account in Sparks' *American Biography,* and looking
through the Fontaine MSS. in the library at Cornell
and the writings of Thomas Jefferson. The task absorbed him: by April 1 he was composing his first
chapter, for (like Woodrow Wilson) he worked up
each set of facts as he went along. On August 7 he
had finished the first eight chapters—to the end of
the Continental Congress, when he knocked off for
a month at the seaside. By November he had finished
the revision of chapter ten.[3] It seemed to him he had

never worked so well or been so steadily free from interruptions. He was temporarily halted later in November by the absence of books, but William Wirt Henry, grandson of Patrick Henry, sent him what he lacked, and placed at Tyler's disposal, besides, his rich mass of manuscript material. He also lent the historian Henry's fee-books as a lawyer. In fact, William Wirt Henry was invaluable.

By December 4 Tyler was pushing rapidly on to the conclusion—"had a great flow of composition,"[4] "brain at full tilt."[5] By the end of the year he was almost done, but there were interruptions. He was spurred on again by a letter from Morse saying that he wanted to begin printing at once if he could persuade the publishers to use an unfinished manuscript.[6] On January 18 Tyler finished a final revision of the first fifteen chapters, which he sent to Morse.[7] January 21 he "pitched into *Patrick* like fun"; he had got down as far as 1781–4.[8] But Morse, aghast at the size of the manuscript, wired him to know how much more he proposed to write, and there was endless correspondence back and forth. Tyler stood by his guns: if the work was not acceptable, it might be returned, or he would shorten the remaining chapters, but he would not cut down what he had done.[9] On March 21, 1887, he finished the first draft of the final chapter: "his death, which I have just described, seemed very real and personal to me;

and my eyes were moist as I wrote."[10] Two days later he finished the final revision. He had worked himself into a cold and felt the need of dawdling, but he had confidence in what he had done.[11] One afternoon in September, as he was about to mow the lawn, the express company's wagon drove up to bring him the first ten copies of *Patrick Henry*.

The reception of the volume was, on the whole, highly favorable, albeit Tyler detected "a low growl from the Jeffersonians in the *Richmond dispatch*."[12] George Bancroft paid him "on the whole the most valuable compliment I ever had," writing that "you have said all that there was to be said; you have said it thoroughly well; you have rejected all the trash called tradition which cannot stand the test of historic criticism,"[13] and later sent him his portrait.[14] White was pleased, and the newspapers were favorable, if sometimes "flippant and trashy."[15]

In truth, Tyler had done a good, sound job; of all his books it is the only one still in print. Albert Bushnell Hart, reviewing it in 1887, remarked that "it is not too much to say that the real Patrick Henry for the first time stands before us. . . . More perhaps than any other of the *American Statesmen Series,* it places before us a clear view of a man as he lived, and of his connection with the times."[16] Edward Channing remarked that it was "still a stimulating and useful book";[17] and in his revision

of an earlier biography of Henry (published originally in 1907, and re-published in 1929), Mr.
George Morgan leans heavily on Tyler at many
points, and corrects him in few.[18] The publication
of *Patrick Henry: Life, Correspondence, Speeches*
in three volumes by William Wirt Henry in 1891
merely amplified and substantiated Tyler's analysis,
for the two men had worked sympathetically together, and Tyler had paid cordial tribute to Henry
in his preface.[19]

The book was in truth a triumph for that "better
method in the study of history" which had led to
the founding of the American Historical Association. The rhetorical school was waning, and one of
the chief tasks of the historians of Tyler's generation
was to re-examine the mythology which inhabited
the American Valhalla. Of these mythological cre-
ations Henry, thanks to William Wirt, was one of
the principal characters; a thousand school boys
knew by heart the passage about "George the Third
may profit by their example" and the passage about
"Give me liberty or give me death." For Wirt's
Sketches of the Life and Character of Patrick Henry,
first published in 1817, though it does not meet the
test of historical accuracy, meets and triumphantly
passes the test of artistic vitality. Wirt did not pre-
tend to exhaust the materials, which he found scanty
and meagre; and, a busy man, he was able to devote

only portions of his time to the book. But on the basis of such researches as he could make, he wrote a really great work of fiction based on history; he created Patrick Henry. And Tyler, wiser than some subsequent writers, did not crush Wirt for his fictions, but tactfully praised him for what he was able to do:

> Any one who will take the trouble to ascertain the enormous disadvantages under which Wirt wrote, and which, as we now know, gave him great discouragement, will be inclined to applaud him for making so good a book, rather than to blame him for not making a better one.[20]

Tyler liked rhetoric, skilfully handled, and Wirt at his best was a skilful rhetorician.

To the correction of the popular concept of Patrick Henry, Tyler was able to marshal a variety of first-hand evidence which might well have made Wirt despair. Through the kindness of William Wirt Henry he was given copies of all of Patrick Henry's official letters extant in the files of the Department of State at Washington, besides the mass of supplementary material which Henry's grandson had patiently brought together. And Tyler had at his disposal Force's *American Archives,* useful in placing Henry against the background of his time, together with the collected writings of the "fathers," however inadequate the texts of these might occasionally be. Finally, there was Jared

Sparks' *Correspondence of the American Revolution,* and the innumerable notes Tyler had collected for the continuation of his literary history. If the Cornell professor lacked the economic point of view from which a writer like Parrington or Beard analyzes Patrick Henry and the social facts which determined his views, it must be remembered that the first task of his generation was to correct the egregious errors which had accumulated in American political history. Economic determinism as a key to the past, with all the virtues and all the faults of that point of view, still lay slumbering in the womb of time; six years were to elapse before Frederick J. Turner was to read his epochal paper on the significance of the frontier in American history.

Tyler's task, then, was to disentangle the real Patrick Henry from the myths which had gathered about him. In general, these myths were three. The first one, most indelibly imprinted on the popular consciousness, was the myth of the uneducated rhapsodist with a tongue of flame inspired by heaven in the cause of political righteousness. Jefferson had strongly influenced Wirt in the creation of this picture:

> From what has already been stated, it will be seen how little education had to do with the formation of this great man's mind. He was, indeed, a mere child of nature, and nature seems to have been too proud and too jealous of her work, to permit it to be touched by the hand of art.

She gave him Shakespeare's genius, and bade him, like Shakespeare, to depend on that alone.[21]

Tyler brought this picture to the acid test of fact and dissolved it into air by showing that Henry not only quizzed his grandmother in Latin, but carried on a conversation with a French envoy in that tongue.[22] The "better method" had led him to the Fontaine manuscripts at Cornell, which, of course, Wirt could not have seen.

In order to make Henry's success more dramatic, Wirt had taken the view that the first three years of Henry's legal career had been years of failure and that his admission to the bar had been a *tour de force* of native intelligence. Wirt's picture is skilful:

Of the science of law, he knew almost nothing: of the practical part he was so wholly ignorant, that he was not only unable to draw a declaration or a plea, but incapable, it is said, of the most common or simple business of his profession, even of the mode of ordering a suit, giving a notice, or making a motion in court. It is not at all wonderful, therefore, that such a novice, opposed as he was by veterans, covered with the whole armour of the law, should linger in the background for three years.[23]

Whatever might be true of the manner of Henry's being admitted to the bar, Tyler showed on the basis of the evidence furnished him by William

Wirt Henry that the hero had, in three years, charged fees in 1185 cases, in striking contrast to Jefferson, who, in the first four years of his practice, did less than half as much business.[24]

But it was Henry the orator who drew from Wirt his liveliest and most inaccurate passages. Wirt's description of the first Continental Congress has all the charm of an old steel engraving:

The meeting was awfully solemn. The object which had called them together was of incalculable magnitude. The liberties of no less than three millions of people, with that of all their posterity, were staked on the wisdom and energy of their councils. No wonder, then, at the long and deep silence which is said to have followed upon their organization; at the anxiety with which the members looked around upon each other; and the reluctance which every individual felt to open a business so fearfully momentous. In the midst of this deep and deathlike silence, and just when it was beginning to be painfully embarrassing, Mr. Henry arose slowly "and delivered himself of an oration on the grievance of the colonies." Rising, as he advanced, with the grandeur of his subject, and glowing at length with all the majesty and expectation of the occasion, his speech seemed more than that of mortal man.[25]

Inevitably Wirt found that a man capable of this sort of thing was incapable of ordinary business: "when called down from the heights of declamation, to that severer test of intellectual excellence," Henry was "completely thrown into the shade."[26] But Tyler quietly points out that, after the meeting was organized, Henry arose for "a plain and quiet handling of a mere 'detail of business' ";[27] and, moved to unusual sarcasm, the biographer destroys the legend in this incisive passage:

Surely, no mere declaimer however enchanting, no sublime babbler on the rights of man, no political charlatan strutting about for the display of his preternatural gift of articulate wind, could have grappled in keen debate, for all those weeks, on the greatest of earthly subjects, with fifty of the ablest men in America, without exposing to their view all his own intellectual poverty, and without losing the very last shred of their intellectual respect for him.[28]

In place of the Roman Fathers sitting in "awfully solemn" state, Tyler, extracting pertinent passages from John Adams' diary, reveals the very human delegates meeting in taverns, drinking punch and eating sprats, and gossiping about each other.[29] To Wirt, and to most Americans then and since, Henry's famous speech in the Virginia convention of 1775 was the focal point of the Revolution; Henry arose "to guide, . . . almost to create the destinies of a nation."[30] The historians knew better; and Tyler, without derogating from Henry's fame, showed that his resolutions echoed similar resolutions adopted elsewhere in the colonies.[31]

But perhaps the boldest of Tyler's corrections was his treatment of Henry's repudiation of the Consti-

tution; and it is in his discussion of this episode in
the orator's career that the professor of American
history comes closest to economic interpretation.
Henry had been a staunch unionist during the war,
but he could not accept the Constitution because he
feared the ascendancy of the Northern States. Why
this dramatic reversal? Tyler showed the profound
influence upon Henry of Jay's proposal that the
Confederation surrender the navigation of the Mississippi to Spain in return for commercial advan-
tages which would benefit mainly the North. To
Henry a gulf seemed to yawn under his feet. If such
an idea could be seriously discussed under the Articles of Confederation, what might not a new constitution, written under Northern influence, bring
forth? Henry resolutely refused to attend the Philadelphia convention in consequence. Furthermore, as
Henry had fought the war to gain certain inalien-
able rights which the new Constitution (as yet un-
amended) did not guarantee, Tyler showed that his
dissatisfaction, his agitation for a Bill of Rights was
the chief force which led to the first ten amend-
ments:

> Those amendments were really a tub to the whale; but
> then that tub would not have been thrown overboard at
> all, had not the whale been there, and very angry, and
> altogether too troublesome with his foam-compelling tail,
> and with that huge head of his which could batter as well
> as spout.[32]

The reader of the *Patrick Henry* volume seldom meets those happy "literary" passages which are part of the charm of *The History of American Literature,* but they are not wholly omitted, albeit Tyler's style is soberer and more "professional." There are, however, picturesque moments: the "little provincial world" of Henry's youth

with an occasional clergyman, pedagogue, or legislator, small planters and small traders, sportsmen, loafers, slaves and the drivers of slaves, and, more than all, those bucolic Solons of old Virginia, the good-humored, illiterate, thrift-less Caucasian consumers of tobacco and whiskey, who, cordially consenting that all the hard work of the world should be done by the children of Ham, were thus left free to commune together in endless debate on the tavern porch or on the shady side of the country store. . . .[33]

This passage is from the beginning of the book. Tyler's portrayal of Patrick Henry's death has a swift, sympathetic, picture-making quality:

Then Patrick Henry said, "Excuse me, doctor, for a few minutes"; and drawing down over his eyes a silken cap which he usually wore, he prayed, in clear words, a sim-ple childlike prayer, for his family, for his country, and for his own soul then in the presence of death. Afterward, in perfect calmness, he swallowed the medicine. Meanwhile, Dr. Cabell, who greatly loved him, went out upon the lawn, and in his grief threw himself down upon the earth under one of the trees, weeping bitterly. Soon, when he had sufficiently mastered himself, the doctor came back to

his patient, whom he found calmly watching the congeal-
ing of the blood under his finger-nails, and speaking words
of love and peace to his family, who were weeping around
his chair. Among other things, he told them that he was
thankful for that goodness of God, which, having blessed
him through all his life, was then permitting him to die
without any pain. Finally, fixing his eyes with much tenderness on his dear friend, Dr. Cabell, with whom he
had formerly held many arguments respecting the Christian religion, he asked the doctor to observe how great a
reality and benefit that religion was to a man about to die.
And after Patrick Henry had spoken to his beloved physician these few words, in praise of something which, having never failed him in all his life before, did not then
fail him in his very last need of it, he continued to breathe
very softly for some moments; after which they who were
looking upon him saw that his life had departed.[34]

This is perhaps the finest single paragraph that
Moses Coit Tyler ever wrote.

The book was done, and while the creative mood
was upon him, once his fatigue was over, he turned
ambitiously to the next volumes of the *History* which
he had promised himself to complete. Would it be
a history of American literature during the Revolutionary period, or would it be a history of the
Revolution itself? His mind was divided; sometimes
it seemed to dwell "kindly upon the plan of writing
a history of the revolution somewhat after the
method of Lecky,"[35] and once, in October, 1887, he
met Charles Kendall Adams coming out of his office

and walked with him for half an hour, asking whether he should write a history or a life of Washington, or get out an edition of Washington's writings. Adams voted for a biography of Washington as the first task, and for the history in the second place. Tyler went home to think it over, deciding finally to resume work on the history.[36]

At the age of fifty-two Adams was now president of Cornell, embarking upon seven years of administrative turmoil. Both White and Adams had confided in Tyler during the negotiations which led to White's resignation and Adams' succession to the throne.[37] It seemed to Tyler that Adams was the "incarnation of character and good sense,"[38] though he did not follow Adams' advice about a life of Washington; walking with the new president, whose face had a drowsy expression, due to a peculiar droop of the upper eyelids, and listening to his slow and ponderous utterance,[39] Moses could not foresee that with this old friend he was to carry on the one bitter personal conflict of his life.

The history was not, however, to be continued immediately, for Tyler was looking forward to a sabbatical leave in 1888–89. In truth he sorely needed a vacation. Ever since April, 1888, what he took to be his "lazy, obstructive, mulish liver" had been troubling him.[40] The Tylers were going to Germany, and Moses, not dreaming of conflict with

Adams, had been getting up German in his spare time. He looked forward eagerly to the change. Anxiously chronicling the threat of a European war, he sorrowed over the death of "the good Emperor William of Germany" and grew alarmed over Boulanger—"the French people are children."[41] Perhaps his liver accounted for the gloomy views he took: in sombre succession he recorded the deaths of Matthew Arnold and Roscoe Conkling, nor did Goldwin Smith's account of Canadian politics add to his cheerfulness: "the face of the world seems troubled."[42] But all things come to him who waits —even commencement, which was held on a June day that was excessively hot, and Tyler wrote late that night that he was leaving his study for "fifteen months—perhaps forever. The clock strikes eleven as I write this."[43] The next day they left Ithaca, and presently the *Werra* brought them to Bremen by way of Southampton.[44]

There was something heroic in Tyler's purpose in going abroad at the age of fifty-three with the aim of mastering German sufficiently well for him to attend university lectures in Germany and to discover the enchantments of the German university system which had so fascinated Michigan, Johns Hopkins, and Cornell. German gave him great trouble; sometimes he despaired of mastering it; but by January he was reading Gellert with facility; by

February he was capable of finding *Lichtenstein* "a charming romance";[45] and by March he was reading *Soll und Haben*. He toiled terribly, but when he heard his first German lecture, he was delighted to be "able to follow it in substance," and by the end of their stay in Germany, he was having no difficulty with the language—no small triumph for an American college professor prematurely old.[46] Save for an attempt to attend lectures at the University of Berlin in October, he mainly confined his university experiences to Leipzig where the Tylers remained from the end of October to the end of February; and as he grew more at ease in the language, so that he could move easily among the learned, he filled the pages of his travel diary with inimitable sketches of German professors, such as only Tyler could draw.[46a] Once he returned to his old dream of writing an American historical novel on the subject of Bacon's rebellion;[47] he possessed at any rate one of the novelist's necessities, an eye for portrait-painting. Here, for example, is his swift, sure sketch of Professor Delitsch:

At twelve went to hear the elder Delitsch. A large room, many students. He came in with tottering steps and the movement of old age; wears no glasses; seems to be nearly eighty; his voice was too feeble for the room; and in the early part of the lecture his face was turned away from the class, and part of the time he talked to the blackboard. We could hear only a murmur of indistinguishable sounds. Some of the students were laughing at the absurdity of the performance. He wrote on the blackboard names of certain Israelitish kings. Then read slowly the leading propositions of his lecture; but the class often scraped the floor for repetition, which he seldom gave them. The scraping was met by hisses.[48]

Sometimes Tyler felt like an old man, but he knew he was not as old as that.[49]

On the whole it was one of his best years, albeit broken by one or two sorrows—the death of his beloved Bishop Harris, of which he learned in August, and the defeat of Cleveland, which troubled him a good deal.[50] Sometimes he felt "unaccountably depressed" by the defects of his own character, the littleness of what he had done,[51] but, as he wrote his mother (now eighty-one): "Never before have I been able to work for so many hours a day, with brain and body, and feel so little fatigue."[52] All kinds of ambitions were stirring in him, among them the desire to be at the *History* again, which the reading of a notice of Richardson's *American Literature* revived.[53] But in Germany he could do little;[54] after the Tylers went to England (about the middle of May, 1889), he went to work in earnest at the British Museum, getting up a good deal of information about Sir William Berkeley and his times.[55] (The ghost of his unwritten novel was still haunting him.) It had been a good year, and he was

eager to get home. The Tylers landed in New York
on September 1, 1889; two days later they were in
Ithaca; and in November he was hard at work on
the *History of American Literature* "from 1765 to
1815."[56] But he had returned from the land of peace
to the country of storm.

The quarrel between Moses Coit Tyler and
Charles Kendall Adams which enlivened the years
1889–91 was one of those distressing personal differences which add to the uncertainties of academic
life, and for its understanding certain facts in the
history of Cornell are necessary. Adams had been
made president on the resignation of White in 1885.
Although the trustees and the faculty parted with
White regretfully and desired him to continue some
connection with the university, however tenuous,
there can be no doubt that a master-hand was needed
at Cornell if the institution was ever to become what
its founders had intended.[57] White had been requested to recommend a successor, and his choice
had fallen on the Michigan professor, who, however, was given only twelve of the fifteen votes of
the Board.[58] Adams took office, there is no doubt,
with that "painful sense of solicitude" of which he
spoke[59] at his inauguration, but with an implied
mandate to remake Cornell. That he succeeded in
the general outlines of his task is shown by the increased attendance, the brilliant work done by men

who came to Cornell during his administration, and
the increase in the resources and departmentaliza-
tion of the institution. But organic changes are not
made without mental anguish; and Adams had an
unhappy faculty of antagonizing some men, and of
sticking to his own point of view in the face of
determined opposition from others. A student of his
at Michigan wrote in later years that Adams' ambition there was "accountable for a good deal of
jealousy, or, if that be unfair, criticism and misgiving among some of his colleagues. I think he was by
no means always tactful. . . . Adams probably was
too self-confident and eager to move too rapidly,
and he had not the art of winning folks by a gracious
and compelling attractive personality," though "he
was essentially sound and his general views of university character and policy were pretty wide and
generous."[60] If he had come to Cornell with misgivings,[61] his misgivings were unfortunately soon realized: after he left the presidency, he wrote to White
that "I have no desire again to breathe the atmosphere of that place," adding with grim humor that
"until it is changed by one or two funeral ceremonies, I imagine I shall not put my happiness to
so severe a strain."[62] He had been out of the presidency three years when he wrote that, but he had
an unhappy brain for remembrance. Addressing the
New York alumni less than a year after his election

to the presidency, he was tactless enough to tell them
that he felt he had come to swim in a river of
"hungry and open-mouthed crocodiles." (The New
York alumni had sent a delegate to Ithaca at the
time of his election to say that "the interests of the
University would not be subserved by the election
of Professor Adams to the Presidency.")[63] On the
same occasion he made a smart, and totally uncalled
for, allusion to the candidate whom the New York
alumni had favored.[64] When he came into office "he
greatly discouraged the scientific members of our
staff by taking the stand that as the scientific departments here were more strongly developed than
those of Michigan they could be well left as they
were while other parts of the University were built
up."[65] He was probably right, but for the moment
it did not make the scientists very happy.

Apparently during Tyler's absence in Europe,
Adams, in the process of reorganizing the university,
had resolved to re-make the curriculum in history.
From the contemporary point of view the departmental organization was, in truth, somewhat in-
choate. Adams himself held the post of professor of
general history and political science, and Tyler was
professor of American history. In 1886–7 Adams
persuaded ex-President White, who had given his
private library to Cornell,[66] that it would be appropriate to create "The President White School of

History and Political Science" in gratitude, with White as dean. But White, though he did not actively prevent the creation of the "school," declined the deanship,[67] and the matter rested for a while until Adams resolved (without consulting Tyler, or, apparently, any one else) to call Herbert Baxter Adams to the post—a younger man of much vigor, who would build up the proposed school.[68] Tyler was in Europe when he heard these facts, or the rumor of them; and on his return he faced a situation in which he was to be superseded by a younger man and his "department" was to be swallowed by a larger whole, concerning which he had never been consulted. It hurt him to the quick, especially because of Adams: "A very intimate relation, lasting nearly twenty years"[69] was broken through no fault of his own, except the fact that he was growing old. But he persuaded himself it was the path of duty to oppose the president:

A personal war, like this, is at war with my nature. . . . But I am in a path of duty and I must not flinch. I was never in a fight before; and I am not going out of this fight behind,[70]

he grimly assured himself. Faculty meetings became "painful," and once when Adams called at Tyler's home (reading between the lines, one surmises that Adams had some dim, awkward hope of reconciliation and understanding) Tyler was on his dignity and would not melt.[71]

Insurgent professors rebelled, and Tyler joined them.[72] The form of their rebellion was the creation of a university senate composed of the full professors, as a check on the appointive power of the president.[73] On October 30, 1889, it was "provided that in the case of the appointment of a full professor of the university, no election shall be made except upon the nomination of the candidate by a committee composed of the president and all the full professors of the university." On November 4 this body was named the Academic Senate; on November 12, the University Senate; on December 2, it was provided that on the reception from the president of any nomination for a full professorship the senate should ballot yea or nay upon the recommendation, and their action, with any reasons which the senate might see fit to submit, should go to the trustees.[74] One surmises that Adams did not so much mind advising with the senate as that he disapproved of its power of confirming and even originating nominations.[75] On April 12, 1890, Adams took his battle to the executive committee of the board of trustees, trying to get his own men named.[76] At a later meeting he returned to the charge, saying that he could not possibly accomplish anything in regard to the Department of History and Political Science "while Tyler and Tuttle[77] were there."[78] But Henry W. Sage, the "angel" of Cornell, did not approve of Bismarckian methods, and blocked Adams, telling Tyler that the Board "wiped the floor with him."[79]

Adams, however, refused to stay wiped. He had the interests of the university genuinely at heart, and was probably more annoyed by the inability of his faculty to see that this was the case than he was desirous of dictatorial powers. Consequently there was a counter-move toward compromise. Adams suggested to Sage that Tyler be appointed dean of the President White School of History and Political Science, but failed to inform Tyler that he had done so, telling him no more than that White had refused the position. The trustees, on the other hand, ended the power of the University Senate to initiate nominations,[80] and, as Tyler had not been informed of Adams' intention to nominate him in place of White, he did not know what to do. On November 20 he wrote Adams a long letter "touching our relations," and two days later Adams offered to name him for promotion.[81] But Tyler pushed forward in his demands, and on the day following receipt of this letter, he "wrote a letter to C. K. A. in reply to his, stating plainly my need and wish for $4000 salary" if he were to be dean.[82] It was not an unreasonable request, but Tyler wrote in his diary a few days later with remarkable frankness that the

deanship "has tempted me (1) as an escape from a
dean introduced from without (2) as a means of
getting my salary raised,"[83] and it is possible that
finer taste or greater tact might have eased the situation. The day in which he made this entry he
talked with Professors Laughlin and Tuttle, who
were unalterably opposed to deans, and who persuaded him to "cease to be a candidate for the Deanship."[84] But pride, or anger, led him to fail to make
public announcement of this sudden conversion,
and on March 17, 1891, the board of trustees appointed him dean of the President White School
with an additional honorarium of $500. Tyler ac-
cepted.[85] The faculty insurgents immediately set to
work to have the appointment rescinded, not because they disliked Tyler, but because they disliked
deans; a committee of the University Senate appeared before the Board to request a hearing, and
Tyler, the newly created dean, was a member of
the committee! The following day the trustees
rescinded the appointment.[86] Tyler thereby lost his
$500, which was doubtless a piece of Roman virtue,
but one wishes that he had conducted himself in a
more direct and straightforward manner. It was some
compensation to him that, on November 10, 1891,
his salary was increased to $4000,[87] apparently with
Adams' approval. The year before, Tuttle was made
professor of modern European history, despite the

reluctance of Adams, and George Lincoln Burr was
made an associate professor in 1891,[88] so that the
victory of the professorial party was reasonably complete.

It was the sort of squabble from which nobody
emerges with much credit; the trustees failed to
uphold the president, the president had been tactless, the faculty had been "difficult," and Moses Coit
Tyler, the soul of honor and integrity on all other
occasions, had been forced by the logic of events into
devious political ways. On the whole, one is inclined
to think that, once past his initial mistake, Adams
had proved to be the bigger man of the two: he had
put the interests of the university ahead of the sting
of his personal defeat, and he had written Tyler a
letter while the conflict was still smoldering which
drew from its recipient the reluctant admission that
"it expresses every sort of kind feeling for me" and
"opens the way at least for better working relations
between us. What I lack is confidence. But I cannot
refuse such a proffer of good will."[89] One does not
feel that Tyler wholly rose to the level of Adams'
obvious desire to do right. But things healed over,
as they usually do in such cases; and it is perhaps
significant that between May, 1891, and September,
1892, Tyler made but one entry in his diary, and that
this entry records a private walk and talk with
Adams in May, 1892, when Adams told his old

friend that he had made up his mind to resign the presidency and accept the presidency of the University of Wisconsin. It is pleasant to record that eight years later Adams suggested to Frederick J. Turner that Tyler be invited to lecture at the University of Wisconsin during the summer session of 1900, Tyler receiving the invitation about nine months before his death.[90]

CHAPTER X

TYLER's experience in German universities may be regarded as the precipitant which, after one or two false starts, eventually brought forth *The Literary History of the American Revolution*. Before going to Europe Tyler had played with the idea of writing a book to be called "Vivi Memorabiles," which was "to be American History unfolded in a series of Biographies, each being as short as a rigorous exclusion of minor matters would permit."[1] The "Vivi Memorabiles" was never written, but *Three Men of Letters,* besides being "an incidental product of the research which I made . . . when working upon my 'History of American Literature during the Colonial Time,' "[2] may be regarded as a fragment of the modern Plutarch which once kindled his enthusiasm. He toyed with the idea of an historical novel, dealing with Bacon's Rebellion, as we have seen, but got no farther than writing the opening of the story.[3] But his main occupation after returning to Cornell from his sabbatical year, and aside from his university duties and his squabble with Adams, was the *History*. "I am very happy to be in my private study and to be at my history once more," he recorded on November 22, 1889,[4] and if he was sometimes "somewhat dejected by the mediocrity of my materials for American literary history between 1765 and 1815,"[5] he lured himself on by concentrating on the Connecticut wits, especially Barlow, who interested him tremendously. Writing came hard, probably because his standards were higher than ever,[6] but by the end of January, he had written his discussion of the author of *The Columbiad,* and, despite illness, had passed on to the other Connecticut Wits. ". . . a reading of several chapters written some years ago, restores me somewhat my courage, and gives me hope that a true, honest, scientific, and yet attractive piece of work can be built over that territory," he confided to his diary.[7] Writing was his refuge from the jangle in the university: "it cheers, but does not inebriate,"[8] he thought; and during the spring vacation he ran down to New York and New Haven to hunt up material on the Wits in the Lenox, Astor, and New York Historical Society Libraries, and at Yale, where he found the Ezra Stiles manuscripts unexpectedly rich.[9] He also learned that Professor Sumner did not like the regnant Yale president, which, in view of the Adams controversy, must have been comforting.

Amidst the inevitable interruptions and digressions—faculty meetings, bishops, German books, talks with Goldwin Smith, who thought that literature was on its death-bed—the college year drew to its close with much solid work accomplished.[10] Tyler finished writing up his Trumbull material (amid certain Carlylean groanings) on July 10, and began on Humphreys the next day. The "Barlow" paper he was very fond of; he decided to offer it to *The Atlantic Monthly,* but Horace E. Scudder returned it, a refusal which depressed him: I "feel the lack of balance in my judgment, my liability to self-delusion thro' the colored light in which I often view things." He was fifty-five now, "an elderly man, with the cool, mournful sob of autumn sounding about him," and inclined to indulge in self-pity.[11] In the fall, lecture-making done, he plugged steadily on, noting with anxious care the state of his health, and chronicling the nights when he "had a wonderful sleep."[12] One traces him step by step through his labors on Timothy Dwight until May, 1891, when the diary suddenly ceases until September, 1892, save for the one entry chronicling President Adams' decision to go to Wisconsin.

But with Adams' departure, and the election of Jacob Gould Schurman to succeed him on May 18, 1892, *incipit vita nova!* Professor George C. Caldwell, speaking for the faculty at Schurman's inauguration, roundly told the incoming president that

It is not to be supposed, we trust, that . . . there is to be no direct communication between individual members of the Faculty and of the Board of Trustees, on subjects of mutual interest . . . a large part of the important communications from the one body to the other, or from its individual members, must pass through your hands. The Faculty may justly expect that every such communication shall be faithfully and fairly presented; and we are sure that a right so plain and equitable will be fully and cheerfully conceded by you.

The new Cæsar bowed and kissed the rod like a good constitutional monarch, saying:

Gentlemen of the Faculty, it is your privilege as it is your duty, to settle our educational problems in the way you think best.[13]

and Tyler smiled happily, and buckled down to real work:

I am going to nail myself down now and henceforth to work on History of American Literature till it is done. Many things have been settled in my mind the last year. Concentrate. Simplify. Persevere. Must get back to the method in the old Hillcroft study.[14]

And for 1892–3 his diary records, amid incidental discouragements and interruptions and some preaching and occasional bad health, mostly the steady, Roman march of his labors. By April 18 he had completed chapters I–IV of the final draft.

One can watch him at work and observe his methods if one traces his way of treating Francis Hopkinson, on whom he labored in the spring and summer of 1893. On June 19 he commenced by reading over the lecture on Hopkinson which he had been delivering at various times for the last eight years, doubtless adding touches here and there in that interval. Most of the research on Hopkinson had been completed; and his task was mainly one of revision. From that date until July 5 he "wrought"—a favorite word with him[15]—at revising his material, writing each morning in his study from eight-thirty until one o'clock, but confining his efforts to Hopkinson's career before 1776. On June 29 he "was a long time in a turmoil of dissatisfaction with some sentences which would not take shape to suit me," but after working for sixteen days, four and one-half hours a day, he succeeded in satisfying himself that the sixty-one pages of manuscript had been adequately revised. He then turned to Hopkinson's career after 1776, feeling at first an obligation to hurry, since the previous material had occupied him so long, but finding that the inner man refused to be drugged with specious excuse:

I can never do any literary work, unless an inward arbiter smiles approval. So, I fling overboard once more every calculation founded on the almanac and plod patiently and slowly along the path which I must take.[16]

On July 14 he had added thirty more pages to his discussion of Hopkinson. In *The Literary History*

of the American Revolution these ninety-one manuscript pages are reduced to fifty pages of print; it
had taken Tyler a month, not to write, but to revise his discussion; and he went over it again before
sending it off to the publisher. Never was a literary
history more solidly "wrought." (He deserved a vacation, and he took a trip to the sea-shore with his
family.) Upon this miracle of patience his modest
comment is:

> It presents a pretty complete view of Hopkinson's liter-
> ary services to the Revolution, and shows their importance
> in a light stronger than ever before indicated, I think.[17]

Some time before October, 1894, he changed his
mind about the date he would use for his *terminus ad
quem*. Hitherto he had intended to end with 1815
in order to include in his work the essays on the
Connecticut Wits on which he had labored after his
return from Europe, but he now decided that 1783
would be a better stopping place. What, then, would
he do with the chapters on the Wits, wrought with
such loving care? He mulled the matter over in his
mind, and on October 16, 1894, "last night, being
wakeful for many hours, there came to me a flash of
an idea: to precede the publication of my big Revolutionary volume by a pretty little book containing
three elaborately finished chapters which will not go
into it."[18] At first he thought of calling the book

"Three dissimilar men," but on second thought chose the title, *Three Men of Letters*. On October 27 he sent the manuscript to Putnam while he was suffering from a cold (his health troubled him a good deal now); he read the page proofs the very last of the year; and he received printed copies in January, 1895.[19]

Three Men of Letters includes an essay on Berkeley, written earlier than the other two essays, and two discussions devoted respectively to Timothy Dwight and Joel Barlow. It is a book of great charm and insight. The essay on Berkeley in particular is written with a tender sympathy which springs from Tyler's reverence for the churchman rather than from his interest in the philosopher: his aim was always men, not metaphysics. The unity of the volume consists in the fact that all three men are, in their various ways, associated with Yale College; and in their contributions to the growing intellectual life of America. Despite Tyler's absorption in the Barlow essay, this discussion seems to be slightly inferior to the other two, though one notes the amusing accuracy of its title: "The Literary Strivings of Mr. Joel Barlow." The personality of Barlow does not shine through the material, either because Tyler failed to divine the man or because, by failing to emphasize Barlow's relation to the French Revolution, he failed to find the key to his intellectual development. The essay on Dwight, touched as it is with irony and humor, is one of the pleasantest of Tyler's studies. But the Berkeley essay is a little gem—"the cream of the whole," as White wrote him in a tenderly appreciative letter,[20] and the book has remained an important interpretation. There is little in Sainte-Beuve finer than Tyler's portrait of Berkeley.

After the completion of *Three Men of Letters* Tyler surveyed the list of 203 names he had compiled for possible inclusion in his history. Twenty-two men were "done," and he commenced to weed out the lesser names. On October 15, 1894, there were 97 names left; on December 31 the list had dwindled under severe and judicious pruning to 49, and he had chosen as his title, "The Literary History of the American Revolution." He hoped to finish the book by July 31, 1895.[21] But on January 1, 1895, he had to postpone this date to "the closing day of this year,"[22] and in January, 1896, he was still at work on John Dickinson and Thomas Jefferson, and was hurrying. The effect of this penultimate haste is, unfortunately, evident, the discussion of Jefferson in the *History,* for example, being well-nigh wholly confined to his state papers, especially the Declaration. On June 24, 1896, after spending three weeks on the final revision of chapter XI (British Tea as a Political Intoxicant in America), Tyler finished that unit—"the longest time yet out on any chapter in this labor of revision."[23] Sometimes he felt he was racing with the spectre of ill health—which, indeed, he was. But on the day before election day, November, 1896, he wrote in his diary: "Yesterday I finished the thirty-nine chapters, and sent them to Putnam by express. They weighed just nineteen pounds! I feel as if I had lost something—a baby perhaps—and I can hardly realize my full freedom."[24] The preface of the first volume he dated January 24, 1897; the dedication was to Jeannette. On April 30, 1897, while he was wrestling with a call to the Emily Sanford professorship of English at Yale, he received the "first copy of first volume of my new book."[25] The preface to the second volume is dated July 19, 1897, and he did not see the completed work until his return from his trip to England in the autumn of 1897, when he found on his desk in Ithaca two octavo volumes of 1048 pages in all, entitled *The Literary History of the American Revolution*.[26]

This second great work is neither quite a continuation of the *History of American Literature, 1607–1765,* nor quite a complement of it, but something of both, as well as an innovation in the treatment of American literary history, facts which, together with the gap of time between the appearance of the first and second volumes of the new work, may account for the difference in reception accorded the

masterpiece of Tyler's later years by contemporary
critics. The first *History* had surveyed one hundred
fifty-eight years of intellectual development; the second was confined to eighteen; and though in point
of date the one is the continuation of the other, the
change in the formula of the title is indicative of a
change in point of view. The first work had traced
the unfolding of the American mind; the second
rehearsed a drama, a conflict of views:

There would, perhaps, be no injustice in describing this
book as the product of a new method, at least of a method
never before so fully applied, in the critical treatment of the
American Revolution. The outward history of that famous
procedure has been many times written, and is now, by a
new breed of American scholars, being freshly rewritten in
the light of larger evidence, and under the direction of a
more disinterested and a more judicial spirit. In the present work, for the first time in a systematic and a fairly
complete way, is set forth the inward history of our Revolution—the history of its ideas, its spiritual moods, its mo-
tives, its passions, even of its sportive caprices and its
whims, as these uttered themselves at the time, whether
consciously or not, in the various writings of the two
parties of Americans who promoted or resisted that great
movement.
The plan of the author has been to let both parties in the
controversy—the Whigs and the Tories, the Revolutionists
and the Loyalists—tell their own story freely in their own
way, and without either of them being liable, at our
hands, to posthumous outrage in the shape of partisan im-
putations on their sincerity, their magnanimity, their patriotism, or their courage.[27]

This is plain warning of his intention to treat Greeks and Trojans without discrimination. Moreover, Tyler belonged to a generation of historians strongly dominated by the race-consciousness theory of history, especially of "Teutonic" history; a sincere patriot and a warm admirer of Great Britain,[28] he deplored the "race-feud" which he believed to exist between the two countries. It seemed to him that the "prayerful obstinacy in baleful leadership" of George III

brought to England the loss of her most valuable dependency, and to the English-speaking race a disruption that should bear for unborn millions on both sides of the Atlantic a legacy, perhaps an endless legacy, of mutual ill-will.[29]

His book was intended to counteract the effects of this legacy:

I now greatly mistake the case, if one practical consequence of this history, so far as it may find readers at all, shall not be eirenic, rather than polemic,—namely the promotion of a better understanding, of a deeper respect, of a kindlier mood, on both sides of the ocean, among the descendants of those determined men who so bitterly differed in opinion, so fiercely fought, and, in their anger, so widely parted company, a century and a quarter ago.[30]

Charles Kendall Adams saw the point and congratulated him on his achievement in a rather magnificent letter,[31] but Tyler's Jovian calm was beyond the comprehension of run-of-the-mine reviewers on both sides of the Atlantic, the English notices insisting that he was anti-English,[32] and the Americans being puzzled by his apparently equal enthusiasm for Whig and Tory alike.[33] The way of the peacemaker is not always blessed.

One result of this historic impartiality, and one of the greatest contributions of the *Literary History,* is the sound and sympathetic presentation of the Loyalists' side of the struggle, for in this work Tyler was not committed to any postulates about the "American mind," and could therefore treat the Tories in terms of their own contemporaneity, unmindful of the ignominy which the rhetorical historians had attached to their cause. He began by presenting the Tory theory in regard to the right of Parliament to tax the colonies, and if his statement seems familiar enough to the reader of Beard or other modern historians, it must be remembered that it was Tyler who helped to make it so.[34]

. . . the historic meaning of the word representation, as the word had always been used in English constitutional experience, seemed fairly to justify the Loyalist contention, that the several organized British communities in America, as an integral part of the British empire, were to all intents and purposes represented in the British parliament, which sat at the capital as the supreme council of the whole empire, and exercised legislative authority co-extensive with the boundaries of that empire.[35]

Having thus fairly presented the Loyalist cause, Tyler allows the Tories to speak their minds freely in regard to certain characteristics of the patriots commonly overlooked in the history books. The patriots had protested against British tyranny, yet when they themselves attained power, they made the mob into a tyranny quite as obnoxious. And they were inconsistent. To free themselves from the constitutional monarch, King George, they called in the absolute monarch, King Louis. Tyler quoted the Tory prophets on this delicate point, adding:

> Certainly, it is not easy for us Americans, more than an hundred years after that dreadful prophecy was uttered, and after every atom of its dire burden has been falsified by the facts of actual experience, to realize how awful, in 1779, was the possibility that it might be exactly fulfilled, and with what an ineffable anxiety, with what a sinking of the heart, with how horrible a dread, it must have been read by many thousands of Americans at a time when no mortal man could know whether or not it would come true.[36]

His was a necessary, a sympathetic, and a solid achievement in historical reconstruction,[37] and his insight was certainly the stronger by reason of his sentiment for the mother country, his love of tradition, and the association of the Tory cause with the Anglican church.

So his primary purpose was to re-live the past, to

plunge himself and his readers into the emotional and intellectual conflict of the time. Once again, but more richly, he was writing *Kulturgeschichte;* his preface to the first volume admirably states his aim:

The proceedings of legislative bodies, the doings of cabinet ministers and of colonial politicians, the movements of armies, are not here altogether disregarded, but they are here subordinated; they are mentioned, when mentioned at all, as mere external incidents in connection with the ideas and the emotions which lay back of them or in front of them, which caused them or were caused by them. One result of this method, also, is an entirely new distribution of the tokens of historic prominence—of what is called fame—among the various participants in that very considerable business. Instead of fixing our eyes almost exclusively, as is commonly done, upon statesmen and generals, upon party leaders, upon armies and navies, upon Congress, upon parliament, upon the ministerial agents of a brain-sick king, or even upon that brain-sick king himself, and instead of viewing all these people as the sole or the principal movers and doers of the things that made the American Revolution, we here for the most part turn our eyes away toward certain persons hitherto much neglected, in many cases wholly forgotten—toward persons who, as mere writers, and whether otherwise prominent or not, nourished the springs of great historic events by creating and shaping and directing public opinion during all that robust time; who, so far as we here regard them, wielded only spiritual weapons; who still illustrate, for us and for all who choose to see, the majestic operation of ideas, the creative and decisive play of spiritual forces, in the development of history, in the rise and fall of nations, in the aggregation and the division of races.[38]

In this preface are summarized some of Tyler's favorite ideas—the search for a fundamental principle in history, his belief in the efficacy of ideas, that happy fusion of "historical" history and literary history which he had spent his life to search out. He painted the drama of events as it appeared to the participants but with prophetic asides from the wings by the author. If critics were disappointed that he did not give "a consistent general statement of the author's theory of the Revolution,"[39] they overlooked his interest as a dramatist in the interplay of forces. He was writing philosophical history, but not of the usual kind.

The Literary History of the American Revolution, the product of some twenty years of reflection, study, and research is, it needs scarcely to be said, a monument to American scholarship. To the apparatus of the former history, Tyler added a bibliography which *The Nation* reviewer rightly hailed as "the most important catalog of books on the subject yet compiled."[40] His innate New Englandism appears in the disproportionate lack of emphasis given to Southern writers and newspapers, a fault noted by a number of reviewers,[41] and in the case of Jonathan Carver's *Travels* he made tremendous errors, of commission and omission, viewing the work of a plagiarist as the product of a belated Elizabethan, and neglecting four essays, all written before Tyler's discussion appeared, which would have set him right.[42] Though he read and discussed Adair's *History of the American Indians,* from which Carver stole, Tyler missed the incriminating evidence. But, these errors aside, he was a stylist (at least in the better parts of this huge study) still emphatically himself. The striking portraitures in which he excelled flash upon many a page—Francis Hopkinson meeting John Adams in the studio of Charles Wilson Peale; Philip Freneau, a broken old man, dying in the snow of a swampy meadow near Monmouth; Ezra Stiles among his books and scientific apparatus, "descriptive of the omnivorous appetency of his mind"; James Otis haranguing in the Old Town House in Boston before the judges "in full wigs, bands, and robes of scarlet."[43] On the other hand, both by reason of the material, some of it abstract political reasoning, and by reason of his own weariness, larger areas of the *Literary History* fail to rise out of a kind of dogged competence.

But it was—and is—a great book, the crown of his career. He was an old man now, and his work was done. A few more years of teaching, the publication of another book, compounded of his earlier writings, the mellow glow of his deservedly great reputation around him, the faithful Jeannette, and the amusements of letter-writing—these were the pleasant concomitants of an Indian summer singularly beautiful and untroubled. He was one of the demi-gods, and Albert Bushnell Hart, William Dean Howells, George W. Cable, William H. Lecky, Edmund Gosse, Gladstone, Edward Dowden, and others of the great were writing respectful letters about his book.[44] The younger generation viewed him with vast respect, young F. L. Pattee telling the publishers that "every page shows traces of great research among original documents. It seems exhaustive. . . . I am singing its praises right and left."[45] Charles Kendall Adams, all passion spent, was longing for a visit from him and his wife;[46] and at sea, in the interval between the publication of the first and second volume, Tyler was happily dreaming of writing his novel once more—"if I live?" But something troubled him—"I wonder if I shall live? Constantly am I haunted this year by the thought of sudden death."[47] He did not tell Jeannette when he had thoughts like these. When he returned from England, it was to the stimulus of a friendly chorus over the second volume, and that was heartening.

His humor never deserted him, even during the troubles with Adams. One of Tyler's most delightful letters, addressed to the editor of *The New York Tribune,* was written at the age of sixty-five gravely to reprove that august journal for "the extraordinary image" of him which the paper had published. His rector, he said, thought he ought to murder the *Tribune* editor, and "you will agree with me, that when a minister of religion begins to prompt one of his parishioners to homicide, the case must be an aggravated one." Instead of homicide, "I content myself for the present by asking you to accept a copy of my latest photograph, and to be so good as to hold it up for a moment by the side of the portrait which you have innocently sent to your readers as mine." He said solemnly that the derision showered on him by reason of the *Tribune* engraving had brought on "Lenten humility . . . a general loss of appetite, and . . . much fasting and prayer." A delightful letter;[48] unfortunately the reply of the *Tribune* editor has not been preserved.

One of the ideas which interested Tyler most was the creation of an historical journal for printing articles on history; out of it had grown *The American Historical Review*. Two groups of historians, one at Harvard and one at Cornell, arrived independently at the idea of founding such a magazine, the Cornell group being composed of Professor H. Morse Stevens, Professor G. L. Burr, and Professor Tyler. On the prospectus calling upon historians to organize in support of the enterprise, Tyler's signature was one of the six "representative signatures";[49] and when in the first number of the new magazine (October, 1895), the editors affirmed the policy that

the three criteria for contributions should be freshness and originality of treatment, accuracy in scholarship, and literary merit,[50] Tyler was happy; he
had been asked to contribute to the first number, in
company with Henry Adams, John Fiske, von
Holst, and other leading historians.[51] In truth, he
was among the honored elder statesmen: once,
when he reviewed a life of Thomas Hutchinson by
James K. Hosmer, Hosmer wrote him that

you were the one scholar in America who was best equip-
ped to sit in judgment on such a book as mine. Your few
strong words let me know I have succeeded: I really need
nothing more.[52]

The country flung itself into the Spanish-Ameri-
can War; imperialism became blatant, and Theodore Roosevelt was doing picturesque things in
Cuba, but the Tylers peacefully toured Canada in
the summer of 1898. Moses was elected a member
of the Virginia Historical Society,[53] and various
other honors were heaped upon him—an LL.D.
from New Brunswick University in 1900; membership in the American Philosophical Society, membership in the Colonial Society of Massachusetts,
membership in the Authors' Club of New York
City, membership in the Educational Council of the
Chautauqua System of Popular Education. In 1899
he was made second vice-president of the American

Historical Association, in 1900 he was made first vice-president, and in the natural course of things (happy close!) he would have been elected president when the Association met in Ann Arbor in January, 1901, if he had lived.

And there were various interesting jobs to do and to refrain from doing. Perhaps one of the hardest refusals Tyler had to make was when President Timothy Dwight of Yale University ("dear old Tim")[54] wanted to make him the Emily Sanford professor of English there. How hard it was to refuse! For a while he could think of nothing else, and, unable to take his nap after luncheon the day he received Dwight's letter, he "went down town and took a long ride."[55] That was in April, 1897; he and Jeannette talked it over, and decided they had better visit New Haven, and he "wrestled in much anguish with this problem."[56] But they returned unconvinced of the wisdom of the move; he was too old now, and he "wrote a loving letter to dear old Tim, sorrowfully telling him that the call to Yale comes too late! Did I ever dream that I could refuse a call to old Yale?"[57] The day he mailed this letter, he received the first copy of the first volume of the *Literary History,* and that was something, but he read with sadness a letter from Professor A. M. Wheeler telling him that his decision was right because "a man who has reached our time

of life" ought not "to tear himself out of his nest,"
and adjuring him that they must "hold together
somehow during the years that remain, and try to
meet often enough at least to keep green the memories of the earlier time."[58] Ah! that earlier time!
The Beecher's Bibles and the Divinity School, and
Owego and Poughkeepsie, and the Civil War! How
far away it all seemed! When he visited New Haven
again in June, he could not get into the old house
where he used to have a room, and a big class was
going to the ivy planting, just "as we did forty years
ago."[59]

Not that Moses was not as active as ever. In 1898
Putnam published for him his *Glimpses of England,* composed of the best of the essays and sketches
he had written during his first visit to England. On
January 7 of that year, furthermore, he received a
letter from J. T. Morse, saying that his *Patrick
Henry* was to be republished and asking for any re-
visions he might care to make, and Tyler, with his
usual thoroughness, gave the "text a minute revision from beginning to end" and made "numerous
changes both in its substance and its form."[60] Finally, during these last years of his life he took up seriously once more his idea of an American Plutarch or
"Vivi Memorabiles," a biographical study of American statesmanship which he planned to make an
"interpretation of American history through the

lives of great Americans."[61] The *Literary History* being out of the way, he began serious study in November, 1897, after his return from Europe. He began with his old idol, Charles Sumner, for he planned to begin with the nineteenth century and work back to Columbus. Among other figures he planned to treat the statesmen of the South as well as those of the North, for he was older now, and incapable of referring to embattled Southerners as he had during the hectic fifties. This new attitude may be gleaned from a rejected preface to *Glimpses of England*:

As to our once-erring brethren of the South, I have long since come to see that, great as was their mistake in opinion, they were as sincere and as honorable as ourselves; and I am sure that I could never again bring myself to apply to them and to the great practical wrong they did, the harsh expressions which, in the heat of those angry days, so easily leaped from our pens and our tongues.[62]

He had lived through too much waving of the bloody shirt, he had seen too much of the Gilded Age still to possess his youthful faith in democracy; and in this same preface he wrought the latest version of his final political beliefs:

In our own country . . . have taken place, during the same period [since the sixties] changes quite as great, at least in political tone and mood; so that, instead of the exuberant confidence which was felt by us, thirty years ago, in the practical success of the purely democratic forms of government and which had then been stimulated into vivid expression by the stupendous triumph of armed democracy in 1865, there has now come upon us a period of depression, certainly of gloomy anxiety, as to the working of our own political system,—a system nominally controlled by the people but actually controlled by a small number of irresponsible and inaccessible chiefs, called bosses, who, after the old device of the Roman Cæsars, now exercise over us nearly unqualified despotisms under the names and forms of constitutional liberty. In the deep anxiety into which many of us are thrown by this later, this subtler, this more fundamental, and more deadly, assault upon free institutions in America, I am conscious that I suffer with my brethren; and while I still hold unflinchingly to my early faith in the ultimate capacity of even the mass of men for the direct management of their own governments, I am forced to hold this faith with more forbearance than once I felt toward those who are not able to hold it at all;—for I now realize, as I did not when some of these letters were written, that the full development even of American capacity for self government is still far off, and only to be reached by us after much more blundering, and loss, and shame, and sorrow.[63]

One of his chapters was to be on John Tyler, the descendant of one of the three original Tyler brothers from whom he himself had sprung, but when he wrote the Virginia Tylers for material, the Southerners did not respond as he had hoped they would.[64] It was too bad; had he been permitted to complete his book, had he given to the South the same sympathetic interpretation he had given the loyalists in the Revolution, he would have been again a pioneer. Even Andrew D. White advised him against including Calhoun and Jefferson Davis.[65] Tyler pondered gravely, examining his style and counselling himself to

avoid diffuseness; non-essentials; melodious conventionalism. Re-write each life patiently; cut it down; compress. The model is Tacitus, rather than Plutarch.[66]

The Tylers spent eight months of 1899 in rest and travel in the south of Europe, where he observed the idiocies of the tax system and looked respectfully at F. Marion Crawford.[67] On returning to Ithaca, he plunged again into his task. (He had seen Theodore Tilton, now permanently domiciled in Paris—"if we never meet again in this life . . . your recent visit was . . . an episode I shall not forget").[68] It was the major occupation of his last two years, interrupted, of course (was he never to be free from side-issues?), by trips to Boston and speeches at Chautauqua in "sizzling, boiling, roasting, frying weather" and by a long visit to Madison, Wisconsin, diversified by gargantuan bicycle rides.[69] He wrote, half-savagely, in May, 1900:

I long to read—to read—to read—not with a lecture or other pot-boiler in view, but a true piece of work,—the slow building up of these American Lives.[70]

But it was not to be, despite the fact that nobody dared to interrupt his morning hours.[71] All that re-

mains among his manuscripts of this admirable plan
is a study of John Randolph of Roanoke, with its
characteristic Tyler opening—Randolph taking the
oath of office as a representative in Congress. The
manuscript includes a characterization of Randolph,
a sketch of his career, and a discussion of Randolph's
ideas. Tyler was writing at his best:

> His speeches were without system, or logical continuity:
> each was a succession of thoughts as they occurred—topics
> presented allusively by jerks and starts—reminding one
> rather of the literary method of Sterne, with not a little
> also of Sterne's sprightliness. To say that at such or such a
> time he spoke on any particular subject, would not be do-
> ing him justice,—he always spoke on many subjects.[72]

"John Randolph of Roanoke" is a fragment only,
but into this fragment has gone all that Tyler had
experienced in sixty-five years—his observations of
men and things, the nice fusion of historical thoroughness with literary finish he had achieved, the
insight, the lurking humor, the intuitive grasp of
the personality he was studying in the setting of its
time. Had the book been completed of which the
essay was to form a part, it would have been a remarkable series of portraits. But this was not to be.

The realization that death was near did not greatly trouble him. "Much of the things I have toiled
for in life now appear to me, as I approach the period of old age, to be mere froth and scum."[73] He

was not, in truth, old, but he had lived strenuously, he had burned out before his time, he had become a patriarch in middle life, an old man who complained now and again of being tired, one who moved slowly during his final days. How much he had to look back upon! Marshall and Burlington and Union City and Detroit—each called up its separate pictures. And Ann Arbor in its early years, and Yale, and Andover, and then his marriage to the faithful Jeannette! His pastorates, and then the breakdown! Dio Lewis—and England—and those uncertain months from which Haven had finally rescued him. And then the great mistake of going to New York on *The Christian Union*. But then his triumphal recovery from this error—Michigan, Cornell, his books, his fame! He had made many mistakes, but he had lived a rich and full life, and it was time to draw to an end, to take in sail. And so, full of honors, Tyler died on Friday, December 28, 1900.[74] Cornell and Michigan mourned him, and in the American Historical Association it was as if a great tree had fallen amid a younger forest, so patriarchal had Tyler become.

He was buried the following Sunday in the lot he had long ago chosen. And presently there was created in the west transept of the Sage Chapel on the campus of Cornell a stained-glass window, an allegorical figure showing History as a venerable sage with a white beard, and beneath it one reads the words: "In loving memory of Moses Coit Tyler." To Tyler the bearded figure would have seemed right and just, for to him history was venerable. Why not? Was not Tyler's generation the bearded generation?

THE LIFE OF MOSES COIT TYLER

APPENDIX

APPENDIX

THE following list of Tyler manuscripts and of published works by Tyler is believed to be reasonably complete. It does not include his contributions to newspapers except when important.

A. THE TYLER MANUSCRIPTS

Mr. Willard Austen, Tyler's son-in-law and Librarian of Cornell University, was appointed Tyler's literary executor. The MSS. are preserved in the Library at Cornell University. In addition, there is a small group of letters to Mr. and Mrs. Moncure D. Conway in the William L. Clements Library; the manuscript of an address on temperance entitled "Address delivered by Moses Tyler on taking his seat as Worthy Archon of Chrystal Fount Section No. 5 C. of T. Detroit, July 7, 1851," in the Burton Historical Library, Detroit; and undergraduate essays in the manuscript magazine, *The Sybil*, vol. IX, in the University of Michigan Library.

Author's copies of books by Moses Coit Tyler:
> The Cornell collection includes all of these except *The Omnibus* (which is in the Clements Library), *The New Gymnastics as an Instrument in Education*, *The Direct Study of English Masterpieces*, *The Direct Study of English Masterpieces: Shakespeare Course.*

Published articles by Moses Coit Tyler:
> There are many separate copies of articles, and journals containing articles, by Tyler scattered among the papers.

Projected books:
> During his last years Tyler made plans to publish four books composed of articles written during his earlier years. They are as follows:

Fragments (Paragraphs) Round the Table.
> This contains 26 clippings from the columns he conducted in *The Christian Union* (1873-4), and two clippings from *The Golden Age* (1871).

Men, Women and Books: A Miscellany of Views and Reviews.
This contains 48 articles selected from his contributions to *The Independent, The Christian Union, The Nation, The Golden Age, Youth's Companion, Political Science Quarterly,* and *Yale Review.* There are also the MS. of a speech, "Woman Is a Person," delivered at the Woman's Suffrage Association in 1870, a copy of the speech delivered at the dedication of Sage College for Women in 1873, and the MS. of a Memorial Day Address given in 1871.

Folder with no title containing 15 articles from *The Independent,* and *The Christian Union.*

Folder with no title containing 11 articles from *The Brooklyn Union, The Nation,* and *The Independent.*

The printed material listed above is included in the list of books and articles in the bibliography which follows below.

Essays and addresses in MS:
"John Randolph of Roanoke."
  The one chapter which Tyler completed for his "Vivi Memorabiles."
"The Two Washingtons: the Mythical and the Real."
"The Old English Ballads."
"The Early Colleges and College Builders of America."
  The three foregoing are lectures.
"The Moral Significance of the Name America."
  A prospectus with notes, in an unfinished condition.
"The American Revolution as a Wit-Combat: Illustrated from the Writings of Francis Hopkinson."
  Material substantially reproduced in the *Literary History of the American Revolution.*
"General Garfield."
  Published in *The Golden Age.*
"The Historic Name of Our Country."
  A lecture.
"Heaven Fights on the Side of Great Principle."
  Commencement address at Yale in 1857.
Rejected preface to *Glimpses of England.*

Sermons in MS:
"The Millennium," "The Two Sons in the Parable," "Hope a Duty," "Christian Manliness," "The Idea of Prayer,"

"Prayer: The Opposition of Scientific Theories," "The Passive Virtues," "The Many-sidedness of God," "The Crime of Pontius Pilate," "The Call of Matthew," "The Day of Judgment," "Christianity a Missionary Religion," "Forgetting God," "Our Father," "The Pharisee," "Life's Burdens and the Bearing of Them," "St. Thomas" (2), "Fellowship with God in Labor," "Something Wrong with Human Nature," "Almost Persuaded," "Christianity a Power as Well as an Idea," "The Optimism of Christianity," Ordination Address to the Candidates.

Manuscripts collected by Moses Coit Tyler:

A large scrapbook containing the following:

John Trumbull MSS.

Selections made in 1881 from MSS. in possession of the Woodbridge family in Detroit. See *Literary History of the American Revolution,* vol. I, p. 188, footnote.

Letter from Vice-President John Adams to his former pupil Judge Trumbull, New York, April 2, 1790.

Sketch of Joseph Stansbury from the MS. of his son Arthur Joseph Stansbury; copied by Fred N. Wines, grandson of the poet. Tyler received it from Mrs. Jeannie Stansbury Holden.

Nathaniel Niles MSS.

Copies.

Will of William Fielding of New York City, 1766.

Abbé Raynal, "Nouvelle Angleterre."

Original MSS.

Autograph of John Randolph, of Roanoke.

Letter from W. W. Henry concerning John Randolph, 1898.

Patrick Henry material.

Letters from W. W. Henry on Patrick Henry's residence.

Letter from W. W. Henry regarding Virginia Resolutions of 1765.

W. W. Henry's letter on the Convention, March, 1775.

Copy of Patrick Henry's will.

Sketch of Edward Fontaine by his daughter, Susette.

Letter from Daniel Webster to Governor Woodbridge, 1841.

Letter from Daniel Webster to Governor Woodbridge, Dec. 20, 1841.

Letter from Colonel J. Lewis Peyton on Patrick Henry.

Letter from W. A. Trumble to his brother.

Autographs of Charles Sumner, Vice-President Colfax, J. G.
   Blaine, Senator Thurman, Senator Chandler.
Passport of Moses Coit Tyler, 1863, signed by Wm. H. Seward.
Letter from Philip Freneau to James Madison.
   Copy.

The Correspondence of Moses Coit Tyler:
Nine volumes of neatly filed letters written to him by others
   from 1854 to 1900.
Family Letters from Moses Coit Tyler, 1865–99.
Letters of Moses Coit Tyler.
   Copies of letters written by him, 1874–8.
Letters of Moses Coit Tyler to his children.
Index to the Correspondence of Moses Coit Tyler.
   Compiled by Mr. Willard Austen.

Thirty-five Diaries covering the years 1859–1900.

Eight Commonplace Books covering the years 1853–81.
Scrapbooks:
   Critical Notices, American Literature during the Colonial Time.
   Personal Letters, American Literature during the Colonial Time.
   Press Notices, Literary History of the American Revolution.
   Personal Letters, Literary History of the American Revolution.
   Critical Notices, Patrick Henry.
   Personal Letters, Patrick Henry.
   Notices, Three Men of Letters and Glimpses of England.
   M. C. Tyler, Miscellaneous.
   Personal Records, 1853–75.
   Personal Records, 1879–97.
Diary of Charles Tyler, 1858.
Notes for Genealogy.
Tyler Family Papers (2), 1779–1842; 1843–99.
Tyler Family Records.
Autobiography of Mary Greene Tyler, 1884.
Genealogy of the Family of Elisha and Freelove Harris.
Letters regarding Thomas Jackson, 1875.

B. BOOKS BY MOSES COIT TYLER

Our Solace and Our Duty in This Crisis. Poughkeepsie, 1861.
*The New System of Musical Gymnastics as an Instrument in
   Education.* London, 1864.
The Omnibus. London, 1865.

The New Gymnastics as an Instrument in Education. Cambridge, Mass., 1869.

The Brawnville Papers. Boston, 1869.

The Direct Study of English Masterpieces. Ann Arbor, 1875.

The Direct Study of English Masterpieces: Shakespeare Course. Ann Arbor, 1877.

A History of American Literature, 1607–1765. 2 vols. New York, 1878, 1879, 1890, 1897.

A Manual of English Literature. By Henry Morley. Revised by Moses Coit Tyler. New York, 1879.

In Memoriam: Edgar Kelsey Apgar. Edited by Moses Coit Tyler. Ithaca, 1886.

Patrick Henry (American Statesmen Series). New York and Boston, 1887, 1888. Rev. Ed., 1898, 190?, 1908, 1917.

Three Men of Letters. New York and London, 1895.

The Literary History of the American Revolution, 2 vols. New York and London, 1897.

Glimpses of England. New York and London, 1898.

C. CONTRIBUTIONS TO BOOKS AND PERIODICALS

Many of the following articles were not signed by Tyler, but are known from the Tyler papers to be his. No conjectural attributions have been made in this list.

"The Reverend Thomas Spencer." *Quinby's Monthly Literary Miscellany,* Sept., 1852.

"Vassar Female College." *The New Englander,* XXI, Oct., 1862.

"Introduction." Dio Lewis, *The New Gymnastics for Families.* London, 1864.

"Musical Gymnastics as an Instrument in Education." *The Herald of Health,* VI, Aug., 1865.

"Mason Jones in England." *The Independent,* XVII, July 6, 1865.

*"John Stuart Mill on the Stump." *The Independent,* XVII, Aug. 17, 1865.

"A Bundle of English Items." *The Independent,* XVII, Sept. 21, 1865.

"A Letter from Old Plymouth." *The Independent,* XVII, Nov. 30, 1865.

"The Spurgeon Brothers." *The Independent,* XVIII, Jan. 11, 1866.

*"American Reputations in England." *The Nation,* II, Jan. 18, 1866.

* Titles thus marked were reprinted in *Glimpses of England.*

*"Joseph Mazzini." *The Independent,* XVIII, Feb. 8, 1866; *The Herald of Health,* VII, May, 1866.

"The Birthplace of Wilberforce." *The Independent,* XVIII, Feb. 22, 1866.

*"A Sunday in Wales." *The Nation,* II, March 22, 1866.

*"A Peep at the Cardiff Consulate." *The Independent,* XVIII, April 12, 1866.

*"The Honorable and Reverend Baptist W. Noel." *The Independent,* XVIII, May 3, 1866.

*"Mr. Mill in the House of Commons." *The Nation,* II, May 11, 1866.

*"The New Reform Movement in England." *The Independent,* XVIII, May 24, 1866.

"The Dio Lewis Gymnastics in England." *The Herald of Health,* VII, June, 1866.

*"Spurgeonism." *The Independent,* XVIII, June 7, 1866.

"Several Things." *The Independent,* XVIII, June 14, 1866.

*"Mr. Gladstone." *The Independent,* XVIII, July 19, 1866.

*"The Accusation Against Mr. Gladstone." *The Independent,* XVIII, July 26, 1866.

*"The House of Commons I." *The Independent,* XVIII, Aug. 16, 1866.

*"The House of Commons II." *The Independent,* XVIII, Aug. 23, 1866.

*"English Pluck." *The Herald of Health,* VIII, Aug., 1866.

"Muscular Christianity." *The Herald of Health,* VIII, Sept., 1866.

"Henry Vincent the English Orator." *The Independent,* XVIII, Sept. 6, 1866.

"Concerning a Muscular Christian." *The Herald of Health,* VIII, Oct., 1866.

*"The House of Commons III." *The Independent,* XVIII, Oct. 11, 1866.

"The Two Englands." *The Independent,* XVIII, Oct. 25, 1866.

*"Mr. Disraeli." *The Independent,* XVIII, Nov. 1, 1866.

*"Lord Brougham." *The Independent,* XVIII, Nov. 8, 1866.

*"John Bright." *The Independent,* XVIII, Nov. 22, 1866.

*"The Career of John Bright." *The Independent,* XVIII, Dec. 6, 1866.

*"Earl Russell." *The Independent,* XIX, Jan. 31, 1867.

"England" (a sonnet). *The Independent,* XIX, March 7, 1867.

"Introduction." Dio Lewis, *The Musical Gymnastics*. London, 1867.

†"Minutes of the Brawnville Athletic Club I." *The Herald of Health*, IX, April, 1867.

"Minutes of the Brawnville Athletic Club II." *The Herald of Health*, IX, May, 1867.

"Have We a Fault Among Us." *The Independent*, XIX, May 2, 1867.

"The Growth of a Nation." *The Independent*, XIX, May 23, 1867.

*"John Bright as an Orator I." *The Nation*, IV, May 30, 1867.

*"John Bright as an Orator II." *The Nation*, IV, June 13, 1867.

*"Queen Victoria I." *The Independent*, XIX, June 13, 1867.

*"Queen Victoria II." *The Independent*, XIX, June 27, 1867.

"Minutes of the Brawnville Athletic Club III." *The Herald of Health*, IX, June, 1867.

"Minutes of the Brawnville Athletic Club IV." *The Herald of Health*, X, July, 1867.

*"London." *The Nation*, V, July 4, 1867.

"Concerning You." *The Independent*, XIX, July 11, 1867.

"Minutes of the Brawnville Athletic Club V." *The Herald of Health*, X, Aug., 1867.

"Minutes of the Brawnville Athletic Club VI." *The Herald of Health*, X, Sept., 1867.

"Cornell University." *The Independent*, XIX, Sept. 5, 1867.

"Minutes of the Brawnville Athletic Club VII." *The Herald of Health*, X, Oct., 1867.

"Minutes of the Brawnville Athletic Club VIII." *The Herald of Health*, X, Nov., 1867.

"Minutes of the Brawnville Athletic Club IX." *The Herald of Health*, X, Dec., 1867.

"Standing by Thackeray's Grave." *The Herald of Health*, XI, January, 1868.

"Minutes of the Brawnville Athletic Club X." *The Herald of Health*, XI, Jan., 1868.

"Minutes of the Brawnville Athletic Club XI." *The Herald of Health*, XI, Feb., 1868.

"Wanted: A New Lecturer." *The Independent*, XX, Feb. 13, 1868.

"Minutes of the Brawnville Athletic Club XII." *The Herald of Health*, XI, March, 1868.

† This series of papers became *The Brawnville Papers*.

"One of Mr. Lincoln's Old Friends I." *The Independent*, XX, March 12, 1868.

"One of Mr. Lincoln's Old Friends II." *The Independent*, XX, March 19, 1868.

"Henry Vincent." *The Independent*, XX, June 11, 1868.

"To the Democrats." *The Independent*, XX, June 11, 1868.

"The Popular Lecture." *The Independent*, XX, June 18, 1868.

"George Dawson, The English Lecturer." *The Independent*, XX, July 23, 1868.

"Carpet Baggers." *The Independent*, XX, July 30, 1868.

"Stump Speaking." *The Independent*, XX, Aug. 6, 1868.

"Enthusiasm for Alma Mater." *The University of Michigan Magazine*, III, Dec., 1868.

*"How They Manage Their Lectures in England." *Putnam's Magazine*, III, N. S., Jan., 1869.

"Latter-Day Blockheads." *The Independent*, XXI, July 29, 1869.

"The Eclipse of the Pulpit." *The Independent*, XXI, Aug. 12, 1869.

"Prof. Watson's Party of Observation." *The Independent*, XXI, Aug. 19, 1869.

"The Burning of Alabama University." *The Independent*, XXI, Oct. 28, 1869.

"Protestant Cullenism." *The Independent*, XXI, Nov. 4, 1869.

"Fragmentary Manhood." *The Independent*, XXI, Nov. 18, 1869.

"Theodore Tilton as a Poet." *Western Monthly*, II, Dec., 1869.

"The Holy Grail" (book review). *The Independent*, XXII, Jan. 20, 1870.

"Light in the West." *The Independent*, XXII, Jan. 27, 1870.

"The National Army in the South." *The Independent*, XXII, Feb. 17, 1870.

"Out of Her Sphere." *The Independent*, XXII, Feb. 24, 1870.

"No Mute Inglorious Milton" (book review). *The Independent*, XXII, April 28, 1870.

"Mr. Emerson as a Teacher of Eloquence." *The Independent*, XXII, May 5, 1870.

"The Literary Labors of Charles Sumner." *The Independent*, XXII, May 12, 1870.

"Mr. Mulford's Treatise on Politics" (book review). *The Independent*, XXII, May 19, 1870.

"The Studies of Old Age." *The Independent*, XXII, May 26, 1870.

"Statesmen Never in Office." *The Independent*, XXII, June 2, 1870.

"A Poet of the Golden Gates" (book review). *The Independent*, XXII, June 16, 1870.

"The Gentlemen from Asia." *The Independent*, XXII, July 21, 1870.

"One Saint Less." *The Independent*, XXII, July 28, 1870.

"Letter from Michigan University." *The Independent*, XXII, Dec. 8, 1870.

"Affairs at the University of Michigan." *The Nation*, XI, Dec. 8, 1870.

"Gentlemen and Scholars in Politics." *The Independent*, XXII, Dec. 22, 1870.

"Our Public Men in Private." *The Independent*, XXIII, Jan. 12, 1871.

"First Impressions of the Senate." *The Independent*, XXIII, Jan. 19, 1871.

"A Glimpse of the House of Representatives." *The Independent*, XXIII, Jan. 26, 1871.

"New Year's Day at the Capitol." *The Brooklyn Union*, Jan., 1871.

"Charles Sumner and the President." *The Brooklyn Union*, Jan., 1871.

"Chat About the Present Congress." *The Brooklyn Union*, Jan., 1871.

"Renewal of the San Domingo Battle." *The Brooklyn Union*, Jan., 1871.

"President Grant in Good Cheer." *The Brooklyn Union*, Jan., 1871.

"The Suspension of an Old and Well-worn Subject." *The Brooklyn Union*, Jan., 1871.

"The Loan of a Pair of Eyes." *The Brooklyn Union*, Jan. 12, 1871.

"Strangers in Washington." *The Brooklyn Union*, Jan. 12, 1871.

"The Function of the Critic." *The Golden Age*, I, March 4, 1871.

"Charles Sumner Editing Himself." *The Golden Age*, I, March 4, 1871.

"A Vice-President Who May Be More." *The Golden Age*, I, March 4, 1871.

"A Few Photographs of Notable Heads." *The Golden Age*, I, March 18, 1871.

"Mr. Darwin's Stunning Book." *The Golden Age*, I, March 18, 1871.

*"The Home and Grave of Coleridge." *The Golden Age*, I, March 25, 1871.

"A Chat About Swinburne." *The Golden Age*, I, April 1, 1871.

"The President Awaking at Mid-Day." *The Golden Age*, I, April 1, 1871.

"One of Our Weak Points." *The Golden Age*, I, April 15, 1871.

"Concerning a Man Who Will Be Better Known" (book review). *The Golden Age*, I, April 15, 1871.

"Sex Among Nouns." *The Golden Age*, I, May 6, 1871.

"The University of Michigan." *Old and New*, IV, July, 1871.

"President White and the New York Tribune." *The College Courant* (Yale), XI, Sept. 14, 1872.

"President Andrew D. White as a Politician." *The Independent*, XXIV, Sept. 26, 1872.

"Speech of Moses Coit Tyler." *Proceedings at the Laying of the Corner Stone of the Sage College for Women of Cornell University*. Ithaca, 1873.

"The Pope and His Little Difficulty." *The Christian Union*, VII, Jan. 22, 1873.

"The Outlook." *The Christian Union*, VII–X, March 5, 1873–Sept. 9, 1874.

"Books and Authors." *The Christian Union*, VII–X, March 5, 1873–Sept. 9, 1874.

"A Tale of Ten Heroes." *The Christian Union*, VII, March 5, 1873.

"A Cobbler Mending a Kingdom." *The Christian Union*, VII, April 2, 1873.

"The Scientist and the Tobacconist." *The Christian Union*, VII, April 16, 1873.

"The Sage College for Women." *The Christian Union*, VII, May 28, 1873.

"The Newspaper of Today." *The Christian Union*, VII, June 18, 1873.

"The Commencement Carnival." *The Christian Union*, VIII, July 2, 1873.

"Agassiz on Penikese Island." *The Christian Union*, VIII, July 16, 1873.

"Jonathan's Sentiments Towards John." *The Christian Union*, IX, Feb. 11, 1874.

"Poor Jacks." *The Christian Union,* IX, March 25, 1874.

"Lincoln and Seward." *The Christian Union,* IX, April 1, 1874.

"The Land of the Sagas." *The Christian Union,* IX, April 8, 1874.

"Washington's Coach and Six." *The Christian Union,* IX, April 15, 1874.

"Agassiz the Teacher." *The Christian Union,* IX, April 29, 1874.

"The Centennial and the Baptists." *The Christian Union,* IX, May 6, 1874.

"A Star in the West." *The Christian Union,* IX, May 20, 1874.

"George W. Sterling." *The Christian Union,* X, Aug. 5, 1874.

"President Hopkins on the Prayer-Gauge." *The Christian Union,* X, Aug. 12, 1874.

"Our Educational Blunder." *The Christian Union,* X, Aug. 19, 1874.

"A Commercial View of Christian Missions." *The Christian Union,* X, Sept. 9, 1874.

"Mr. Bancroft's Last Volume." *The Independent,* XXVI, Dec. 3, 1874.

"The University of Michigan." *Scribner's Monthly Magazine,* XI, Feb., 1876.

"A Bridge Builder." *The Literary World,* XVI, June 27, 1885.

"Christianity and Manliness." *The Christian Union,* XXXII, Nov. 5, 1885.

"Dean Berkeley's Sojourn in America, 1729–31." W. S. Perry, *The History of the American Episcopal Church,* I, IV. Boston, 1885.

"The Evolution of the Free Public Library in America." *Catalogue of the Sage Library of West Bay City, Michigan.* West Bay City, 1886.

"Advice to Boys Preparing for College." *Youth's Companion,* March 11, 1886.

"Doyle's Puritan Colonies" (book review). *The Literary World,* XIX, March 3, 1888.

"Address by Moses Coit Tyler, LL.D." *Exercises at the Opening of the Library Building Cornell University.* Ithaca, 1891.

"A Half Century of Conflict, by Francis Parkman" (book review). *Political Science Quarterly,* III, Nov., 1892.

"A New Study of Patrick Henry" (book review). *Yale Review,* I, Feb., 1893.

"The Party of the Loyalists in the American Revolution." *American Historical Review,* I, Oct., 1895.

"The Life of Thomas Hutchinson" (book review). *The Nation,* LXII, March 26, 1896.

"President Witherspoon in the American Revolution." *American Historical Review,* I, July, 1896.

"The Declaration of Independence in the Light of Modern Criticism." *The North American Review,* CLXIII, July, 1896.

"The Educational Value of History." *Library of Universal History,* I, New York, 1898–9.

NOTES

NOTES

CHAPTER I

[1] Paraphrased from the copy made by Moses Coit Tyler from MS. of his father, Elisha Tyler, at Detroit in 1857. In Tyler Family Records, I.—And in Mrs. Austen, *Moses Coit Tyler* (Garden City, 1911), p. 3, hereafter referred to as Mrs. Austen. The tradition is also noted by Lyon G. Tyler, *The Letters and Times of the Tylers* (Richmond, 1884), vol. I, p. 41. For a gallant attempt to derive the family from Wat Tyler, see *ibid.*, pp. 36–41. The three brothers are believed to have emigrated from Shropshire, perhaps as early as 1640, certainly by 1653. See the sketch of Tyler's ancestry compiled by Professor George Lincoln Burr of Cornell University in the *New England Historical and Genealogical Register*, vol. 55 (1901), pp. xciii–xcv; and for corroborative detail see James Savage, *A Genealogical Dictionary of the First Settlers of New England* (Boston, 1860), vol. IV, pp. 354–6. I have seen only certain pages of the official Tyler genealogy.—*J.*

[2] Savage, *op. cit.* He paid church rates in North Andover to the First Church, to which Mrs. Anne Bradstreet belonged. *Official Report of the First American Tyler Reunion* (Chicago, 1897).—*J.*

[3] Thomas Hutchinson, *History of Massachusetts Bay* (Boston, 1795), vol. II, p. 32.

[4] *First Congregational Church of Preston, Connecticut, 1698–1898* (published by the Society, 1900), pp. 81–2. In 1687 Hopestill was granted liberty in Andover to "set up a shop in ye street near his house" as a blacksmith.—*J.*

[5] *Ibid.*—*J.*

[6] See the declaration signed by Mary Osgood, Mary Tyler, Hannah Tyler, and three other women in Charles W. Upham, *Salem Witchcraft with an Account of Salem Village,* etc. (Boston, 1867), vol. II, part ii, pp. 402–4; and cf. pp. 404–7. Hannah (or Johanna) was the daughter of Mary, born in 1681. Together with Martha Tyler, her sister, she confessed to being "lead into that dreadfull sin of witchcraft" by Abigal Faulkner under date of Sept. 17, 1692. *Records of Salem Witchcraft Copied from the Original Documents,* vol. II, pp. 134–5; and cf. pp. 127–8.—*J.*

⁷ *Publications of the Colonial Society of Massachusetts; Transactions, 1904–1906,* vol. X, pp. 23–4.—*J.*

⁸ *First Congregational Church, op. cit.*—*J.*

⁹ *D. A. R. Lineage Book,* vol. 60, p. 211.—*J.*

¹⁰ See the tax list in the appendices to Daniel L. Phillips, *Griswold—A History* (1929).—*J.*

¹¹ Phillips, *op. cit.,* p. 366, following the State Records.—*J.*

¹² Clipping from *Detroit Free Press,* Feb. 5, 1894, in the Burton Historical Library, Detroit.—*J.*

¹³ Tyler MSS. Letter from Mary Greene Tyler to Moses Coit Tyler, April 17, 1884.—The children were Charles Coit, born Dec. 30, 1830; Rowland Greene, born Jan. 4, 1832; Susannah Greene, born May 24, 1834; Moses Coit, born Aug. 2, 1835 (all in Griswold); Olive Coit, born in Marshall, Mich., July 3, 1837; Edward Scott, born in Burlington, Sept. 1, 1839; John, born in Burlington, July 19, 1841; Samuel Coit, born in Detroit, Nov. 9, 1846; Harris Greene, born in Detroit, Nov. 5, 1852. Of these Samuel Coit did not survive infancy, and Harris Green lived only until 1856. Data corrected from the Tyler genealogy.—*J.*

¹⁴ Phillips, p. 165. The barn was destroyed by a storm in 1901. —*J.*

¹⁵ Cf. J. W. Barker, *Connecticut Historical Collections . . .* (New Haven, 1836), pp. 310–11. The engraving of Jewett's City on p. 310 reveals the rural simplicities of this "flourishing village." —*J.*

¹⁶ Speaking of his father's letters, Moses Coit Tyler wrote: "It is tragic to think that in his early life he longed to go to college, to take a profession, and that his father and mother refused, apparently, on the ground that he was the only son and must stand by them on the farm. . . . He was a high-minded man always." (Quoted by Mrs. Austen, p. 4.) Elisha wrote his son afterwards that "I proposed this [moving west] to my father. He said he was too old to remove [he was sixty-eight when he died]; that duty required me to remain during his life; that when he died I might go if I chose. I accordingly remained on the old homestead, always wishing to go to a more fertile region, but saw no way to do it and keep peace in the family and discharge what I believed to be a duty." (*Ibid.*) Elisha's interest in manufacture is to be inferred from the fact that in Constantia he was interested in a furnace factory, and in Marshall, in a flour-mill. *Ibid.,* p. 5.—*J.*

¹⁷ The details are from H. G. Spafford, *A Gazetteer of the State*

of New York, published in 1824. A dozen years could not, however, have made a profound change.—*J.*

[18] See the account of Calhoun County by O. C. Comstock in *Report of the Pioneer Society of the State of Michigan,* 1877–8, vol. II (1880), pp. 192–202.—*J.*

[19] See, for a graphic account of pioneer Michigan, Mrs. Mary Clavers (Mrs. Caroline Matilda Kirkland), *A New Home—Who'll Follow? or, Glimpses of Western Life,* fifth edition (New York, 1855). The details can be readily verified from the accounts of the early settlers published by the Pioneer Society of Michigan in their volumes of *Reports.*—*J.*

[20] See the quotations from Hoffman in *Michigan History Magazine,* vol. IX (1925), pp. 413–37.—*J.*

[21] It later failed.—*J.*

[22] Hoffman (*op. cit.*) speaks of a flour-mill already erected in 1833. This had been erected in 1832 by George Ketchum. *History of Calhoun County,* p. 52.—*J.*

[23] Tyler MSS. Letters from Mary Greene Tyler to Moses Coit Tyler, Oct. 11 and Nov. 18, 1884.

[24] W. J. Tucker, *My Generation* (Boston, 1919), p. 21.

[25] Thomas F. Gordon, *Gazetteer of the State of New York* (1836), pp. 105–9.—*J.*

[26] Elisha could not apparently afford the faster and more luxurious packets, which kept an average speed of three or three and one-half miles an hour, and which were more comfortably furnished. See Seymour Dunbar, *A History of Travel in America* (Indianapolis, 1915), pp. 847–71; and note the pictures *passim* pp. 179–205.—*J.*

[27] Utley and Cutcheon, *Michigan as a Province, Territory and State* (New York, 1906), vol. III, p. 117. For a description of the rolling stock see B. M. Cutcheon, "Fifty Years of Growth in Michigan," *Report of the Pioneer Society of the State of Michigan,* vol. XXII, p. 488.—*J.*

[28] Tyler MSS. Letter from Elisha Tyler to his mother, August, 1837.—For a graphic account of a similar journey to Marshall made the same year by A. D. P. Van Buren, see "Pioneer Annals of Calhoun County," *Report of the Pioneer Society of the State of Michigan,* vol. V, pp. 237–59. Even the territorial road was occasionally impassable.—*J.*

[29] Burke A. Hinsdale—I. N. Demmon, *History of the University of Michigan* (Ann Arbor, 1906), pp. 15–17.—*J.*

[30] Asa B. Cook, Arza Robinson and Sidney Ketchum had built a stone flour-mill on the Kalamazoo River. *History of Calhoun County, Michigan* . . . (Philadelphia, 1877), p. 52.—*J.*

[31] Burlington was first settled in 1832; the first corn and wheat were grown in 1833; and there was no tavern until David Dexter opened one in 1835. In fact, the township was just being organized, and Burlington did not officially become a village until the Tylers left it in 1842. *Ibid.,* pp. 157–8.—*J.*

[32] On March 3, 1837, Elisha Tyler bought land in section 25 of Burlington township from Elihu Covey, which he sold to Otis S. Tufant on June 4, 1842. On March 29, 1837, he bought land located in Burlington and Tekonsha townships from Daniel Prindle and wife, which he sold to Homer C. Hurd and Edward L. Rogers on Nov. 16, 1839. Letter from Frank M. Eddy, Register of Deeds, Calhoun County, April 21, 1832.—*J.*

[33] Silas Farmer, *The History of Detroit* . . . (Detroit, 1884), p. 336.—*J.*

[34] Tyler MSS. Letter from Elisha Tyler to Doctor Greene, May, 25, 1842.

[35] Details from Detroit city directories for 1845, 1846, 1852–3, 1853–4, 1856–7, preserved in the Burton Historical Library, Detroit.—*J.*

[36] Farmer, *op. cit.,* p. 494. A reproduction of the oil painting is sketched on p. 495.—*J.*

[37] *Fiftieth Anniversary of the Organization of the First Congregational Church and Society of Detroit, Michigan* . . . (Detroit, 1894), p. 166. However, Elisha was not re-elected.—*J.*

[38] Letter in the Woodbridge papers, Burton Historical Library. —*J.*

[39] Farmer, pp. 492–5. Six city blocks burned in 1849, and there were picturesque minor calamities. After 1850–51 fire-risks increased with the introduction of camphene, "a highly inflammable mixture of alcohol, turpentine, and camphor gum," an illuminating fluid expected to rival gas, which had interesting results in the way of explosions.—*J.*

[40] The song may be found in Farmer, *op. cit.,* p. 509, with other effusions of the local muse.—*J.*

[41] *Detroit in 1837. Recollections of Thomas W. Palmer* (Detroit, 1922), p. 26.—*J.*

[42] Buffalo robes.—*J.*

[43] This was written in 1850. Farmer, *op. cit.,* p. 931.—*J.*

[44] Clarence M. Burton, *History of Detroit, 1780–1850, Financial and Commercial* (Detroit, 1917), p. 155.—*J*.

[45] C. M. Burton, *The City of Detroit, Michigan, 1701–1922,* vol. II, pp. 1068–70.—*J*.

[46] Details from Farmer, the two Burton histories, Palmer, etc. A graphic picture of Detroit in the forties is to be found in George B. Catlin, *A Brief History of Detroit in the Golden Days of '49,* issued by the Detroit Savings Bank in 1921.—*J*.

[47] See the editorial from *The Detroit Gazette* quoted in Farmer, p. 740, eulogizing the improvement wrought by the new system.—*J*.

[48] This rests upon the assertion of Mr. William D. Wilkins (p. 457) in his "Traditions and Reminiscences of the Public Schools of Detroit" in *Report of the Pioneer Society of the State of Michigan,* vol. I (1877), pp. 448–69. This able account should be supplemented by chapter lxxv of Farmer.—*J*.

[49] Elisha wrote just before his death: "In all my pecuniary transactions I have used my better judgments (*sic*) to secure a fortune, but now have to lament that at the age of sixty-two I find myself and family poor, and nothing very prosperous at hand for the future of any of us. From my present standpoint I can look back and see how some of my mistakes occurred which have proved so disastrous, and can as easily see how a different course would have given me possession of millions." Mrs. Austen, p. 4. The likeness to Colonel Sellers is obvious. Elisha is a well-nigh classic case of pioneer psychology.—*J*.

[50] Quoted by Mrs. Austen, pp. 5–6.—*J*.

[51] A cousin wrote in 1849: "I think Moses has the most intellectual face in the family. He is determined to be a scholar. We shall hear from him some time." Mrs. Austen, p. 6.—*J*.

[52] Elisha, as we have seen, was one of the first trustees. The rest of the family soon joined: Mary with her husband in 1844; Rowland G. Tyler in 1846; Charles, Susannah Moses, and Olive in 1848; Edward S. Tyler in 1855; etc. *Fiftieth Anniversary of the Organization of the First Congregational Church and Society of Detroit, Michigan,* p. 166.—*J*.

[53] He was graduated from Middlebury College in 1835; shortly thereafter entered Andover; and transferred to the Yale Theological Seminary in 1837, being graduated in 1838. His first pastorate was in Thomaston, Conn., 1839–48. *Catalogue of the Officers and Students of Middlebury College......1810 to 1900.* (Middlebury, 1901), p. 12.—*J*.

[54] *Op. cit.*, pp. 12–13.—*J.*

[55] *Op. cit.*, p. 13.—*J.*

[56] In the winter of 1851 he conducted "the only missionary concert of prayer" in Detroit. *Fiftieth Anniversary*, etc., p. 87.—*J.*

[57] Kitchel gave the "Memorial Address" at the quarter-centennial, and the "Communion Address" on the Fiftieth Anniversary, of the founding of the church, both preserved in the Burton Historical Library.—*J.*

[58] See the list of missionary graduates of Middlebury noted by President Samuel W. Boardman in his "Anniversary Address" in *A Record of the Centennial Anniversary of Middlebury College* (1901), pp. 32–80; and see also the prominent Yale missionaries in Anson Phelps Stokes, *Memorials of Eminent Yale Men* (New Haven, 1914), 2 vols.—*J.*

[59] Funeral discourses by Doctor Kitchel for the mighty William Woodbridge, and for his wife, daughter of John Trumbull of Connecticut, are preserved in the Burton Library, the latter address in particular dwelling with painful literalness upon the sickbed and the tomb. He devoted the "Memorial Address" mentioned above to a mournful enumeration of the church dead.—*J.*

[60] *Fiftieth Anniversary*, pp. 52–3. From the "Historical Address" by George M. Lane.—*J.*

[61] Farmer, *History*, p. 675.—*J.*

[62] *Fifty Years*, p. 34.—*J.*

[63] Typical contributions by Kitchel. See issues of the *Monthly Literary Miscellany* for March, June, July, Aug., and Oct., 1851.—*J.*

[64] *Ibid.*, Dec., 1851.—*J.*

[65] Farmer, *History*, pp. 839–40.—*J.*

[66] The authority for the first statement is the unpublished MS. "Address" noted below; for the second, *Quinby's Monthly Literary Miscellany*, April, 1852, p. 192, one of the protean transformations of Wellman's publication.

[67] Fifteen MSS. pages, half-size, entitled "Address delivered by Moses Tyler on taking his seat as Worthy Archon of Chrystal Fount Section No. 5 C. of T. Detroit, July 7, 1851," preserved in the Burton Historical Library.—*J.*

[68] The school records of Romeo were destroyed by fire in the seventies.—*J.*

[69] Tyler MSS. Letter from Elisha Tyler to Moses Coit Tyler, Dec., 1850.

[70] Tyler MSS. Letter from Elisha Tyler to Moses Tyler, Dec. 6, 1850.

[71] Tyler MSS. Letter from Elisha Tyler to Moses Tyler, Feb. 2, 1851.

[72] Farmer, *History*, p. 676. It began publication May 17, 1851, and continued less than a year. There is no file in the Burton Library.—*J.*

[73] Tyler MSS. Letter from Charles Tyler to Moses Tyler, Aug. 2, 1851.

[74] *Quinby's Monthly Literary Miscellany*, Sept., 1852, pp. 386–9.—*J.*

[75] *Catalogue of the Corporation, Officers and Students in the Department of Medicine, Arts and Sciences, in the University of Michigan, 1852–53* (Detroit, 1853), p. 23.—*J.*

[76] Elizabeth M. Farrand, *History of the University of Michigan* (Ann Arbor, 1885), p. 49. Mr. Almendinger [Allmundinger] also served as assistant librarian (*Proceedings of the Board of Regents, 1837–1864*, p. 372) but only in 1847–8 (*ibid.*, p. 402).—*J.*

[77] Lincoln's *Livy*, Krebb's *Guide*, Eschenburg's *Manual of Roman Antiquities*, Owen's *Homer's Odyssey*, Bourdon's *Algebra*, Eschenburg's *Manual of Greek Antiquities*, Legendre's *Geometry*, Horace's *Odes*, Owen's *Xenophon's Anabasis*, according to the catalogue of 1851–2, which also stipulates a botany and a zoology. But one of the first minutes for 1852 in the manuscript *Records of the Faculty of the University of Michigan* (*A*), preserved in the Registrar's Office, shows that the faculty under Tappan had already modified the Freshman course.—*J.*

[78] The regulations of the University *Catalogue* for 1852, under which Moses entered, pp. xvi–xvii.—*J.*

[79] Reproduced in Wilfred B. Shaw, *History of the University of Michigan*, and in the Hinsdale-Demmon *History.*—*J.*

[80] Details from Shaw, Hinsdale-Demmon, and the printed catalogues for 1852 and 1853.—*J.*

[81] In 1851–2 the whole student body, including "five honorary members of Medical College," numbered 159; in 1852–3, 222.—*J.*

[82] Andrew Ten Brook, *American State Universities and the University of Michigan*, p. 197.—*J.*

[83] *Tributes to James Robinson Boise* (Privately printed, 1895), pp. 29–30.—*J.*

[84] Ten Brook, *op. cit.*, p. 208 note; p. 213.—*J.*

[85] *University of Michigan Regents' Proceedings . . . 1837–1864,* p. 513.—*J.*

[86] *Records of the Faculty of the University of Michigan (A),* Oct. 18. Prayers had been at half-past five, and were later (Nov. 8) changed to eight o'clock.—*J.*

[87] Byron M. Cutcheon's description in Shaw, p. 50.—*J.*

[88] "Historical Statement of my Connection with the University" by Doctor H. P. Tappan, in *University of Michigan Regents' Proceedings . . . 1837–1864* (Ann Arbor, 1905), p. 1160.—*J.*

[89] The *Regents' Proceedings* (pp. 517; 519) lists only Barnard and Adams (probably Reverend William Adams, Yale, 1827), as having received formal offers. President Tappan states that Bancroft declined appointment *(ibid.,* p. 1119); and the Hinsdale-Demmon *History* (p. 41) says that the secretary of the regents corresponded with Potter and Nott.—*J.*

[90] *Ibid.,* p. 512.—*J.*

[91] Tappan's "Historical Statement," *loc. cit.*—*J.*

[92] *Catalogue of . . . the University of Michigan, 1852–53* (Detroit, 1853), p. 21.—*J.*

[93] *Records of the Faculty of the University of Michigan (A).*—*J.*

[94] *University of Michigan, 1871–1896: The Quarter-Centennial Celebration of the Presidency of James Burrill Angell, LL.D., June 24, 1896* (Ann Arbor, 1896), pp. 230–1.—*J.*

[95] Details from a file of *The Washtenaw Whig* for 1852–3.—*J.*

CHAPTER II

[1] The MS. "Examination Book" preserved in the Registrar's Office of the University of Michigan records Moses Coit Tyler as having passed all his Freshman *and* Sophomore examinations from 1852 through 1853–4. But this is clearly in error. A letter of Charles Tyler's in the Tyler papers, under date of April 29, 1853, indicates that Moses had left the University of Michigan; and the records of Yale, as quoted to me in a letter from the Registrar there, are conclusive that he spent only the academic year 1852–3 in Ann Arbor.—*J.*

[2] Tyler MSS. Letter from Samuel Coit to Moses Tyler, May 19, 1857. Charles Coit of Norwich may also have assisted, in view of the dedication in Tyler's *History* already referred to.—That Samuel Coit had a strong family feeling is evident from the fact that he

paid for the completion of the Coit genealogy, left unfinished in
1867. *New England Historical and Genealogical Register,* vol.
XXIX, p. 125. Samuel Coit's father was the brother of Moses Tyler's grandmother. Coit was born in 1819, and was therefore thirty-
four years old in 1853. He had been clerk in the Phoenix Bank,
Hartford, teller in the Farmers and Mechanics Bank, and teller in
the Hartford Bank (after 1848), and was to become secretary of
the Ætna Life Insurance Company (1855) and president of the
American Silver Steel Company. He was a member of the First
Church of Hartford. This information, gleaned from the city
directories, was kindly furnished by Mr. J. Emerson Greenaway
of the Hartford Public Library.—*J.*

[3] Tyler MSS. Personal Records, 1853–75.

[4] *Proceedings of the American Association for the Advancement of Science. Seventh Meeting, Held at Cleveland, Ohio, July,
1853* (Cambridge, 1856), "Executive Proceedings," p. 273.—*J.*

[5] *Op. cit.,* pp. xvii, xviii.—*J.*

[6] *Ibid.,* p. xix. However, there was trouble over an unauthorized
printing of the "Proceedings" by a Cleveland publisher. See the
"Executive Proceedings," last pages.—*J.*

[7] *Op. cit.,* pp. 270–72. I have been able to consult only the files
of *The Evening Post, Weekly.* It is possible that Tyler won more
space in other editions, and in the *Journal of Commerce.*—*J.*

[7a] Students were not officially matriculated until they had
passed their examinations. Though Tyler was admitted in September, he was not officially a member of the collegiate body until
March 31, 1854. Letter of Anne S. Pratt, June 10, 1932.—*J.*

[8] Tucker, *My Generation,* p. 34, cites figures.

[9] [Timothy Dwight], *Memories of Yale Life and Men* (New
York, 1903), p. 193.—*J.*

[10] [Timothy Dwight.] *Theodore Dwight Woolsey, D.D., LL.D.
Memorial Address before the Graduates of Yale University, June
24, 1890* (New Haven, 1890), p. 20.—*J.*

[11] Dwight, *Memories,* pp. 194–5.—*J.*

[12] *Ibid.,* p. 192.—*J.*

[13] Dwight, *Memories,* pp. 18–19. A Scripture passage was read,
the president prayed, the freshmen departed first, the seniors
bowed to the president, and all walked out. See also Dwight's
Address, p. 24; and on Woolsey see also Anson P. Stokes, *Memorials of Eminent Yale Men,* vol. I, pp. 237–46.—*J.*

[14] In 1856 Theodore T. Munger, a sympathetic observer, thought
that although Taylor "exercises a positive power upon you" and

"makes you think for yourself," he disgusted many with his dogmatism. Stokes, vol. I, p. 66. On Taylor see further below. —*J*.

[15] Stokes, vol. II, p. 33.—*J*.

[16] Stokes, vol. II, p. 49.—*J*.

[17] Stokes, vol. I, pp. 336–44.—*J*.

[18] Dwight, *Memories,* pp. 101–3. The facts concerning the Yale faculty are gleaned from Dwight, Stokes, Charles F. Thwing, *A History of Higher Education in America* (New York, 1906), chap. xii; F. B. Dexter, *Sketch of the History of Yale University* (New York, 1887); *Catalogue of the Officers and Graduates of Yale University in New Haven, Conn., 1701–1892* (New Haven, 1892).—*J*.

[19] "The younger men [tutors] . . . when they differed in sentiment from the older ones, did not hesitate to give utterance to their independent thoughts . . . I recall some memorable controversies in which I took an active, or even a leading part, in opposition to the men of greatest influence in the older section of the board [of instruction]." Dwight, *Memories,* p. 107. See the whole chapter. The differences developed over problems of discipline and over the amount of formality between students and faculty members consonant with good management.—*J*.

[20] While Bushnell's sermons before the undergraduates were not disturbing, Connecticut theology was in a state of high tension from 1855 to 1859. (Dwight, *Memories,* p. 85). Bushnell's views were expressed in two discourses on "Christian Nurture" in 1847, a volume entitled *God in Christ* (1849), and one entitled *Christ in Theology* (1851). He stressed the family as a mold of Christian character, minimizing baptismal regeneration, revivals, and a mechanical conception of theology; and he took a quasi-mystic view of the Trinity in opposition to the official rationalism. Various unsuccessful attempts were made to try him for heresy. Consult Theodore T. Munger, *Horace Bushnell: Preacher and Theologian* (Boston, 1899), and chapter I of John Wright Buckham, *Progressive Religious Thought in America: A Survey of the Enlarging Pilgrim Faith* (Boston, 1919).—*J*.

[21] "The Theological Department of our University in September, 1858, was in a very depressed condition, and the outlook for its future was quite discouraging." Dwight, *op. cit.,* p. 253. Dwight attributes the decline to the outmoded theology of Taylor and to lack of funds, and says that "for several years before the date I mentioned, the number of students in attendance had

been steadily decreasing." (p. 254.) The percentage of ministerial graduates at Yale from 1836 to 1850 was only 22.23 per cent of the graduates as compared with 31.65 per cent for the previous fifteen years, and with 27.44 per cent, the average for the 149 years of Yale's existence from 1702 to 1850. See George P. Fisher, *A Discourse Commemorative of the History of the Church of Christ in Yale College during the First Century of its Existence* (New Haven, 1858), p. 95.—*J.*

[22] "Every student of the years between 1840 and 1858 whose mind turned with interest towards religious subjects will remember the voluntary meetings in what was called the Theological Chamber in the old Lyceum Building, which were held on Sunday evenings, immediately after the supper hour, and which were addressed by Professor Goodrich . . . he had extraordinary power in the line of speaking called for in such assemblies. He was most interesting and quickening in his thought, most impressive in his manner and bearing, and most urgent, as well as eloquent, in his presentation of Christian truth and duty." And also rhetorical "in a high degree." Dwight, *Memories,* p. 86.—*J.*

[23] Two professorships in chemistry were founded in the late forties, geology was given a separate professorship in 1850, as was metallurgy in 1855; a chair of civil engineering was established in 1852; the Medical School was undergoing a process of thorough reorganization in the decade; a graduate division, known as the Department of Philosophy and the Arts, founded in 1847, included "various new courses in Philology, Philosophy, and Science," usually offered by younger men; a chemical laboratory was opened in the president's house, which Woolsey did not choose to occupy; and instruction in chemistry and engineering was given in the "Yale Scientific School" after 1854, the foundation of the Sheffield Scientific School, so named in 1860. Franklin B. Dexter, *Sketch of the History of Yale University,* pp. 65–77. The rise of laboratory science and of technological subjects inevitably minimized the importance of the older curriculum.—*J.*

[24] In the twenties some thirty-two southern students, members of the Linonian Society, withdrew in protest against the election of a northern student to the presidency, founding the Calliopean Society as a strictly southern literary and debating group, which flourished to 1853. Clarence Deming, *Yale Yesterdays* (New Haven, 1915), p. 144. A year later Moses Tyler wrote his aunt, noting the denunciations heaped on Yale by "the more influential journals of the South" in consequence of faculty opinion on the

Kansas-Nebraska question, and good feeling was not increased in the college by the "singular fact that at no time since the foundation of old Yale itself have there been so many Southern students presented for admission." (Moses Coit Tyler to Mrs. Dorcas Greene, Sept. 12, 1854, in Mrs. Austen, p. 7.)—*J.*

[24a] W. T. Harris, who entered Yale in 1854, withdrew as a junior, "full of dissatisfaction with the course of study, and impatient for the three 'moderns'—modern science, modern literature, and modern history." "How I Was Educated," *The Forum,* vol. I, p. 560. He was also passing through a period of religious doubt, which Yale did nothing to help. Stokes, *op. cit.,* vol. I, p. 274.—*J.*

[25] Dwight, *Memories,* p. 62.—*J.*

[26] Information on Tyler's Yale career has been kindly furnished by Alfred K. Merritt, Registrar of Yale College, in a letter of March 28, 1932.—*J.*

[27] Deming, *Yale Yesterdays,* pp. 7-8.—*J.*

[28] William Rey, *L'Amérique Protestante: Notes et Observations d'un Voyageur* (Paris, 1857), tom. ii, pp. 51-2.—*J.*

[29] J. D. B. De Bow, *Statistical View of the United States . . .* (Washington, 1854), p. 371.—*J.*

[30] Deming, *Yale Yesterdays,* pp. 21-2.—*J.*

[31] Lady Emmeline Stuart Wortley, *Travels in the United States, etc., during 1849 and 1850* (London, 1851), vol. I, p. 123; p. 128. "The former repeat very plainly the sound that gives them their name, in a most positive and authoritative manner; and after a little time, you will hear others apparently replying 'Katy-didn't'." —*J.*

[32] The Yale Registrar informs me that his four-year average on the scale of 400 was 282; and that his rank was number 36 in his class of 100.—*J.*

[33] He won two prizes for excellence in English composition, and one prize for declamation, as a sophomore. And see note 41 below.—*J.*

[34] Rey, *op. cit.,* vol. II, p. 53. "Il m'a semblé que de tantes les obligations de culte frequent pesait le plus aux élèves."—*J.*

[35] *Ibid.,* pp. 55-6.—*J.*

[36] See Nettleton, *The Book of the Yale Pageant,* pp. 73-4; and Deming, *Yale Yesterdays,* pp. 53-7.—*J.*

[37] Nettleton, *op. cit.,* p. 76.—*J.*

[38] From Deming, *op. cit.,* p. 46.—*J.*

[38a] Letter from Miss Anne S. Pratt, Reference Librarian of

Yale University Library, June 1, 1932, who kindly looked up the records.—*J.*

[39] Stokes, *op. cit.,* vol. I, pp. 167–8. Stedman won the sophomore composition prize later awarded to Tyler.—*J.*

[40] Personal Records, 1853–75. Tyler "reported" these lectures in January, 1854.—*J.*

[41] Details from Stokes and Deming. For White's disillusionment, see *Autobiography of Andrew Dickson White* (New York, 1905), vol. I, pp. 26–7.—*J.*

[42] He was one of thirty-seven elected to Phi Beta Kappa. In the way of prizes he received honors in English composition during his Sophomore year (third prize the second term; tied for first prize the third term); and tied for third place in declamation. In his Junior year he was one of twenty-two orators at the Junior Exhibition out of a class of 111. As a Senior he did not deliver one of the twenty-four orations, but one of the ten "Dissertations," apparently an inferior honor. For the reception of his commencement dissertation see *post,* p. 56. Details from *Phi Beta Kappa General Catalogue* (Somerville, N. J., 1922), and the Yale College *Catalogues* for 1855–6, 1856–7, and 1857–8.

[43] When Dwight was an undergraduate, "all that was then [1845–9] offered in the line of instruction in English during the earlier part of the College course was under the charge of tutors, and was limited to more or less regular exercises in English composition . . . The criticisms . . . were of no significant value or importance." Instruction was casual. Professor Larned, appointed in 1839 to the chair of Rhetoric and English Literature, confined himself to rhetoric, lecturing to successive senior classes on the British orators. Doctor Erasmus D. North, whose relation to the faculty was tangential, was instructor in elocution up to 1854, when he resigned. He was a friend of the poet Percival, who built a house in New Haven with only one door (in back) to signify that he wished to be let alone. This seems to have been North's closest contact with living letters. As a teacher, he had no power of discipline. Dwight, *op. cit.,* pp. 152–5; 202–7.—*J.*

[44] Tyler MSS. Commonplace Book, II, p. 26.

[45] Tyler MSS. Commonplace Book I.

[46] When he suggested to Samuel Coit that he might become a pedagogue, Coit replied: "I have never supposed you would teach school, but have fully intended you should continue your course of preparation for the ministry." Tyler MSS. This was during Moses' Senior year (1857). On his early teaching see *post,* p. 57.

[47] In 1837 the Old-School faction in the Presbyterian Assembly excommunicated 533 churches and more than 100,000 communicants because of their "liberalism." The four exscinded synods (in New York and Ohio), with later adherents, constituted about four-ninths of the Presbyterian faith. The excommunicated synods were generally anti-slavery, and the vote was put through by the virtually solid support of southern Presbyterianism. Leonard Woolsey Bacon, *A History of American Christianity* (New York, 1898), pp. 296-7.—*J.*

[48] *Ibid.*, p. 296.—*J.*

[49] *Ibid.*, p. 303.—*J.*

[50] See the letter to Mrs. Dorcas Green, quoted in Mrs. Austen, p. 7.—*J.*

[51] Tyler MSS.

[52] Tyler MSS. Personal Records, 1853-75. The date of the St. Clair meeting is unknown, but must obviously have been in the summer.

[53] *Ibid.*

[54] Albert J. Beveridge, *Abraham Lincoln, 1809-58* (Boston, 1928), vol. II, p. 434.—*J.*

[55] It is interesting to note that the idea contained in Carlyle's epigram clung to Tyler all his life, reappearing in 1897 in *The Literary History of the American Revolution,* vol. I, p. 515.

[56] Clippings from these journals are preserved in the Tyler MSS. Personal Records, 1853-75. The New Haven *Journal and Courier* called him the best orator, and the Boston *Transcript* agreed.

[57] Mrs. Austen, p. 8.—*J.*

[58] Tyler MSS. Letter from A. W. Skinner to Moses Coit Tyler, Sept. 22, 1858. Moses' financial straits are to be inferred from the fact that as late as March 3, 1860, he owed Yale College $93.94. Letter from the Treasurer of Yale College to Moses Coit Tyler. —*J.*

[59] At Tyler's request Bailey recommended him to Mr. Russell, who was in charge of similar classes at Andover, saying that Tyler "is my best pupil, my best instructor in Elocution." Tyler MSS. Letter from Professor Mark Bailey to Professor Russell, Sept. 24, 1858. Nothing seems to have come of the recommendation.

[60] See Mrs. Austen, p. 9. He had found it impossible to go home during the summer of 1858.—*J.*

[61] Tyler MSS. Commonplace Book III.

[62] Just after removing to Andover he wrote home: "It seems to me that the older I grow the more sacred become the names of home and dear kindred. I sometimes get to musing of past years, of the long, long ago, at Burlington and Union City, and the Phillips House at Detroit, and the pottery and copper stock, and of all those scenes, sad and happy which filled up my childhood. And then the last six years [1852–8] appear to me like a dream, and I wake up and find all things changed, our home broken up, our beloved father and Eddy gone from us. . . ." Moses Tyler to his mother, Oct. 24, 1858, in Mrs. Austen, p. 10. The "pottery and copper stock" apparently refers to two abortive undertakings of Elisha Tyler in Detroit, the "Stone Ware" factory, and a later enterprise. "Eddy" is Edward Scott Tyler, who died in 1856. I have not been able to identify the Phillips House. —J.

[63] The conjecture that Tyler went to Andover to have his faith stabilized under Park is strengthened by an examination of that worthy's "A Discourse delivered before the Convention of the Congregational Ministers of Massachusetts, in Brattle Street Meeting House, Boston, May 30, 1850" (Andover, 1850; reprinted from *Bibliotheca Sacra* for July, 1850). This address is designed to show the superiority of the theology of the intellect over the theology of feeling, and is perfectly definite and self-assured. "The theology of the intellect conforms to the laws, subserves the wants and secures the approval of our intuitive and deductive powers. It includes the decisions of the judgment, of the perceptive part of conscience and taste, indeed of all the faculties which are essential to the reasoning process. It is the theology of speculation, and therefore comprehends the truth just as it is, unmodified by excitements of feeling. Of course it demands evidence, either internal or extraneous, for all its propositions" (p. 4). Park contrasts this view with theology "impervious to argument, reckless of consequences, and dependent on an ill-balanced state of the sensibilities found in a letter to Doctor Henry Ware, Jr." One reads the letter quoted by Park and discovers with some amusement that it is signed by R. W. Emerson. "Argument," says Park, "is wasted upon him." (See note C, pp. 41–2.) The intellectual self-confidence of such a theologian is bound to have a certain appeal.—J.

[64] Mrs. Austen, p. 9.—J.

[65] Andover sprang into being as the creation of the eastern Massachusetts orthodoxy, Hopkinsian Calvinists and Old Calvin-

ists joining in uneasy union to put down Unitarianism and to re-
vive the militant missionary spirit of the fathers. The institution,
to 1846, was largely shaped by Professor Leonard Woods, who
had denounced Channing's sermon at the ordination of the Reverend
Jared Sparks in *Letters to Unitarians,* published in 1820. See Wil-
liston Walker, *A History of the Congregational Churches in the
United States (American Church History Series)* 3d edition,
(New York, 1894), pp. 335 ff.—*J.*

[66] Professor Taylor of Yale, to whom reference has been made
earlier, in 1828 preached a *Concio ad Clerum* at a Yale commencement, in which he argued that sin does not consist in any
attribute of the soul, nor in imputed sin due to the fact that men
are the children of Adam, but in man's free choice of the wrong
object—a doctrine also held by his colleague, Eleazer Fitch. In
Dec., 1829, this theological novelty was severely overhauled by the
Reverend Bennet Tyler, then of Portland, Maine. There is, he
argued, no time at which the sinner is not supremely selfish and
depraved—straight Edwardean theology. Andover enlisted enthusiastically on Tyler's side. See Walker, *op. cit.,* pp. 355–61;
and Emerson Davis, *The Half Century* (Boston, 1851), pp.
364–71.—*J.*

[67] Walker, p. 353.—*J.*

[68] *The Constitution and Statutes of the Theological Seminary,
Andover* (Andover, 1839), pp. 17–20.—*J.*

[69] *Ibid.,* pp. 27–30.—*J.*

[70] "It is strictly and solemnly enjoined, and left in sacred charge,
that every article of the above said Creed shall remain entirely
and identically the same, without the least alteration, addition,
or diminution." *Ibid.,* p. 23.—*J.*

[71] Harriet Beecher Stowe writes her husband from Andover
in 1852: "I had no idea this place was so beautiful"; and later:
". . . a number of us climbed Prospect Hill and had a most
charming walk." Five years later: "I never saw Andover look so
beautiful; the trees so green, the foliage so rich." Charles Edward Stowe, *Life of Harriet Beecher Stowe, compiled from her
Letters and Journals* (Boston, 1890), pp. 185; 186; 324.—*J.*

[72] "The rain, for which the parched earth and the dust-browned
city have been begging all the week, is coming down in thin, fine
drops, distilling itself silently and yet swiftly with an incessant
flow. Oh, how it comes! It is a glorious old northeaster, a watery
emblem of constancy and perseverance." Moses Tyler to his
mother, Mrs. Austen, p. 9.—*J.*

[73] C. E. Stowe, *op. cit.,* p. 324.—*J.*

[74] Harriet Beecher Stowe to Mrs. Follen, Feb. 16, 1853, in C. E. Stowe, *op. cit.,* pp. 197-8.—*J.*

[75] Harriet Beecher Stowe to her sister Catherine, July, 1857, in C. E. Stowe, *op. cit.,* p. 321.—*J.*

[76] *Ibid.,* pp. 185-6.—*J.*

[77] See the biographical sketch in the *Dictionary of American Biography.*—*J.*

[78] Diary entry quoted in Mrs. Austen, p. 38.

[79] Commonplace Book II in the Tyler MSS. includes a record of Tyler's reading at the Yale Theological Seminary and at Andover. It begins with lectures on Jewish history. Then follow a few pages devoted to Lockhart's *Scott,* Shaw's *Outlines of English Literature,* Irving's *Salmagundi,* and Walton's *Life of Hooker.* Then, after some knotty material from Taylor's lectures, one finds the caption, "The Waverley Novels," and there follow notes on Carlyle, Hazlitt, Thackeray, Dickens, Hawthorne, Bancroft, Mahon, etc.

[80] Mrs. Austen, p. 38.—*J.*

[81] See the "Introductory Note" to Mrs. Stowe's *Oldtown Folks,* vol. I (Boston, 1896).—*J.*

[82] C. E. Stowe, *op. cit.,* pp. 339-40.—*J.*

[83] Mrs. Austen, pp. 14-15.—*J.*

CHAPTER III

[1] Tyler MSS. Letter from Noah Porter to Moses Coit Tyler, March 8, 1858.

[2] Tyler MSS. Letter from Horace Bushnell to Moses Coit Tyler, March 30, 1858.

[3] Mrs. Austen, p. 11.—Tyler MSS. Diary for 1859. He delivered his first sermon August 14. This diary runs from Aug. 11 to Oct. 15.—*J.*

[4] J. H. Mather and L. P. Brockett, M.D., *A Geographical History of the State of New York* . . . (Utica, 1851), pp. 255-6.—*J.*

[4a] Washington Gladden, *Recollections* (Boston, 1909), pp. 56-64; 85-6.—*J.*

[5] *Ibid.,* pp. 57-9; 87.—*J.*

[6] Both letters are in Mrs. Austen, pp. 11-13.—*J.*

[7] "One blue horse, four years old, with one watch eye and a great proclivity to oats; saddle, bridle, and whip, currycomb and

brush; one overalls and shirt; half a bushel of oats, more or less hay; an old pair of boots; a shovel, a lamp; an old straw hat; a few quires of sermon paper, an inkstand and some matches in a safe; about a quarter of a cord of wood, and a large circle of mourning friends." *Ibid.,* p. 12.—*J.*

[7a] Charles Coit Tyler owned a store in Detroit. The mother, however, was living in Ypsilanti. Tyler MSS. Letter from Moses Coit Tyler to his uncle Edward, Oct. 10, 1859.—*J.*

[8] John G. Nicolay and John Hay, *Abraham Lincoln: A History* (New York, 1890), vol. II, p. 211.—*J.*

[9] *Recollections,* p. 88.—*J.*

[10] On May 15, 1860. *Congregational Quarterly,* vol. II, p. 346 (July, 1860).—*J.*

[11] Tyler MSS. Letter from the Committee of the First Congregational Church to the Reverend Moses Tyler, July 18, 1860.

[12] When Tyler took over the Owego church, it had a membership of 178 (statistics as of May 1, 1859), *Congregational Quarterly,* vol. II, p. 120 (January, 1860). When he left it the congregation had shrunk to 128 (statistics as of May 1, 1861). *Ibid,* vol. IV, p. 95 (January, 1862).—*J.*

[13] Tyler MSS. Letter from Committee to Tyler, Dec. 26, 1860.

[14] A new church was erected in 1860. *The Congregational Year-Book: 1911 . . .* vol. 33 (Boston, 1911), p. 338.—*J.*

[15] The Poughkeepsie church numbered 151 members on May 1, 1859; on May 1, 1862, after two years of Tyler's ministrations, the membership was 182—a modest success. Statistics from the *Congregational Quarterly* for appropriate years.—*J.*

[16] To the "First Congregational Methodist Church," a body seceding from the Methodist. The call came in 1860; he was installed on November 15, 1861. See *Recollections,* pp. 89 ff.; and *Congregational Quarterly,* vol. III, p. 71 (January, 1861). Tyler preached at Gladden's ordination. *Recollections,* p. 98.—*J.*

[17] "The New England Zone" in *Congregational Quarterly,* vol. II, pp. 341–8 (October, 1861).—*J.*

[18] *The Traveller's Steamboat and Railroad Guide to the Hudson River* (New York, 1857), p. 44.—*J.*

[19] John W. Barber, *Historical Collections of the State of New York . . . with Geographical Descriptions of the Counties, Cities, and Principal Villages, throughout the State . . .* (New York, 1851), p. 86.—*J.*

[20] Tyler MSS. Letter from Helen Lossing to Moses Coit Tyler, Feb. 21, 1862.

[21] Barber, *op. cit.—J.*

[22] A copy, dated Poughkeepsie, 1861, is preserved in the Tyler papers.

[23] Tyler MSS. Letter from C. S. Henry to Rev. Moses Tyler, April 19, 1861.

[24] Mrs. Austen, p. 13.—*J.*

[25] Mrs. Austen, *op. cit.* Tyler had visited John within the Union lines beyond Alexandria in June. Tyler MSS. Letter from Moses Coit Tyler to Susannah G. Tyler, June 22, 1861.—*J.*

[26] *Ibid.—J.*

[27] Mrs. Austen, p. 14. The letter is dated Nov. 14, 1862.—*J.*

[28] Tyler MSS. Commonplace Book III.

[29] Letter from Moses Tyler to his uncle, Nov. 14, 1862. In Mrs. Austen, pp. 14–15.

[30] *Ibid.—J.*

[31] Matthew Vassar's statement to the first board of trustees; in *Historical Sketch of Vassar College, Founded at Poughkeepsie, N. Y., January 18, 1861* (New York, 1876), p. 4.—*J.*

[32] Matthew Vassar to the trustees, June 28, 1866. In J. M. Taylor and Elizabeth H. Haight, *Vassar* (New York, 1915), p. 30. —*J.*

[33] Quoted in *The New Englander,* vol. XXI, p. 733 (October, 1862).—*J.*

[34] Vol. XXI, pp. 725-45.—*J.*

[35] Tyler MSS. Letter to Rev. Moses Tyler from the Secretary of Vassar College, Nov. 4, 1862.

[36] Mrs. Austen, p. 14. Tyler's interest in the education of women was a life-long interest, but the sources of this sudden outburst are not at all clear, except as the radical movements of the time were linked together, and an interest in abolition was likely to connote sympathy with the women's rights movement. Whatever its origins, Tyler's interest never waned, as subsequent events proved. Annotations on the margins of his books testify to the lively quality of his zeal. Reading a letter from Jefferson to Washington from Paris in 1788 (*Works,* ed. H. A. Washington, vol. II, New York, 1853), a passage descriptive of the influence of women in the French government, Tyler writes on the margin: "Tremendous fact." Or again, reading *Romola,* which he bought in 1869, he notes of an early passage that it is "a fine satire on the popular intellectual disparagement of woman's brain." In the second volume of Darwin's *Descent of Man* (New York, 1871), he annotated Darwin's comparison of the mental powers of the

sexes: "The coming era, both through natural and sexual selections, will tend to diminish the inequalities between men & women, by raising the latter to the level of the former," and on his copy of the Ellis edition of Anne Bradstreet (Charlestown, 1867) he noted sardonically (p. 83) "Surprise then at woman's ability."

[37] Tyler MSS. Letter from Moses Coit Tyler to his uncle, Nov. 14, 1862.—*J.*

[37a] Mrs. Austen, p. 15.—*J.*

[38] Mrs. Austen, p. 16.—*J.*

[39] Mrs. Austen, pp. 16-17.—*J.*

[40] See Mrs. Austen, pp. 15-22.—*J.*

[40a] He became editor of *Religion and Social Service,* and of *The Literary Digest,* and died August 18, 1901. Information kindly supplied by Mr. Willard Austen.—*J.*

[41] Moses Coit Tyler, "The Dio Lewis Gymnastics in England," *The Herald of Health,* June, 1866, p. 177.

[42] There is a brief account of Lewis in *The National Cyclopædia of American Biography* (New York, 1900), vol. X, p. 181.—*J.*

[43] In Tyler's *The Brawnville Papers,* devoted to Lewis's cause, Henry reads a part of a dialogue on gymnastics between Socrates and Glaucon to the reading circle; and Doctor Drugger, who represents conservative medicine, sneers: "Don't for God's sake, throw Plato's mantle over that stupendous humbug [Lewis]!" Tyler then defends Lewis as an intelligent follower of Plato. *The Brawnville Papers* (Boston, 1869), pp. 33-43.—*J.*

[44] Fred E. Leonard, *Pioneers of Modern Physical Training* (New York, 1919), pp. 86-7.—*J.*

[45] Dio Lewis, *The New Gymnastics for Men, Women, and Children* . . . 7th ed. (Boston, 1864), p. 96.—*J.*

[46] *Ibid.,* p. 17.—*J.*

[47] *Ibid.,* p. 18. See Dio Lewis, "A Word about Normal Schools," *The Herald of Health,* May, 1866; and Moses Coit Tyler, "The Dio Lewis Gymnastics in England," *ibid.,* June, 1866.—*J.*

[48] *Op. cit.,* pp. 5-6.—*J.*

[49] Tyler MSS. Letter from Moses Coit Tyler to his uncle, Nov. 14, 1862.

[50] Tyler, "The Dio Lewis Gymnastics," *op. cit.*

[51] Tyler MSS. Personal Records, 1853-75. The substance of this article reappears in *The Brawnville Papers,* pp. 154-5.—*J.*

[52] Tyler MSS. Memorandum Book I.

[53] *The Brawnville Papers,* p. 163.—In his article on Vassar,

Tyler had noted approvingly the place given physical exercise in the curriculum. The passage in *The Brawnville Papers* occurs in a discussion of "Muscular Christianity," which mentions Thomas Arnold, Charles Kingsley, Dean Stanley, and Thomas Hughes as exemplars of the movement.—*J.*

[54] He read it in the summer of 1863. Tyler MSS. Commonplace Book III, p. 115.

[55] His enthusiasm for Kingsley was tempered by disgust that "the author of 'Alton Locke' should become the apologist of Governor Eyre, the champion of a pro-slavery rebellion, and a toady to Toryism!" *The Brawnville Papers*, p. 154.—*J.*

[56] *Ibid.*, pp. 74–8; 115–19 and *passim.*—*J.*

[57] *Ibid*, p. 66.—*J.*

[58] *Ibid.*, pp. 159–60.—*J.*

[59] Telescoped and inaccurately quoted from Book II of "The Advancement of Learning." See *Works of Francis Bacon*, ed. Spedding, Ellis, and Heath, vol. VI (New York, 1869), p. 252.—*J.*

[60] *The Brawnville Papers*, pp. 54; 133; 163.—*J.*

[61] *Ibid.*, pp. 129–30.—*J.*

[62] *Ibid.*, pp. 48–9; 60; 71; 73; 132; 186.—*J.*

[63] From Tyler's lecture, "The New Gymnastics as an Instrument in Education" (p. 254), conveniently reprinted on pp. 243 ff. of Dio Lewis, *The New Gymnastics for Men, Women and Children*, 17th ed. (Boston, 1878).—*J.*

[64] Cf. *The Brawnville Papers*, pp. 185–95.—*J.*

[65] Some time in 1863, presumably before he left the United States, Tyler applied for, and received, an M.A. degree from Yale. The *Catalogue* for 1862–3 (p. 41) states that "every Bachelor of Arts of three years' or longer standing may receive the Degree of Master of Arts on the payment of five dollars, provided he shall, in the interval, have sustained a good moral character." Miss Anne S. Pratt of the Yale University Library kindly informs me that the degree was given to virtually all ministers and teachers in these years. It was also about this period that Tyler formally adopted the use of his middle name at the suggestion of a member of the Coit family.—*J.*

CHAPTER IV

[1] Lytton Strachey, *Queen Victoria* (New York, 1921), p. 302. —*J.*

[2] Letters in the Tyler MSS., and the correspondence between Moses Coit Tyler and Moncure Daniel Conway in the William L. Clements Library, indicate that Mrs. Tyler, the children, and Susannah reached England in October, 1863, but the time of their return is not clear, except that it was before March, 1866. The Tyler genealogy (item 5951) indicates that, after spending two years in Europe, Susannah returned to die in Warwick, R. I., Aug. 28, 1865. It is not improbable that Mrs. Tyler, the children, and Susannah returned together some time before this date. But writing Conway from Ann Arbor, Feb. 23, 1879, Tyler speaks of twelve years having elapsed since he, Tyler, had left London, and thirteen years since his wife came away. Since Tyler left London early in December, 1866, this can not be taken literally, though it seems to point to Mrs. Tyler's return late in 1865.—*J.*

[3] Diary letter quoted in Mrs. Austen, p. 23.—*J.*

[4] Mrs. Austen, p. 24. Charles Edward Brown-Séquard was born in Mauritius in 1817 and died in 1894. He was a cosmopolitan and restless soul, a brilliant research worker, and a distinguished physician, living at various periods in France, the British Isles, the United States, and elsewhere. He was regarded as the rival of Claude Bernard. When Tyler met him, he had lectured brilliantly in London, Edinburgh, Dublin, and Glasgow, and had been made a Fellow of the Royal Society, a Fellow of the Royal College of Physicians, and physician-in-chief in the recently established hospital for paralyzed and epileptic patients in London. See the biographical sketch by D'Arcy Power in *Dictionary of National Biography,* First Supplement, vol. I, pp. 319–21.—*J.*

[5] *The Weekly Record,* July 15, 1863, reprinted in Dio Lewis, *The New Gymnastics,* etc., 17th ed. (Boston, 1878), pp. 277–80. —*J.*

[6] The Liverpool *Albion,* Dec. 21, 1863, reprinted in Lewis, *op. cit.,* pp. 276–7.—*J.*

[7] Mrs. Austen, pp. 24–5.—*J.*

[8] *Ibid.*—*J.*

[9] Mrs. Austen, p. 49.—*J.*

[10] Tyler MSS. Letter from the College of Preceptors to Moses Coit Tyler, April 9, 1864. The lecture was printed (Cambridge,

Mass., 1869), and a copy is to be found among the Tyler papers.
—It can be found more conveniently in the appendix to the edition
of Dio Lewis, noted above.—*J.*

[11] *A New System of Musical Gymnastics,* p. 28.

[12] Dio Lewis, *op. cit.,* p. 272.—*J.*

[13] *Ibid.,* pp. 274–6.—*J.*

[14] In January, 1864. *Ibid.,* p. 281.—*J.*

[15] In March, 1864. *Ibid.*—*J.*

[16] Feb. 8, 1864. *Ibid.,* pp. 282–3.—*J.*

[17] March 26, 1864. "Mr. Tyler's genius is well directed towards
awakening an interest in the neglected subject of physical culture." *Ibid.,* p. 284.—*J.*

[18] Mrs. Austen, p. 25.—*J.*

[19] Mrs. Austen, p. 26.—*J.*

[20] Lewis, *op. cit.,* pp. 243–67.—*J.*

[21] *Ibid.,* p. 286.—*J.*

[22] Mrs. Austen, p. 25.—*J.* Tyler MSS. Letter to Moses Coit
Tyler from the Greenwich Society for the Diffusion of Useful
Knowledge, Nov. 17, 1864.

[23] Tyler MSS. Letters to Moses Coit Tyler from various institutes and lyceums.

[24] January, 1866. Tyler MSS. Diary, 1864–6.

[25] The date of this meeting is fixed as May 7, 1863, by a comparison of Tyler's *Glimpses of England,* p. 38, with the *Autobiography: Memories and Experiences of Moncure Daniel Conway* (Boston, 1904), vol. I, pp. 416–7.—*J.*

[26] Tyler, *Glimpses,* pp. 38–9.—*J.*

[27] *Ibid.,* pp. 42–53.—*J.*

[28] Diary, Dec. 21, 1864. Mrs. Austen, pp. 26–7.—*J.*

[29] Mrs. Austen, pp. 27–8. Feb. 11, 1865.—*J.*

[30] *Glimpses,* p. 19.—*J.*

[31] *Ibid.,* p. 174.—*J.*

[32] Essays on these subjects form the substance of the *Glimpses*
volume. The Tyler-Conway letters show Tyler's affectionate regard for Conway.—*J.*

[33] *Glimpses,* p. 1.—*J.*

[34] *Ibid.,* p. 11. He also described London in his poem, *The Omnibus,* 1865, for which see below, pp. 104–5.—*J.*

[35] Mrs. Austen, pp. 26; 27. Robert Browning was a neighbor,
and Tyler asked him for his autograph. Tyler-Conway Letters.
—*J.*

[36] Mrs. Austen, pp. 28–9.—*J.*

[37] Mrs. Austen, p. 30; *Glimpses,* pp. 234–41.—*J.*

[38] *Glimpses,* p. 240.—*J.*

[39] "A Sunday in Wales," *Glimpses,* pp. 223–33.—*J.*

[40] Mrs. Austen, p. 29.—*J.*

[41] Mrs. Austen, pp. 30–1.—*J.*

[42] Mrs. Austen, p. 33.—*J.*

[43] *Glimpses,* pp. 253–76.—*J.*

[44] See in *Glimpses* the essays entitled "On Certain English Hallucinations Touching America" and "American Reputations in England."—*J.*

[45] See the comparative table of fees in England and the United States, *Glimpses,* pp. 265–70.—*J.*

[46] Tyler MSS. Letter from Charles A. Dana to Moses Coit Tyler, July, 1854.—Tyler's financial plight may be inferred from a letter to Mrs. Conway, dated 337 Strand, Aug. 17, 1866, in which he says he is short of funds to send Jennie and the children "a lot of things" and asks for help.—*J.*

[47] Tyler MSS. Letter from same to same, July 29, 1865.

[48] Founded in 1845 as *The Water Cure Journal* under the editorship of Joel Shew, this paper continued to advocate simplicity in hygiene and medicine. The curious will find as the leading article in the opening issue "Confessions and Observations of a Water Patient" by Bulwer-Lytton, an essay thought to be so valuable that it was reprinted serially, beginning April, 1863. In 1862 the magazine became *The Hygienic Teacher and Water Cure Journal,* and in 1863, *The Herald of Health.* In that year it was bought by Dr. R. T. Trall and published by him in New York City.—*J.*

[49] Trall did not change the policy of the paper, the purpose of which he characterized as "to lay broad, deep, and enduring foundations of the True Mental Philosophy, and to apply it to the harmonious and highest development of the Human Being." *Herald of Health,* New Series, vol. I, no. 1, January, 1863, p. 6. Dio Lewis was a regular contributor, most of *The New Gymnastics* appearing serially in this magazine.—*J.*

[50] The essay on Joseph Mazzini was reprinted in *The Herald of Health* in May, 1866, from *The Independent;* "The Dio Lewis Gymnastics in England" was the leading article for June, and is a complement to Tyler's first contributed lecture; "English Pluck" appeared in August; "Muscular Christianity" in September; and "Concerning a Muscular Christian" in October, 1866. The subject of the last is Thomas Hughes. The essays on Mazzini and

on English pluck were reprinted in *Glimpses of England.* Tyler's pay, if any, must have been small.—*J.*

[51] "Mason Jones in England."—*J.*

[52] Tyler MSS. Letter from Oliver Johnson to Moses Coit Tyler, Aug. 9, 1865.

[53] Except two, "Have We a Fault Among Us?" and "The Growth of a Nation" (March 7 and May 2, 1867), which, however, are tangentially related to the English theme.—*J.*

[54] Thursday, July 6, 1865.—*J.*

[55] ". . . to promote and develop a higher standard of criticism" *The Nation,* vol. I, no. 1, July 6, 1865, p. 10; and to promote "the maintenance and diffusion of true democratic principles in society and government, and the advocacy and illustration of whatever in legislation or in manners seems likely to promote a more equal distribution of the fruits of progress and civilization." From the original prospectus, quoted in Rollo Ogden, *Life and Letters of Edwin Lawrence Godkin* (New York, 1907), vol. I, p. 237.—*J.*

[56] Tyler MSS. Letter from Wendell Garrison to Moses Coit Tyler, Sept. 10, 1865.

[57] The difficulty of identification arises from the anonymity which shrouds most of the earlier articles in *The Nation.* The five that are certainly Tyler's are, in addition to the one mentioned in the text, "A Sunday in Wales" (March 22, 1866); "Mr. Mill in the House of Commons" (May 11, 1866); and two articles on John Bright (May 30 and June 13, 1867).—*J.*

[58] Tyler MSS. Letter from the *Cincinnati Daily and Weekly Commercial* to Moses Coit Tyler, Sept. 14, 1865.

[59] *Glimpses,* p. 136.—*J.*

[60] *Ibid.,* p. 136.—*J.*

[61] *Ibid.,* p. 66.—*J.*

[62] *Ibid.,* p. 71.—*J.*

[63] Tyler MSS. Commonplace Book IV.

[64] Tyler MSS. Letter from Moses Coit Tyler to his wife, March 1, 1866.

[65] Tyler MSS. Letter from Moses Coit Tyler to his wife, Sept. 15, 1866.

[66] *The Nation,* vol. III, no. 53, July 5, 1866, p. 4. "His repertory embraced lectures on America, literature, history, and education, some of the titles being 'Muscular Christianity,' 'American Orators and Oratory,' 'Richard Brinsley Sheridan,' 'American Wit and Humor,' etc., etc." (Tyler sent clippings direct to *The Nation.*)

[66a] Clipping preserved in Tyler MSS. Personal Records, 1853–75. The paragraph was copied by various other papers.—*J.*

[67] Tyler MSS. Letter from Oliver Johnson to Moses Coit Tyler, Dec. 24, 1866.

[68] Tyler MSS. Personal Records, 1853–75.

[69] *The Independent,* June 28, 1866.

[70] Tyler MSS. Letter from Moses Coit Tyler to his wife, cited above.

[71] Tyler MSS. Letter from W. A. Howard to Moses Coit Tyler, Aug. 23, 1866.—This concerns an address scheduled for February, 1867. Mrs. Austen quotes a letter (p. 34) which may point to a previous Detroit lecture in January.—*J.*

[72] Tyler MSS.

[73] Mrs. Austen, p. 34.—*J.*

[74] Mrs. Austen, p. 34.—*J.*

[75] See the account in Andrew D. White, *Autobiography* (New York, 1905), vol. I, chaps. xvii–xx.—*J.*

[76] Tyler MSS. Letter from Andrew D. White to Professor Müller, Dec. 10, 1866.

[77] Waterman Thomas Hewitt, *Cornell University: A History* (New York, 1905), vol. I, p. 183.—*J.*

[78] Tyler MSS. Letter from Moses Coit Tyler to his wife, April 18, 1867.

[79] Tyler MSS. Same to same, July 7, 1867.

[80] Tyler MSS. Letter from Erastus O. Haven to Moses Coit Tyler, July 4, 1867.

[81] Tyler MSS. Letters from Moses Coit Tyler to his wife, July 27 and July 31, 1867.

[82] The appointment was announced in the president's report of Sept. 24, 1867, and confirmed later. See *Proceedings of the Board of Regents of the University of Michigan, 1864–70* (Ann Arbor, 1870), pp. 224; 227.—*J.*

CHAPTER V

[1] *University of Michigan. Catalogue of the Officers and Students for 1867–8, with a General Description of the University* (Ann Arbor, 1868), *passim.*—*J.*

[2] Details from Hinsdale-Demmon, *History of the University of Michigan,* pp. 41–56; and Wilfred B. Shaw, *The University of Michigan, passim.*—*J.*

[3] O. W. Stephenson, *Ann Arbor: The First Hundred Years* (Ann Arbor, 1927), p. 332.—*J.*

[4] *Ibid.,* p. 179.—*J.*

[5] *Ibid.,* pp. 354–5.—*J.*

[6] Details from Stephenson, pp. 203–5.—*J.*

[7] Hinsdale-Demmon, p. 56.—*J.*

[8] Mrs. Austen, p. 37.—*J.*

[9] *Chapin's City Directory of Ann Arbor for 1868* (Adrian, Mich., 1868) gives his residence as the south side of North between State and Division, *Cole and Keating's Ann Arbor Directory for the Year 1872* (Ann Arbor, 1872) gives the number as 36 E. North. Tyler bought land there on May 23, 1870, from Harvey and Alice Cornwell.—*J*

[10] See "Ten Days at the University of Michigan" and "Our Leading Universities" in *The Independent* for Nov. 22, 1866, and Dec. 13, 1866, respectively.

[11] White abandoned teaching by rote, anticipating by some years the method of Henry Adams. See White's *Autobiography,* vol. I, pp. 251–65.—*J.*

[12] *Proceedings of the Board of Regents of the University of Michigan, January, 1864, to January, 1870.* "President's Report," Sept. 29, 1868, p. 279.—*J.*

[13] Doctor Jeremiah W. Jenks, later president of the Alexander Hamilton Institute, wrote of Tyler in *The Michigan Alumnus* for March, 1901 (p. 225): "His students felt that he required exactness and finish in their work, and all shrank from the silent reproof of his manner when slovenly, inaccurate work was presented. Precision, accuracy, truth, he demanded from himself; and he expected them, so far as immaturity would permit it, from his students. . . . He always showed in connection with the management of young men and women, sympathy with youth, tolerance of youthful follies and a confidence in the right impulses and good intentions of University students. While he might be rigid in his just demands for faithfulness, he was no less appreciative and generous in his recognition of good work faithfully done. Many a student can recall a generous word of praise discriminately given which he has felt as a stimulus for many years thereafter. Many also owe him a debt of gratitude for the good memory and sympathetic spirit which enabled him, years after they had passed from his classroom, to give them aid and encouragement in carrying out the plans for their life work."

[14] See Levette Jay Davidson, *A History of College English as a*

Requirement for the A.B. Degree in the United States, a doctoral dissertation (1922) in the University of Michigan Library. "English philology became a weapon with which to combat those defenders of the traditional course who asserted that English could not furnish a discipline comparable to that offered by Latin and Greek."

[15] C. S. Carter, *History of the Class of 1870* (Milwaukee, 1903), p. 227.

[16] *Proceedings of the Board of Regents . . . January, 1870, to January, 1876,* pp. 222–6.—*J.*

[17] The annotations cited are on pp. x; 142; 280 of Tyler's copy of E. O. Haven, *Rhetoric: A Textbook* (New York, 1869).—*J.*

[18] In Tyler's copy of the Shaw-Smith-Tuckerman, *A Complete Manual of English Literature* (New York, 1867), p. 94.—*J.*

[19] Cowper's *Works,* edited by Southey, vol. I, p. 388, last eight lines. Reading Cowper's translation of Homer, Tyler makes some interesting comments. "What radiant courtesy breathes through all this intercourse of these grand characters," he says in one place (*Works,* vol. VIII, p. 235), and of Ulysses' interview (*ibid.,* p. 239) remarks: "Talk about Yankee habits of interrogating strangers!" —*J.*

[20] Tyler read Southey in the summer of 1869 in the edition (in ten volumes) published in Boston in 1864.—*J.*

[21] Comment on a passage, p. 336, in the *Works* of Burns published in Boston (1859).—*J.*

[22] December, 1867, p. 116.—*J.*

[23] Carter, *op. cit.,* pp. 320; 368.—*J.*

[24] *The University of Michigan Magazine,* Dec., 1868, pp. 81–7.

[25] Hinsdale-Demmon, *op. cit.,* p. 55. He embodied these pedagogical advances in *The Direct Study of English Masterpieces* (Ann Arbor, 1875); *The Direct Study of English Masterpieces: Shakespeare Course* (Ann Arbor, 1877).

[26] This statement is based upon an examination of the catalogues of Harvard, Yale, Dartmouth, Princeton, Cornell, and Michigan for the period.

[27] *Catalogue of the College of New Jersey, 1872–73* (Princeton, 1873), p. 21.

[28] *Catalogue of the University of Michigan, 1872–73* (Ann Arbor, 1873), pp. 32–3.

[29] Mrs. Austen, p. 37.—*J.*

[30] Tyler addressed the Students' Lecture Association in Ann Arbor during Oct., 1867, the program for the year including

such names as Charles Sumner, E. P. Whipple, Theodore Tilton, Petroleum V. Nasby, and Wendell Phillips. *The University of Michigan Magazine* included Tyler in remarking that "no speakers have been engaged who have not acquired a national reputation." (Oct., 1867, p. 34.)

[31] Tyler MSS. Letter from Moses Coit Tyler to John Tyler, Jan. 25, 1869.

[32] "*Ann Arbor, Apr. 21, 1872.* I am revising old university lectures and writing new ones, as well as preparing a new lyceum lecture. All this intended work is now done six weeks sooner than I expected." He rewarded himself by reading American history. Mrs. Austen, p. 73.—*J.*

[33] Clipping from *The Grand Rapids Democrat,* Nov. 14, 1867, preserved in the Tyler MSS.—On the other hand *The Chicago Tribune* (Feb. 11, 1867) took him severely to task for exaggerated statements in regard to British educational conditions, and a Rochester paper acidly noted that "to the credit of the audience, two puffs for Garibaldi both failed to elicit a single stroke of applause." Clippings in the Tyler MSS.—*J.*

[34] Clippings in the Tyler MSS.—*J.*

[35] "Let any one quietly look over the history of the American people for the past thirty years, and he will find no figure, on the whole, more remarkable or more interesting than that of Charles Sumner. And above all other American statesmen of his time, not even excepting Lincoln, he towers in that grandeur which comes of a pure, high, impassioned, persistent moral purpose." So wrote Tyler in *The Independent,* May 12, 1870. The first volume of Sumner's *Works* appeared in Boston in 1870, and the set continued publishing until the appearance of the fourteenth volume in 1883. This Tyler carefully read, annotating each volume with comment on Sumner's political positions and on his style, nor did his admiration for the man smother independent judgment. He notes (vol. III, p. 96) that Sumner's "mind spontaneously moves thro' bookish & esp. classic illustrations," and that (*ibid.,* p. 104) "as Lincoln used an anecdote S. [used] a quotation." Although Tyler comments approvingly, "Tremend[o]us summary against slavery" (*ibid.,* p. 106), he notes elsewhere (vol. IX, p. 112) that Sumner's "partisanship in statement [is] shewn in omitting to acknowledge that such menaces were made by anti slavery also," and catches Sumner in other weaknesses. Nevertheless, the general tone of Tyler's comment is eulogistic: "affluence of diction & imagery worthy of Burke" (vol. IV, p. 50); "a gem of per-

fect prose" (of "Tribute to a College Classmate, vol. V, p. 236);
"a superb piece of eloquent argumentation" (vol. VI, p. 278).—*J*.

[36] Mrs. Austen, pp. 48–9.—*J*.

[37] *Ibid.*, p. 49.—*J*.

[38] Mrs. Austen, p. 43. "There are very few public men who
seem consecrated, absolutely honest, pure minded, unselfish."—*J*.

[39] Tyler's comment on J. W. Schuckers, *The Life and Public
Services of Salmon Portland Chase,* which he bought a few years
later.—*J*.

[40] Mrs. Austen, p. 54.—*J*.

[41] Mrs. Austen, pp. 55–63.—*J*.

[42] *Ibid.*, p. 64.—*J*.

[43] *The Education of Henry Adams* (Boston, 1918), p. 280.—J.

[44] Shaw, *op. cit.*, pp. 60–61.—J.

[45] *Proceedings at the Laying of the Corner Stone of the Sage
College for Women at Cornell University* (Ithaca, 1873), pp. 31–7.

[46] Tyler MSS. Personal Records 1853–75. The speech had been
delivered May 10, 1871.

[47] An abstract is printed by Mrs. Austen, pp. 67–70. Tyler
covers the usual brief for the rights of women.

[48] Mrs. Austen, pp. 71–3; 70.—*J*.

[49] Tyler's salary was increased (July 11, 1871) to $2500, to take
effect Oct. 1, 1871. *Proceedings of the Board of Regents . . .
January, 1870 to January, 1876* (Ann Arbor, 1876), p. 137.—J.

[50] Moses Coit Tyler to John Tyler, Nov. 4, 1867. Mrs. Austen,
p. 37.—*J*.

[51] These appeared in *The Herald of Health* from April, 1867,
through March, 1868.—*J*.

[52] Copy preserved in the University of Michigan Library. The
handwriting is identifiable.

[53] "The crudeness of the book vexed and shamed me from the
moment I saw it between two covers; and for years I regularly
destroyed all specimens of it that came into my possession." Autograph note in the author's copy preserved in the Tyler MSS.

[54] These are listed in the bibliography, pp. 281–8.—*J*.

[55] Tyler MSS. Letter from Andrew D. White to Moses Coit
Tyler, Aug. 2, 1869.

[56] *The Independent,* vol. XXI, Nov. 4, 1869.

[57] "Mr. Emerson as a Teacher of Eloquence," *The Independent,*
vol. XXII, May 5, 1870; "Mr. Darwin's Stunning Book,"*The
Golden Age,* vol. I, Mar. 18, 1871; "A Chat about Swinburne," *The
Golden Age,* vol. I, Apr. 1, 1871.—*J*.

[58] Diary, Oct. 14, 1869. In Mrs. Austen, pp. 42–3.—*J*.

[59] Tyler MSS. Commonplace Book VI, vol. I, p. 20.

[60] See Mrs. Austen, pp. 46–7.—*J*.

[61] Tyler MSS. Commonplace Book VI, vol. II, p. 22.

[62] Mrs. Austen, p. 47.—*J*.

[63] Tyler MSS. Letter from Andrew D. White to Moses Coit Tyler, May 22, 1871; letter from Moses Coit Tyler to John Tyler, July 28, 1871.

[64] Tyler MSS. Diary for 1872.

[65] Tyler MSS. Commonplace Book VI, vol. 2, p. 45.

[66] Tyler MSS. Andrew D. White to Moses Coit Tyler, May 13, 1872.

[67] Tyler MSS. The passage occurs also in Mrs. Austen, p. 40, but under an erroneous date.

[68] Mrs. Austen, pp. 37–40.—*J*.

[69] *Ibid.*, pp. 42–5.—J.

[70] *Ibid.*, pp. 44–5. His annotations show that Burke was for Tyler a standard of measurement for political writers.—*J*.

[71] Tyler MSS. Commonplace Books V and VI. For example, he read all of Drummond, Wyatt, Marvell, Surrey, Prior, Gay, Young, and Milton's prose, besides many detached works; Dante, Ariosto, Machiavelli; Froissart; Homer, Hesiod, Herodotus, Xenophon, Thucydides, Pindar. The foreign literature he read in translation.—In his copy of Marvell, Tyler speaks of the influence of the metaphysical poets (p. 71) and notes on the inside cover that Marvell's "satires are intended to rouse Englishmen to a sense of their degradation under the Stuarts; exposing the gross sensualism of the king—his ingratitude & base neglect of duty, the designs of James, & the universal profligacy & corruption of Courts, Legislature & nobility." (*Poetical Works,* Boston, 1857). He thought Milton's *Areopagitica* "a good a/c of what we aim at," but notes that Milton "does not advocate [the] irresponsibility of books." Prior's "To My Lord Buckhurst" Tyler calls "a baseminded poem," and on Surrey he observes generally that "these men of feverish stormy lives have struck off the most vivid pictures of a quiet mode of existence." A passage in Swinburne's *Chastelard* he calls "tremendous," and inside the back cover of his copy (New York, 1866) he jots: "N.B. The copious superb strong Saxon of S[winburne]'s style." He has copiously annotated Skelton, displaying great freshness of judgment in so doing.—*J*.

[72] Tyler MSS. Commonplace Book VI, vol. 2, p. 15 (Oct. 14, 1869).

[73] Tyler MSS. Commonplace Book VI, vol. 2, pp. 7–8.

[74] Mrs. Austen, p. 47.—*J.*

[75] *Ibid.*, p. 48. The date should be Jan. 21, 1870.—*J.*

[76] Tyler MSS. Commonplace Book VI, vol. 1, pp. 43–56.

[77] He wrote White July 16, 1870, that he hoped to be admitted to the bar in a year, and that he wished he had studied it "twelve years ago, instead of wrecking so much of my life and happiness upon the priesthood." Tyler MSS. Commonplace Book VI, vol. 2, p. 23. This was, however, but a passing fancy; Tyler seems at no time to have seriously considered the law as a profession.—*J.*

[78] Tyler MSS. Letter from Carl Schurz to Moses Coit Tyler, Mar. 18, 1871; letter from Charles Sumner to same, Apr., 1871; letter from Schuyler Colfax to same, Apr. 13, 1871. And see the account of an interview with George Willard, delegate to the Philadelphia convention, in Mrs. Austen, pp. 73–4.—*J.*

[79] Tyler elaborately annotated his copy of George Bancroft's *History of the United States* (New York, 1871). Of a passage in vol. I (p. 376) he says that Bancroft's "the equality of opinions before the laws" is a "phrase of Chas. Sumner's relative to citizens," notes (p. 190) that "some nations have an aptitude for arts, music, science, poetry, war, we for govt.," jots "Nullification" against one passage (vol. III, p. 172) and "First for Union! First for Disunion, too!" against another (vol. V, p. 294). Similar comments appear in other books read in this period.—*J.*

[80] Tyler MSS. Commonplace Book VI, pp. 166–7.

[81] Of John W. Draper, *Thoughts on the Future Civil Policy of America* (New York, 1865), Tyler scribbled on the title-page: "This book is a pewter imitation of the golden Buckle." Reading Bancroft (vol. II, p. 48) he notes: "contrary to Buckle's dictum that the personal characters of princes & statesmen have *no* influence on events," and vol. III, p. 397, he annotates: "Suits Buckle!" —*J.*

[82] Tyler MSS. Commonplace Book VI, vol. 2, Aug. 27, 1871.

[83] Tyler MSS. Commonplace Book VI, vol. 1, pp. 175; 176.

[84] Tyler MSS. Diary for 1873; the quotation is found in the "Personal Records" for 1853–75.

[85] Tyler MSS. Diary for 1873. White's advice was largely responsible for Tyler's acceptance. Letter from Moses Coit Tyler to John Tyler, May 21, 1874.

[86] Tyler MSS. Diary for 1873.

[87] Reported to the Regents Mar. 24, 1873. *Proceedings . . . January, 1870, to January, 1876*, p. 264.—*J.*

[88] Tyler MSS. Letter from Moses Coit Tyler to John Tyler, February 18, 1873.

CHAPTER VI

[1] See Paxton Hibben, *Henry Ward Beecher: An American Portrait*, p. 188.—*J.*

[2] John Howard in Algernon Tassin, *The Magazine in America* (New York, 1916), p. 275. Cf. Washington Gladden, *Reminiscences*, pp. 232–5.—*J.*

[3] Quoted in Tassin, p. 279.—*J.*

[4] *Ibid.*—*J.*

[5] Quoted in Hibben, *op. cit.*, p. 226.—*J.*

[6] *The Christian Union*, vol. IX, no. 2, p. 180, March 4, 1874.—*J.*

[7] Quoted in Hibben, p. 227. The offer long appeared at the editorial masthead.—*J.*

[8] Hibben, p. 226.

[9] Tyler MSS. Portions of the year '71, etc.

[10] *Ibid.*

[11] *Ibid.*

[12] Hibben, p. 238.

[13] Mrs. Austen, p. 78. Tyler's office was room 28, Bible House. From March 26, 1873, to May 1 he seems not to have been definitely allocated to any particular office, but in May he moved into room 66. *Ibid.*, p. 80.—*J.*

[14] Note Beecher's pathetic attempts to be jocular as recorded in Mrs. Austen, pp. 77–8; 81–2.—*J.*

[15] "13 May, 1874. My life in New York is very distasteful to me. I hate the newspaper and its work; but I must work on faithfully till I have paid the penalty for my blunders and sins." Mrs. Austen, p. 84. —*J.*

[16] *Ibid.*, pp. 77–8. Despite his association with the principals in the case, Tyler managed to stay out of the scandal with one exception. On Jan. 2, 1876, he told two friends in confidence what he knew of the situation. One of these repeated Tyler's account. This eventually reached *The New York Sun* in garbled version, which printed what purported to be the substance of Tyler's statement, and hinted that Tyler would testify as to Beecher's guilt (*New York Sun*, Jan. 20, 1876). Tyler repudiated the article as "grossly inaccurate," though to himself he admitted its general drift was correct. He then prepared a complete statement of his knowledge of the case with a view to publication, but on the advice of Pres-

ident Angell of the University of Michigan and other colleagues, he never published it. Tyler MSS. Correspondence, vol. II, pp. 239–52; vol. IV, 167–201.—*J.*

[17] *The Christian Union,* March 26, 1873. Most of Tyler's contributions are identified through the Tyler MSS.

[18] In 1869 he copied into his diary a sentence which "utters with great power my present thought on the subject of the method and spirit of culture: 'Sweep away utterly all frothiness and falsehood from your heart; struggle unweariedly to acquire what is possible for every God-created man, a free, open, humble soul: speak not at all in any wise, till you have somewhat to speak; care not for the reward of your speaking, but simply, and with undivided mind, for the truth of your speaking.'" Tyler MSS. Commonplace Book VI, vol. 2, p. 11.—*J.*

[19] *The Christian Union,* June 4, 1873. Tyler's view is, in fact, worked out by Fred Lewis Pattee in his *A History of American Literature since 1870.*

[20] *The Christian Union,* June 24, 1874.

[21] *Ibid.,* March 5, 1873.—Note the likeness to "the golden Buckle."—*J.*

[22] *Ibid.,* March 19, 1873.

[23] *Ibid.,* May 7, 1873. "Had not the *Idylls of the King* been written, *Lars* would not have been written." He repeated this from his marginalia in the book itself.—*J.*

[24] *Ibid.,* July 23, 1873. He is reviewing *Red-Cotton-Night-Cap Country.*

[25] *Ibid.,* April 22, 1874.

[26] *Ibid.,* November 19, 1873.

[27] Thus on April 2, 1873, he said that John Fiske was a positivist. Fiske replied in a letter April 23, saying that "if twelve years' study of the Positive Philosophy has taught me anything, it has taught me that it is utterly impossible, save by the entire distortion and misuse of language, to classify me as a Positivist," and Tyler was compelled to apologize for his "over-hasty classification." *Ibid.,* April 23, 1873.

[28] Written March 5, 1875. In Mrs. Austen, p. 90. Annotations in Tyler's copy of *The Descent of Man* indicate no disagreement with Darwin.—*J.*

[29] A lecture in March, 1873, at Carbondale, Pa., "ends my toils of that kind for this spring," though he had still to give the commencement address at the University of Syracuse in June, for which he chose a topic associated with the "great subject," "The

First Colleges and College Builders of America." Mrs. Austen, p. 78.—*J*.

[30] *Ibid.*, p. 82.—*J*.

[31] *Ibid.*, pp. 79–81; 82–3.—*J*.

[32] On March 15, 1874, he preached on "The Spiritual Uses of Experience" at the Unity Chapel; on March 23, he substituted for his friend, Washington Gladden, in Brooklyn; and on May 31, he preached at the Twenty-third Street Presbyterian Church in New York. Tyler MSS. Diary for 1874.

[33] "I am strongly moved by the attractions of preaching." *Ibid.*, May 12, 1874.

[34] The offer was made May 17, 1874. Mrs. Austen, p. 84.—*J*. Tyler MSS. Letter from Moses Coit Tyler to John Tyler, May 21, 1874.

[35] Mrs. Austen, p. 84.—*J*.

[36] "Had it not been for him, I should not be here now in the most distasteful, exhausting, and ungrateful work I was ever in." Tyler MSS. Letter from Moses Coit Tyler to John Tyler, May 21, 1874.

[37] When his office was moved to room 66 "where I expect to have my study for a year at least," Tyler noted with pleasure that the room had formerly been occupied by Frank Moore, the historian, and that the carpet was the straw-matting used "by dear Horace Greeley in room 63, where he wrote *The American Conflict*. So as a writer of American history I am not without some inspiring associations." Mrs. Austen, p. 80.—*J*.

[38] Tyler MSS. Diary for Portions of the Years '71, etc.; Diary for 1874; Personal Records, 1853–75.

[39] *Ibid.*

[40] *The Christian Union,* March 12, 1873.

[41] *Ibid.*, July 16, 1873.

[42] From a review of Edward A. Freeman, *ibid.*, Oct. 29, 1873.

[43] *Ibid.*, March 5, 1873.

[44] *Ibid.*, June 25, 1873.

[45] Tyler MSS. Letter from Moses Coit Tyler to John Tyler, Jan. 12, 1874.

[46] Tyler MSS. Letter from same to same, April 9, 1874.

[47] See Mrs. Austen, p. 79.—*J*.

[48] Tyler MSS. Letter from James Burrill Angell to Moses Coit Tyler, Aug. 5, 1874.

[49] Tyler MSS. Letter from Moses Coit Tyler to John Tyler, Aug. 13, 1874.

[50] Mrs. Austen, p. 86.—*J.*

[51] Tyler MSS. Diary for 1874; Letter from C. H. Davis to Moses Coit Tyler, Aug. 24, 1874. He was elected to the Middletown position, but did not go.

[52] Tyler MSS. Letter from Oliver Johnson to Moses Coit Tyler, Aug. 28, 1874.

[53] Mrs. Austen, p. 86.—*J.*

[54] *Proceedings . . . January, 1870, to January, 1876*, p. 408.—*J.*

[55] Mrs. Austen, p. 85.—*J.*

[56] Letter of Moses Coit Tyler on the occasion of the quarter-centennial of Angell's presidency, dated from Cornell, June 12, 1896. In *The Quarter-Centennial Celebration of the Presidency of James Burrill Angell, LL.D., June 24, 1896* (Ann Arbor, 1896), pp. 76–79.—*J.*

[57] *Ibid.,* p. 78.—*J.*

[58] *The Reminiscences of James Burrill Angell* (London, 1912), pp. 230–1.—*J.*

[59] *Ibid.,* p. 226.—*J.*

[60] *University of Michigan: The President's Report to the Board of Regents for the Year Ending June 30, 1873* (Ann Arbor, 1873), pp. 9–10.

[61] Shaw, *op. cit.,* p. 71.—*J.*

[62] See, for typical discussion, the *President's Report* cited above, pp. 11–12; and cf. "The Library must be the fountain of strength in a University. If our collection of books were trebled or quadrupled in numbers at once, it would not be at all beyond the real demands of the Institution." *President's Report . . . for . . . 1876* (Ann Arbor, 1876), p. 16. A separate library building was established in 1883.—*J.*

[63] See the important discussion of the relation of the university to the high schools in *President's Report . . . for . . . 1881* (Ann Arbor, 1881), pp. 5–9.—*J.*

[64] Cf. Table II in the Appendix to Shaw, *op. cit.*—*J.*

[65] Shaw, *op. cit.,* p. 69.—*J.*

[66] Cf. Shaw, pp. 74–5.—*J.*

[67] Mrs. Austen, p. 86.—*J.*

[68] *University of Michigan: The University Palladium . . . 1877* (Ann Arbor, 1877), vol. XX, No. 1, p. 24.—*J.*

[69] Mrs. Austen, p. 86.—*J.*

[70] Cf. Irving's annual report, in *President's Report . . . for . . . 1874*, pp. 42–43.—*J.*

[71] *Catalogue of the University of Michigan, 1875–1876*, pp. 37–8.

[72] *University of Michigan: Department of Literature, Science and the Arts, Announcement for 1878–9* (Ann Arbor, 1878), p. 10; *do.* for 1879–80, p. 6; for 1880–1, p. 8.—*J.*

[73] "The lectures were merely chapters from a book at that time unpublished, but we students had the advantage of having the book interpreted to us by the trained, sympathetic voice of the author who had evidently enjoyed to the full the delight of preparing it. The lecture room was filled with students and visitors from the city, and I shall never forget the twinkle in his eyes or the drollery in his voice as he interpreted to us some of the verses of the early rhymesters who may well have been filled with a poetic spirit but who clearly lacked a poet's ear." Jeremiah W. Jenks, "The Rev. Moses Coit Tyler, A.M., LL.D." *The Michigan Alumnus,* vol. VII, No. 62, March, 1901, pp. 221–5. Pattee is in error in stating (*The Reinterpretation of American Literature,* ed. Norman Foerster, New York, 1928, p. 4) that "Tyler's volumes on the Colonial and Revolutionary periods were first put on paper as lectures to college students." The situation was, in fact, reversed.

[74] Although the university catalogue does not list it, in 1879 Tyler, following Adams' example, introduced the second seminar into the University of Michigan, as noted by the Hinsdale–Demmon *History*, p. 71. The date (not given in Hinsdale-Demmon) is clear from Tyler's commonplace book which contains references to his "seminary" during the fall and winter of 1879. The study here, as in the case of the senior course noted in the text, was the direct approach to masterpieces.

[75] Tyler MSS. Commonplace Book VI, vol. 2, p. 123.

[76] Tyler MSS. Commonplace Book VI, vol. 2, p. 65.

[77] Mrs. Austen, p. 103.—*J.*

[78] He also eliminated Morley's off-hand allusions, likely to confuse the American student, and presented the history in bolder outlines in order that the literary movements might be more quickly grasped.

[79] Mrs. Austen, p. 103.—*J.*

[80] Mrs. Austen, p. 104.

[81] Mrs. Austen, pp. 103–4.

[82] *A Manual of English Literature, by Henry Morley . . . Thoroughly Revised . . . by Moses Coit Tyler . . .* (New York, 1879), p. ix.

[83] It was formed by uniting the *University Chronicle* with the *University Magazine.* Shaw, *op. cit.,* p. 215.—*J.*

[84] Vol. X, no. 1, Oct. 12, 1878, p. 11.—*J.*

[85] *The Chronicle,* vol. X, no. iii, Nov. 9, 1878, p. 43.—*J.*

[86] *Ibid.,* vol. X, no. iv, Nov. 23, 1878, p. 50. There is also an extended analysis of the work on pp. 56–7. On Dec. 7, 1878 (vol. X, no. v), *The Chronicle* noted that the American edition had been exhausted ("very flattering to the author") and that an English edition was being brought out, and followed the fortunes of the work for a good while with eagerness. Similar interest was expressed in hte Morley-Tyler *Manual (Ibid.,* vol. X, no. xv, May 17, 1879, p. 226).—*J.*

[87] *Ibid.,* vol. X, no. viii, p. 119; no. xvii, p. 262.—*J.*

[88] *Ibid.,* vol. XI, no. iv, pp. 62–3.—*J.*

[89] *Ibid.,* vol. X, no. xiv, p. 211. "Professor Tyler gave a most interesting lecture on Chaucer at the regular meeting of the class last Tuesday. The talks of the professor on the plays of Shakespeare are always interesting and suggestive. The class study of Shakespeare has been of great value to all who were so fortunate as to elect it." *Ibid.,* vol. X, no. xvi, p. 251, May 31, 1879.

Professor William H. More, Emeritus Professor of History at Syracuse University, kindly contributes this anecdote of Tyler's classroom methods: He was admitted to the course in English masterpieces, though ranking only as a sophomore at the time, in 1879. A senior read his dissertation, and More was appointed by Professor Tyler to criticize the production. This he did, taking occasion to speak of the senior's awkwardness on the floor, which detracted somewhat from the effectiveness of the discussion. When the time came for remarks from the class, a tall senior arose and proceeded to "lambast" the sophomore for having criticized the senior. "I felt pretty thoroughly squelched when he finished."

At the next meeting of the class, Tyler reviewed the dissertation and the criticism, and proceeded to set forth his own views of the masterpiece under discussion. When he had finished, he called the attention of the class to "an unusual episode" that he could not pass by, and proceeded to give the offending senior a verbal drubbing. At the conclusion of Tyler's remarks, the senior arose and "in a fine, manly way apologized to me, to the class, and to Professor Tyler."

Mr. More later entered Cornell while Tyler was there, and found Tyler cordially interested in his career. "I never," he writes, "regretted following his advice." "His was a great soul."—*J.*

[90] *Ibid.,* vol. XI, no. v, Dec. 6, 1879, p. 75.—*J.*

[91] *Ibid.,* vol. XII, no. vii, Jan. 15, 1881, pp. 97; 108.—*J.*

[92] *Ibid.,* vol. XII, no. iii, p. 43, Oct. 30, 1880.—*J.*

[93] *Ibid.,* vol. XII, no. viii, Jan. 29, 1881, p. 125.—*J.*

[94] *Ibid.,* vol. XII, no. xiii, April 16, 1881, p. 193.—*J.*

[95] *Ibid.,* vol. XI, no. viii, Jan. 31, 1880, p. 120.—*J.*

[96] *Ibid.,* vol. XI, no. xii, April 3, 1880, p. 177–8.—*J.*

[97] "Students too often read the masterpieces hurriedly, and when tired from other work, with a view to 'points'; they get the points and little more; the poetry has escaped them. These difficulties could be obviated by following the professor's instructions: read the masterpiece when you are brightest; read it twice—once with appreciation, once critically. These courses are well planned and well conducted; more is left to the student than in any other work; he can do much or little; if he fail of any good result, the fault is his own." *Ibid,* vol. XI, no. xv, May 15, 1880, p. 227.—*J.*

[98] The files of *The Chronicle* are filled with the struggles of the university to secure an appropriation from the legislature for a gymnasium. Tyler served on a faculty committee which drew up a memorial recommending the building to the regents and through them to the legislature. See for typical entries *The Chronicle,* vol. XII, no. v, Nov. 27, 1880, pp. 76–7.

[99] *Ibid.,* vol. X, no. xvii, June 18, 1879, p. 268. Although the professor is anonymous, the reference to "steaming down one of the main walks" and the "broad bosom," taken with other details, is too characteristic of Tyler's well-known mannerisms to leave the identification in doubt.—*J.*

[100] *Ibid.,* vol. XII, no. xvi, May 28, 1881, p. 252.—*J.*

[101] Mrs. Austen, p. 87.—*J.*

[102] Moses Coit Tyler to Dio Lewis (spring of 1875), Mrs. Austen, p. 91.—*J.*

[103] Mrs. Austen, p. 96. In addition to the lot purchased in 1870, he bought adjoining land in two purchases, one on May 1, 1875, and one on March 27, 1880.—*J.*

[104] The grounds are now occupied by the Sigma Phi fraternity, 426 N. Ingalls.—*J.*

[105] Mrs. Austen, p. 89.—*J.*

[106] See Mrs. Austen, pp. 108–10.—*J.*

[107] Presumably Castoria.—*J.* Tyler MSS. Letter from Moses Coit Tyler to Andrew D. White, February 12, 1875.

[108] Tyler's MS. sermons are preserved in the Tyler MSS. As denoting the approbation with which some of them were received, one finds Charles Kendall Adams writing him, Nov. 2, 1874, "God bless you for your noble sermon of yesterday! It helped me, and it must have helped every student in the audience. When it comes

my turn, I am going to resign in your favor; so you must have an extra one in *soak.*" The reference is to the custom of having the faculty members officiate in turn on successive Sundays at a university religious service.—*J.*

[109] Tyler MSS. Diary for 1874.

[110] St. Andrew's, erected in 1869. See Arthur L. Cross, *A History of St. Andrew's Church* (Ann Arbor, 1906).

[111] So he noted in his diary Aug. 6, 1876. Tyler MSS.

[112] See the letter of Moses Coit Tyler to "an avowed anti-Christian" May 16, 1875, in Mrs. Austen, pp. 91–2.—*J.*

[113] Cross, *op. cit.,* pp. 164; 142.

[114] A copy of Stephen H. Tyng, *The Vow Assumed, A Pastor's Address to Those who have been Confirmed* (New York, n. d.), preserved in the Tyler library, shows that Tyler was confirmed on April 27, 1877, by S. S. McCloskey, D.D., Bishop of Michigan. A second copy, also among the Tyler books, shows that Jessie Gilbert Tyler was confirmed on the same day.—*J.*

[115] Tyler MSS. Commonplace Book VI, vol. 2, p. 64.—*J.*

[116] Mrs. Austen, p. 104. Aug. 2, 1879.—*J.*

[117] *Ibid.,* pp. 105; 106.—*J.*

[118] Tyler MSS. Commonplace Book VI, vol. 2, p. 84.

[119] Mrs. Austen, p. 115.—*J.*

CHAPTER VII

[1] The sort of thing that was always distracting Tyler is represented by a request from the U. S. Bureau of Education for an article and special report on "Art Museums in Connection with Public Libraries." Tyler MSS. Letter from the Department of Interior, Bureau of Education, to Moses Coit Tyler, Nov. 13, 1875.—*J.*

[2] Tyler MSS. Letter from George H. Putnam to Moses Coit Tyler, July 12, 1875.

[3] Tyler MSS. Letter from George H. Putnam to Moses Coit Tyler, July 19, 1875.—Tyler's copy of Arnold's *Manual* is still among his books.—*J.*

[4] Tyler MSS. Copies of Letters by Moses Coit Tyler, 1874–5, pp. 145–6.

[5] As a matter of history, Putnam did not receive the last chapter in manuscript until Oct. 18, 1878.—*J.*

[6] Tyler MSS. Copies of letters by Moses Coit Tyler, 1874–5.

[7] The antiquarian and historian later in charge of the Lenox

Library, New York, and in 1875, librarian of the New York Historical Society; author of *The Treason of Charles Lee,* 1860, and *Notes on the History of Slavery in Massachusetts,* 1866.—*J.*

[8] Best known as the author of the *Pictorial Field-book of the Revolution,* 1851–2.—*J.*

[9] Mrs. Austen, pp. 95–6.—Putnam's ready acquiescence in Tyler's widening plans was undoubtedly part of the increasing interest of this publisher in Americana. George P. Putnam had died in Dec., 1872, when George H. Putnam came into control of the business. The fruit of his interest in American history, undoubtedly increased by the favorable reception of Tyler's first two volumes, is seen in the issuing of the present standard editions of the writings of the "Fathers of the Republic" by Putnam's in the eighties. See George Haven Putnam, *Memories of a Publisher, 1865–1915* (New York, 1915), chap. iv.—*J.*

[10] Tyler MSS. Letter from Moses Coit Tyler to Mr. Chaney.

[11] Tyler MSS.

[12] Tyler MSS. Tyler's library eventually numbered about 4000 volumes. After his death it was sold to Peter White, N. M. Kaufman, and E. N. Breitung, who presented it to the Northern State Normal School, Marquette, Mich.—It is among these that one finds the marginalia quoted in this biography.—*J.*

[13] Tyler MSS. Letter from J. B. Angell to Moses Coit Tyler, Aug. 26, 1876.

[14] Tyler MSS. Letter from Addison Van Name to Moses Coit Tyler, Aug. 12, 1876.

[15] Tyler MSS. Diary for 1875.

[16] Tyler MSS. Letter from Moses Coit Tyler to James Redpath, Jan. 25, 1876.

[17] Tyler MSS. Diary for 1876.

[18] The Bradstreet chapter became chapter X, and the Ward material, chapter IX of the finished book.—It is interesting to follow Tyler's methodology in the creation of the finished studies. The whole of the discussion of Ward (*History . . . 1607–1676* [vol. 1], pp. 227–41) lies in germ in comments which Tyler wrote on the inside back cover of his copy of *The Simple Cobler:* "The book contains 1. A ferocious declaration against freedom of conscience & the tolerance of diversity of beliefs. Nothing more savage in the Fathers of the Inquisition. Here is the logic of persecution. [Here Tyler refers to pp. 1–25 of Ward.] 2. A satire, witty, fierce, coarse, uncivil & bitterly eloquent, upon the fashions of women in

N.E.—extravagance in dress, vanity of [undecipherable], etc."
"This book is full of vigor, fire, wit, satire, invective, patriotism
& bigotry." "He was in a panic about new ideas in religion—
progress. He thought the book of truth was finished." "He took
the ground boldly of the crime of heresy—of holding wrong doctrine." "In style marked by the ostentatious quotations, the con-
ceits, the bold & tasteless metaphors, the energy & vivacity of
English prose in the 17th century."

The striking description of Ward's manner quoted above appears in the *History* (vol. I, p. 230) as "intensely vital even yet,
full of fire, wit, whim, eloquence, sarcasm, invective, patriotism,
bigotry." Tyler's reference to the first twenty-five pages of Ward
he develops into the long paragraph beginning on p. 232 of the
History, and the concluding sentence on Ward's style is developed
at length in *History,* pp. 238–9.

In the case of Anne Bradstreet, however, Tyler's ample annotations in his copy (the Ellis edition) have a much more remote
relation to the final text, and much modification has intervened.
Of some twenty important comments scribbled on the margin of
Ellis, only two represent citations actually used in the text [quo-
tation beginning, "We often see stones hang with drops," *History,*
vol. I, p. 281; quotation beginning, "O Time, the fatal wrack," p.
290, *do.*]. Tyler twice calls marginal attention to passages showing the poet's historical learning, but does not use either in the
final discussion. Three or four times he marks passages "Rich"
(apparently ironic), or "Good," but does not cite them in his text.
A note or two on the fact that Anne Bradstreet was a woman poet
in colonial America remains undeveloped. It is also a curious fact
that Tyler fails to note the famous "grasshopper" stanza of "Con-
templations" as anything remarkable, nor does he quote it in his
history. He discusses at length the "braggart speech-making" in
the "Four Elements" (*History,* pp. 283–7), but in his marginalia
there is nothing of this, though in his notes on the "Four Humours" he jots down: "They (*i.e.,* the humors) get hot in debate
& call hard names like lawyers badgering." In writing up his
notes, however, he omitted the "Four Humours" altogether!—*J.*

[19] William Swinton, 1833–92, compiled innumerable textbooks,
as did George Payn Quackenbos, 1826–81, all of them derivative.
The second reference may be to J. D. Quackenbos, 1848–1926.—*J.*

[20] George P. Marsh.—*J.*

[21] Mrs. Austen, pp. 97–9.

[22] Tyler MSS. Letter from G. H. Putnam to Moses Coit Tyler, April 11, 1876.

[23] Tyler MSS. Letter from Moses Coit Tyler to John Tyler, Aug. 10, 1877.—The *Survey* was never written.—*J.*

[24] *Ibid.* Mrs. Austen prints a large section of this letter, pp. 99–100.—*J.*

[25] As exemplifying Tyler's care, one finds in the Tyler MSS. a letter from Charles Ward Dean, librarian of the New England Historic-Genealogical Society, in answer to Tyler's query as to how many children Roger Clap had. The information is embedded in a note in the *History of American Literature, 1607–1765,* vol. I, p. 95: "Pleasant examples of the early New England family meet one at almost every turn in the field of New England biography. The sturdy patriot, Roger Clap of Dorchester, was happy in the possession of fourteen children, among whom were Experience, Waitstill, Preserved, Hopestill, Wait, Thanks, Desire, Unite, and Supply." Thomas Wentworth Higginson wrote, in response to inquiry, that he was not a descendant of Anne Bradstreet; Tyler compiled a list of important descendants of the poetess and inserted it on the last page of vol. I.

[26] See the letter from Moses Coit Tyler to G. P. Putnam, March 8, 1878, printed in Mrs. Austen, pp. 100–1.—*J.*

[27] Tyler MSS. Memorandum from G. P. Putnam's Sons to Moses Coit Tyler, Oct. 18, 1878.

[28] Mrs. Austen, p. 101.—*J.*

[29] He wrote in his diary, after writing the last word in the revised copy of the last chapter, "I thank God for his good help to me in all this long, long labor. . . . Since my return from New York in August my brain has been more severely worked than ever before in my life. But I am marvellously fresh and well." Mrs. Austen, p. 102.—*J.*

[30] Putnam wrote him in an undated letter in the Tyler MSS: "We have not given to any work since 'Irving's Washington,' so much care and advertizing investment."

[31] See Mrs. Austen, p. 102.—*J.*

[32] *Ibid.*—*J.*

[33] *Ibid.*—*J.*

[34] See chapter vi.—*J.*

[35] Vol. XLIII, no. 257, March, 1879, p. 405.—Professor Parrington was still combatting this point of view in 1927: "Our literary historians have labored under too heavy a handicap of the genteel

tradition—to borrow Professor Santayana's happy phrase—to enter sympathetically into a world of masculine intellects and material struggles. . . . The colonial period is meager and lean only to those whose 'disedged appetites' find no savor in old-fashioned beef and puddings." *The Colonial Mind, 1620–1800* (New York, 1927), pp. vi–vii.—*J*.

[36] Charles D. Cleveland, in his *A Compendium of American Literature* (New York, 1858), resenting the British charge that we have no literature, is typical. His book is eminently patriotic, and of American literature he says that its "native growth and development commenced with our Revolutionary period." The whole preface should be read.—*J*.

[37] "Preface," p. iii.

[38] Cf. *The History of American Literature, 1607–1765*, vol. II, pp. 5–63;—and especially the footnote on p. 21.—*J*.

[39] Originally published in two volumes in Philadelphia in 1855. A supplementary volume appeared in 1866.

[40] Tyler MSS. Diary for 1875. He used it more frequently than the notes to the *History* might indicate.

[41] Tyler treats approximately 124 authors; for the same period the revised Duykinck cited approximately 82. According to their preface, "It was considered that, under any principle of selection, the story [of the author's life] should be as briefly told as possible; being confined to the facts of the case, with no more comment than was required to put the reader in ready communication with the author, while matters of digression and essay-writing should be carefully avoided. . . . It is not the purpose to sit in judgment, and to admit or exclude writers according to individual taste, but to welcome all our guests who come reasonably well introduced. . . ."

[42] Henry T. Tuckerman's "Sketch of American Literature" appeared in Shaw's *Outlines of English Literature*, 1852; John Nichol's "American Literature" appeared in the ninth edition of the *Encyclopaedia Britannica*, 1875; Francis H. Underwood's *A Handbook of English Literature: American Authors* appeared in 1872; John S. Hart's *Manual of American Literature*, which appeared almost simultaneously, was reviewed by Tyler (as was Underwood's book) in *The Christian Union* in 1873. See chapter vi, pp. 156–7.

[43] He depended importantly on Isaiah Thomas, *The History of Printing in America*, 1810; Frederic Hudson, *Journalism in the*

United States, 1873; W. B. Sprague, *The Annals of the American Pulpit*, 1859–69; Edward Tuckerman, *America and Her Commentators*, 1864; Jeremy Belknap, *American Biography*, 1794; Samuel L. Knapp, *Biographical Sketches of Eminent Lawyers, Statesmen, and Men of Letters*, 1821; Francis S. Drake, *Dictionary of American Biography*, 1872; Peter Force, *Tracts and Other Papers Relating Principally to the Origin, Settlement, and Progress of the Colonies in North America from the Discovery of the Country Until the Year 1776*, 1836–46, and the collections of the State historical societies. Of course, he took material wherever he found it; but these seem (with Kettell and the revised Duykinck) to have constituted his working library.

[44] *The History of American Literature, 1607–1765*, vol. I, p. vii.

[45] *Ibid.*, p. vi.

[46] *Ibid.*

[47] *Ibid.*, vol. I, p. 5.

[48] *Ibid.*, vol. I, p. 8.—*J*.

[49] Vol. XVII, no. 5, March, 1879, p. 757.

[50] An excellent instance is the long discussion of Puritan life and character which prefaces the treatment of the Puritan men of letters, vol. I, pp. 93–114. Tyler noted that Nicholas Noyes belongs to the "fantastic" or metaphysical school, and placed Anne Bradstreet in the same category (II, p. 39; I, p. 282) but the "evolution of literature" scarcely interested him. See the discussion by W. P. Trent in *The Forum*, vol. XXXI, Aug., 1901, especially p. 756.

[51] From Tyler's article on Sainte-Beuve in *The Christian Union*, March 5, 1873, already quoted.

[52] *History*, vol. I, pp. 137–8.

[53] *Ibid.*, vol. II [pp. 64, 67, 123–30;—*J*.], 192–4.

[54] He accuses Mather of "an intellectual and moral inability to be either accurate or fair," vol. II, p. 83, but Tyler himself employs the *Magnalia* for forty-one quotations and one reference, salting his pages with pat phrases from that "bulky thing." Cf. vol. I, pp. 100, 221, 271, 94, 195, 214, for typical examples.

[55] Mather, Cotton, *Magnalia Christi Americana* (Hartford, 1855), p. 30.

[56] The omission of any discussion of Thomas Morton is an instance.—*J*.

[57] *History*, vol. I, p. 65.—*J*.

[58] *Ibid.*, vol. II, p. 182.—*J*.

[59] See the *History,* vol. I, p. 153; vol. II, pp. 60–1.

[60] The paragraph on Hammond's *Leah and Rachel,* vol. I, pp. 64–5, reads like a bad Fourth-of-July oration; in his own copy of the *History* (now among the Tyler MSS.) he inserted a note to exclude this passage in the next revision.

[61] He interprets *The Burwell Papers literatim,* mistaking irony for assertion; and confuses the two poems on Bacon's death, the first of which is a sincere elegy, and the second of which is ironical. However, he first read the narrative in the corrupt text printed in the *Collections of the Massachusetts Historical Society,* 2d Series, I, 33. The narrative was later reprinted with a correct text in *Proceedings, 1866–1867,* vol. IX, pp. 299–342, and Tyler corrected his readings, without, however, changing his views. See *History,* vol. I, p. 79.

[62] This was in Jan., 1878, preceding the publication of the *History.*

[63] Tyler MSS. *passim.*

[64] Mrs. Austen, p. 103.—*J.*

[65] Mrs. Austen, pp. 112–3.—*J.*

[66] Mrs. Austen, p. 113.—*J.*—On Dec. 31, 1880, Tyler wrote in his diary: "My mind is moving steadily towards a final refusal of the project to go to the Cornell presidency." Tyler MSS. Commonplace Book VI, vol. 2, p. 205. Apparently he destroyed White's second letter announcing a change of intention; Tyler wrote in his diary: "So it is in this world."

[67] Tyler MSS. Commonplace Book VI, vol. 2, p. 217.

[68] Mrs. Austen, p. 116.—*J.*

[69] He lectured at Harvard and before the Rhode Island and New York Historical Societies. Tyler MSS. Diary for 1881.

[70] Tyler MSS. Letter from E. D. Neill to Moses Coit Tyler. Nov. 5, 1878.

[71] He began to go through Drake's *American Biographical Dictionary* and note all the names for the period 1765-1815, with which he might have to deal. Tyler MSS. Commonplace Book VI, vol. 2, 76.

[72] *Ibid.,* pp. 78–9.

[73] Mrs. Austen, p. 106.—*J.*

[74] *Ibid.,* p. 80.

[75] Mrs. Austen, p. 105.—*J.*

[76] Mrs. Austen, p. 106.—*J.*

[77] Tyler MSS. Commonplace Book VI, vol. 2, p. 120.

[78] *Ibid.,* p. 122.

[79] Mrs. Austen, p. 107.—*J.*

[80] Mrs. Austen, p. 107.—*J.*

[81] Mrs. Austen, p. 107.—*J.*

[82] See chapter vi, p. 169.—*J.*

[83] Mrs. Austen, p. 111.—*J.*

[84] Mrs. Austen, p. 114.—*J.*

[85] See chapter vi, p. 173.—*J.*

CHAPTER VIII

[1] Moses Coit Tyler to John Tyler, March 24, 1881, Mrs. Austen, pp. 115–16.—*J.*

[2] Tyler MSS. Andrew D. White to Moses Coit Tyler, March 7, 1881.

[3] Tyler's reply has been lost, but the drift of his letter is evident from the Diary for 1881 in the Tyler MSS.

[4] Tyler MSS. Letter from White to Tyler, April 16, 1881.

[5] Mrs. Austen, p. 116.—*J.*

[6] Clipping from *The Detroit Times* reporting a sermon delivered in Ann Arbor, Jan., 1884, in the Tyler MSS., Personal Records, 1879–97.—The change in his appearance had begun before he left Ann Arbor for Cornell.—*J.*

[6a] Mrs. Austen, p. 117.—*J.*

[7] Tyler MSS. Letter from Andrew D. White to Moses Coit Tyler, April 26, 1881.

[8] Mrs. Austen, p. 117.—*J.*

[9] Tyler MSS. Diary for 1881.—Not May 21, as Mrs. Austen has it, p. 118.—*J.*

[10] *Ibid.*

[11] *Proceedings of the Board of Regents of the University of Michigan,* Jan., 1881, to Jan., 1886, pp. 37–8.—*J.*

[12] *Ibid.,* p. 11.

[13] Mrs. Austen, p. 118.—*J.*—The Diary shows that the first hint came in a letter from George H. Putnam.

[14] Mrs. Austen, p. 119.—*J.*

[15] Mrs. Austen, p. 119.—*J.*

[16] Tyler MSS. Diary for 1881. Mrs. Austen, pp. 121–2, 126–7, 129–30.

[17] From a contemporary account by D. Morris Kurtz, *Ithaca and Its Resources* . . . (Ithaca, 1883), pp. 8–10.—*J.*

[18] O. D. Von Engeln, *Concerning Cornell* (Ithaca, 1917), opp. p. 433.—*J.*

[19] Mrs. Austen, p. 119.—Tyler managed to go through the Trumbull papers at Grosse Pointe on his way to Ithaca.—*J.*

[20] Tyler MSS. Diaries for 1881 and 1882.

[21] The Tylers lived at 5 East Avenue, in a rented house. "Hillcroft" was begun in 1884.—*J.*

[22] Vol. I, chapter xxiv.—*J.*

[23] White, *Autobiography,* vol. I, p. 437; and cf. Hewett, vol. I, p. 185.—*J.*

[24] Hewett, *loc. cit.*—*J.*

[25] White says there was trouble in the governing board, but that no serious damage was done. Hewett, the official historian, is silent as to the nature of the trouble in the board. It is perhaps significant that after 1878 the student body declined in number, and that it did not reach the 1878 figures until 1884–5, at the conclusion of which year White resigned. See Hewett, *op. cit.,* vol. I, pp. 185–6.—*J.*

[26] *Cf.* Hewett, *op. cit.,* vol. III, p. 425.—*J.*

[27] Hewett, *op. cit.,* vol. I, p. 184.—*J.*

[28] Tyler MSS. Diary for 1882.

[29] White, *op. cit.,* vol. I, pp. 419–21; Hewett, *op. cit.,* vol. I, chapters xxi–xxii, *passim.* Hewett estimates the gift at a million dollars; White, at a million and a half. Part of the loss was later made up by others.—*J.*

[30] James Fraser Gluck, *Cornell University: Its Conditions and Needs in 1884. A Report Thereon Made to the Alumni at Their Request* ([Buffalo,] 1884).—*J.*

[31] *Ibid.,* p. 29.—*J.*

[32] *Ibid.,* p. 61.—*J.*

[33] Mrs. Austen, p. 120.—*J.*

[34] *Cornell University Register 1881–1882* (Ithaca. 1881), pp. 10–13.—Lectures on American history had been given before Tyler's coming but no chair had been established. See Hewett, vol. II, pp. 120–2.—*J.*

[35] Quoted in Hewett, *op. cit.,* vol. II, p. 120.—*J.*

[36] Mrs. Austen, p. 121. He returned to Ann Arbor for the purpose.—*J.*

[37] Tyler MSS. Diary for 1881.

[38] *Cornell Sun,* Sept. 2, 1881, in Personal Records, 1879–97.

[39] Professor George Lincoln Burr of Cornell, who was a stu-

dent in Tyler's first course there, found it dull for the reason stated, and so reported to Mr. Casady. Mr. Willard Austen, Tyler's son-in-law, a student of his in 1889, in talking with Mr. Casady, said that he was "the most perfect lecturer" he ever sat under. William H. Glasson, another later student, wrote that "his classes were among the most popular in the university and his students were delighted by the wealth of anecdote and the flashes of wit and humor which illuminated the subject matter of his lectures." "Moses Coit Tyler and Charles Sumner," *The South Atlantic Quarterly,* vol. II, Jan., 1903, pp. 51-2.

[40] Mrs. Austen, p. 123.—*J.*

[41] Oct. 20, 1881. Tyler MSS. Personal Records, 1879-97.

[42] Mrs. Austen, pp. 123-30.—*J.*

[43] Tyler MSS. Letter from J. T. Morse to Moses Coit Tyler, Dec. 17, 1881.

[44] Mrs. Austen. pp. 127-8.—*J.*

[45] Mrs. Austen, p. 131.—*J.*

[46] Mrs. Austen, pp. 131-5.—*J.*

[47] Mrs. Austen, pp. 131-75.—*J.*

[48] Mrs. Austen, p. 175.—*J.*

[49] Glasson, *loc. cit.*

[50] See the picture on p. 49 of Frank C. Perkins, *Cornell University: Her General and Technical Courses* (Buffalo, 1891).—*J.*

[51] *Cornell University: Courses of Instruction in the President White School of History and Political Science, 1894-95* (Ithaca, 1894), p. 12.—*J.*

[52] *Annual Report to the Board of Trustees,* June, 1883.

[53] Tyler MSS. Diaries for 1882 and 1883. The offer of the presidency came in Feb., 1883; the degree on July 12, 1883.

[54] Tyler MSS. Personal Records, 1879-97.

[55] Tyler MSS. Diary for 1883.

[56] Tyler MSS. Diary for 1883. He was ordained April 29.

[57] Mrs. Austen, p. 178.—*J.*

[58] Mrs. Austen, p. 179.—*J.*

[59] *Ibid.—J.*

[60] Tyler MSS. Diary for 1884.

[61] Mrs. Austen, p. 179.—*J.*

[62] *Ibid.,* pp. 181-5.—*J.*

[63] *Ibid.,* p. 189.—*J.*

[64] *Ibid.,* p. 194.—*J.*

[65] *Ibid.—J.*

[66] The paper is summarized in *Papers of the American Historical Association* (New York, 1886), vol. I, pp. 35–7.—*J.*

[67] Inadequately noted in *Magazine of American History,* vol. XIII, pt. i, p. 601.—*J.*

[68] From the summary in *Papers of the American Historical Association,* vol. II, pp. 20–22.—*J.*

[69] Data from the Tyler MSS.

[70] Tyler MSS.

[71] The organizing movements of the association can be followed in *Papers of the American Historical Association,* vol. I, pp. 5–44.—*J.*

[72] Cf. Mrs. Austen, pp. 175, 189. In this connection, there is an amusing comment by Tyler on Bancroft, whom in the main he admired as a stylist. But in the margin of his copy of vol. IV, p. 456, Tyler writes: "He almost bursts with the effort of being grand and eloquent."—*J.*

[73] Tyler MSS. Diary for 1884, pt. I.

[74] Tyler MSS. Diary for 1882.

[75] Mrs. Austen, p. 196.—*J.*

[76] Tyler MSS. Diary for 1884, pt. II.

[77] *In Memoriam: Edgar Kelsey Apgar.* Edited by Moses Coit Tyler, Ithaca, 1886.—*J.*

[78] Mrs. Austen, p. 199.—*J.*

[79] Tyler MSS. Diary for 1886.

[80] Mrs. Austen, p. 188.—*J.*

CHAPTER IX

[1] Tyler MSS. Letters from John T. Morse to Moses Coit Tyler, Jan. 26, 1886; Jan. 29, 1886. Morse offered Tyler the choice between outright sale of his manuscript for $500 and a royalty of 12½ cents a copy.

[2] Mrs. Austen, p. 204.—*J.*

[3] *Ibid.,* p. 205.—*J.*

[4] Mrs. Austen, p. 206.—*J.*

[5] Tyler MSS. Diary for 1886.

[6] Mrs. Austen, p. 206.—*J.*

[7] Tyler MSS. Diary for 1887.

[8] Mrs. Austen, p. 206.—*J.*

[9] Tyler MSS. Diary for 1887.

[10] *Ibid.*

[11] Mrs. Austen, p. 208.—*J.*

[12] *Ibid.,* p. 209.

[13] *Ibid.,* pp. 208–9.—*J.*

[14] *Ibid.,* p. 210.—*J.*

[15] *Ibid.,* pp. 209, 210.—*J.*

[16] *Political Science Quarterly,* vol. II, no. 4, December, 1887, pp. 688, 689–90.

[17] *History of the United States* (New York, 1912), vol. III, p. 8, footnote.

[18] George Morgan, *Patrick Henry* (Philadelphia, 1929), index *sub* Tyler.—*J.*

[19] "In the very front of this book, therefore I record my grateful acknowledgements to Mr. William Wirt Henry; acknowledgments, not alone for the sort of generosity of which I have just spoken, but for another sort, also, which is still more rare, and which I cannot so easily describe—his perfect delicacy, while promoting my more difficult researches by his invaluable help, in never once encumbering that help with the least effort to hamper my judgment, or to sway it from the natural conclusions to which my studies might lead." *Patrick Henry* (Boston, 1887), p. vii.—*J.*

[20] *Ibid.,* p. vi. On the other hand Tyler was perfectly aware of Wirt's deficiencies. He pencilled an amusing note on p. 9 of his copy of the Wirt biography: "Illustrates W's habit of cackling loudly over a very small egg. There is nothing extraordinary about P. Henry ['s] conduct in this."—*J.*

[21] William Wirt, *Sketches of the Life and Character of Patrick Henry,* 10th ed. (Hartford, 1845), pp. 24, 25.—For Tyler's statement that Jefferson led Wirt to color his original theory that Henry received "no mean classical education," see *Patrick Henry,* p. 13.—*J.*

[22] Tyler, *op. cit.,* pp. 14–15.

[23] Wirt, *op. cit.,* p. 36.

[24] Tyler, *op. cit.,* pp. 25–30.

[25] Wirt, *op. cit.,* p. 124.

[26] *Ibid.,* p. 126.

[27] Tyler, *op. cit.,* p. 98.

[28] *Ibid.,* p. 109.

[29] See, for Tyler's defence of his method, the illuminating paragraph on p. 92.

[30] Wirt, *op. cit.,* p. 137.

[31] Tyler, *op. cit.,* pp. 113–22.

[32] Tyler, *op. cit.,* p. 317.—On the problem of the navigation of the Mississippi and Henry's views see pp. 273–7; and for the whole matter, chapters xvii–xix.—*J.*

[33] *Ibid.,* pp. 18–9.

[34] *Ibid.,* pp. 376–7.—*J.*

[35] Mrs. Austen, p. 208.—*J.*

[36] Mrs. Austen, p. 210.—*J.*

[37] Tyler MSS.

[38] Wheeler agrees with this judgment in his remarkably frank memorial address on Adams. See Benjamin Ide Wheeler, "President Adams at Cornell University," in *Memorial of Charles Kendall Adams, Late President of the University* (Madison, 1903), pp. 32, 36–7.—*J.*

[39] Wheeler's description, p. 32.—*J.*

[40] Mrs. Austen, pp. 211, 212.—*J.*

[41] *Ibid.,* p. 212.—*J.*

[42] Mrs. Austen, pp. 212–3.—*J.*

[43] *Ibid.,* p. 214.—*J.*

[44] Tyler MSS. Diary for June 7–July 23, 1888.

[45] Mrs. Austen, p. 242.—*J.*

[46] On Tyler's struggles with the German language see, for typical diary entries, Mrs. Austen, pp. 219, 220, 224, 227, etc.—*J.*

[46a] Some of these may be found in Mrs. Austen, pp. 216, 224ff. —*J.*

[47] *Ibid.,* p. 217.—*J.*

[48] *Ibid.,* pp. 257–8.—*J.*

[49] He was playing lawn tennis in 1887. Mrs. Austen, p. 210.—*J.*

[50] *Ibid.,* pp. 220, 229, 230.—*J.*

[51] *Ibid.,* p. 234.—*J.*

[52] *Ibid.,* pp. 223–4; and cf. 248–9.—*J.*

[53] *Ibid.,* p. 235.—*J.*

[54] *Ibid.,* p. 241.—*J.*

[55] *Ibid.,* pp. 246–8.—*J.*

[56] *Ibid.,* p. 249.—*J.*

[57] The official manœuvres can be followed in *Proceedings and Addresses at the Inauguration of Charles Kendall Adams, LL.D. . . .* (Ithaca, 1886).—*J.*

[58] *Ibid.,* p. 10.—*J.*

[59] *Ibid.,* p. 75.—*J.*

[60] Quoted from an anonymous source by Charles Forster Smith in *Charles Kendall Adams: A Life-Sketch* (Madison, 1924), p. 17.—*J.*

[61] See his letter to Tyler June 9, 1883, when the Cornell appointment in some form was being broached; Smith, *op. cit.,* pp. 15–16.—*J.*

[62] Smith, p. 28.—*J.*

[63] Charles Kendall Adams, *Cornell University: Its Significance and Its Scope* (Ithaca, 1886), p. 4 and note. As this address was presumably printed under Adams' eye, the inclusion of the footnote, from which I have quoted in the text, is especially revelatory.—*J.*

[64] *Ibid.,* p. 6 and note.—*J.*

[65] Professor J. H. Comstock in Smith, *op. cit.,* p. 28.—*J.*

[66] Andrew D. White, *Autobiography,* vol. I, p. 440.—*J.*

[67] Hewett, *Cornell University: A History,* vol. II, p. 114. White says nothing about the deanship in his *Autobiography.*—*J.*

[68] Hewett, *loc. cit.*

[69] Mrs. Austen, p. 249.—*J.*

[70] Tyler MSS. Diary for November, 1889–May, 1890, Jan. 26, 1890.

[71] Mrs. Austen, p. 251.—*J.*—When his dignity was hurt, Tyler could be very cutting. Once in 1900 the treasurer of a club failed to send him a check for a lecture, and he wrote John Bach Mc-Master, who seems to have been guiltless in the matter, that "I am simply amazed and hurt that the necessity remains that I should again write to you on this paltry subject—paltry as regards the pecuniary consideration involved, but not paltry either to me or to your Club as regards so gross a violation of the amenities everywhere recognized among polite people in transactions like those which led to my journey to Philadelphia a month ago." Tyler MSS. Letter from Moses Coit Tyler to John Bach McMaster, May 10, 1900. He was probably ill at the time.

[72] Tyler MSS. Diary for November, 1899–May, 1890.

[73] The official history of the university is discreet on the subject of the senate, but it appears to have originated with the faculty and to have been approved by the trustees. See Hewett, *op. cit.,* vol. I, pp. 193–9. This view is confirmed by the fact that Adams resigned in May, 1892, and the senate ceased to exist on Oct. 6, 1893.—*J.*

[74] Hewett, *loc. cit.*—*J.*

[75] Smith, *op. cit.,* p. 26.—*J.*

[76] Tyler MSS. Diary for November, 1889–May, 1890.—Information given Tyler by Henry W. Sage.—*J.*

[77] Professor Herbert Tuttle, who taught modern European history.—*J.*

[78] Tyler MSS. Diary for November, 1889–May, 1890.

[79] *Ibid.*

[80] Nov. 18, 1890. *Proceedings of the Board of Trustees Sept. 5, 1890–July 26, 1895* (Ithaca), p. 39.

[81] Tyler MSS. Diary for May, 1890–November, 1893.

[82] *Ibid.*

[83] *Ibid.*

[84] *Ibid.*

[85] *Proceedings of the Board of Trustees, op. cit.,* pp. 65, 71.

[86] *Ibid.,* pp. 71, 72.

[87] *Ibid.,* p. 138.

[88] Hewett, *op. cit.,* vol. II, p. 115.

[89] Mrs. Austen, p. 264.—*J.*

[90] Tyler MSS. Letter from F. J. Turner to Moses Coit Tyler, March 8, 1900.

CHAPTER X

[1] Tyler MSS. Diary for 1888, vol. I.—*The Virginia Plutarch,* by Philip Alexander Bruce (Chapel Hill, 1929), represents the type of book Tyler had in mind.—*J.*

[2] Moses Coit Tyler, *Three Men of Letters* (New York, 1895), p. iii. And see Mrs. Austen, p. 250.—*J.*

[3] Tyler MSS. Diary for Jan.–July, 1889.

[4] Mrs. Austen, p. 249.—*J.*

[5] *Ibid.—J.*

[6] *Ibid.,* p. 250.—*J.*

[7] Tyler MSS. Diary for Nov., 1889–May, 1890.

[8] Mrs. Austen, p. 255.—*J.*

[9] *Ibid.,* pp. 256–8.—*J.*—Tyler MSS. Diary for May 15, 1890– Nov. 13, 1893.

[10] The spring of 1890 saw a pale renewal of interest in *The Brawnville Papers,* which, however, he wisely decided not to re- publish.—*J.*

[11] See Mrs. Austen, pp. 261–3.—*J.*

[12] *Ibid.,* p. 265.—*J.*

[13] *Proceedings and Addresses at the Inauguration of Jacob Gould Schurmann, LL.D., to the Presidency of Cornell University, Nov. 11, 1892* (Ithaca, 1892), pp. 3, 15, 22.—*J.*

[14] Tyler MSS. Diary for May 15, 1890–Nov. 13, 1893.

[15] Mrs. Austen, p. 273.—*J.*

[16] Tyler MSS. Diary for May 15, 1890–Nov. 13, 1893.

[17] Mrs. Austen, p. 274.—*J.*—Characteristically, he spent part of his vacation in Boston and Cambridge libraries, getting up some notes on Freneau.

[18] Mrs. Austen, p. 278.—*J.*

[19] Tyler MSS. Diary for Dec., 1893–April, 1898;—and Mrs. Austen, pp. 278–9.—*J.*

[20] Printed in Mrs. Austen, pp. 281–2. It is fair to say that White (no bad judge) was "carried away" with the Barlow essay, though he found fault with it for not giving an account of Barlow's journey to Poland. On the other hand, it is clear that the Dwight and Berkeley essays interested White more deeply.—*J.*

[21] Tyler MSS. Diary for Dec., 1893–April, 1898.

[22] Mrs. Austen, p. 280.—*J.*

[23] Tyler MSS. Diary for Dec., 1893–April, 1898.

[24] Mrs. Austen, p. 287.—*J.*

[25] Mrs. Austen, p. 288.—*J.*

[26] Tyler MSS. Diary of Trip to England July–Sept., 1897.

[27] *The Literary History of the American Revolution* (New York, 1897), vol. I, pp. v–vi.

[28] Among the Tyler letters preserved in the William L. Clements Library is one addressed to Moncure D. Conway from Ann Arbor, Feb. 23, 1879, in which Tyler says that though it is thirteen years since his wife had left London, and twelve years since he had left himself, they still dreamed about returning. The tenor of the love for England expressed by this letter is confirmed by all the records of his British experiences.—*J.*

[29] *Literary History,* vol. II, p. 272.

[30] *Ibid.,* vol. I, pp. ix–x.

[31] Printed by Mrs. Austen, pp. 295–6.—*J.*

[32] See, for example, *The Athenæum,* Dec. 4, 1897, p. 780; *The Academy,* Dec. 18, 1897, p. 543.

[33] See, for instances, Herbert L. Osgood, "The American Revolution," *Political Science Quarterly,* vol. XIII, no. 1, March, 1898, pp. 41–59; and B. A. Hinsdale, *The Dial,* vol. XXIII, Sept. 16, 1897, pp. 143–5.

[34] Previous treatments had been contemptuous, hostile, inadequate, or full of special pleading. Lorenzo Sabine's *Biographical Sketches of the Loyalists of the American Revolution with an Historical Essay* (1864) was the only volume to show a spirit of "historic disinterestedness" (Tyler, *op. cit.,* vol. I, p. 80, note), albeit Sabine proclaimed his Whig affiliations (vol. I, p. 66). Ryerson's *The Loyalists of America and their Times* (1880) was a piece of special pleading intended to offset the deep American bias, and is a mere compilation for the most part. The most important original work on the subject before Tyler's was the chap-

ter on "The Loyalists and Their Fortunes," by George E. Ellis, President of the Massachusetts Historical Society, in Justin Winsor's *Narrative and Critical History of America,* vol. VII, pp. 185–214; of the data gathered here Tyler made ample use. Much superior is William Kingsford's *The History of Canada* (1894), which gives a very sane and scholarly account of the Loyalists. Kingsford and Tyler both depend upon Ellis. Tyler depended for much Loyalist literature on Frank Moore, *Songs and Ballads of the American Revolution,* 1856; his *Diary of the American Revolution,* 1859; and his *Illustrated Ballad History of the American Revolution,* 1876; and on Winthrop Sargent's *The Loyalist Poetry of the Revolution,* 1857; and his *The Loyal Verses of Joseph Stansbury and Doctor Jonathan Odell,* 1860. Paul Leicester Ford rather unnecessarily deplored Tyler's dependence upon Sargent in a review of Tyler in *The American Historical Review,* vol. II, no. 4, July, 1897; and vol. III, no. 2, January, 1898.—*J.*

[35] Tyler, *op. cit.,* vol. I, p. 307.

[36] *Op. cit.,* vol. II, p. 77.

[37] And was so recognized by many of his colleagues. To the first number of *The American Historical Review* Tyler had contributed a general statement of his point of view (without discussion of the Loyalist men of letters) entitled "The Party of the Loyalists in the American Revolution."

[38] Vol. I, pp. vi–vii.

[39] Hinsdale, *loc. cit.,* p. 145.

[40] Vol. LXVI, no. 1705, March 3, 1898, p. 172.

[41] See *The Nation, supra;* and vol. LXIV, June 10, 1897, pp. 438–9; *The American Historical Review,* vol. II, July, 1897, pp. 738–40; and vol. III, January, 1898, pp. 375–7; *The Independent,* vol. XLIX, Nov. 4, 1897, p. 17.

[42] "It is an interesting illustration of the elusiveness of much important historical information that not one of these four destructive criticisms of Carver's *Travels* ever caught Professor Tyler's eye during his many years of reading in American literature." E. G. Bourne, "The Travels of Jonathan Carver," *The American Historical Review,* vol. XI, Jan., 1906, pp. 287–302.

[43] Vol. I, pp. 162–4; 171–2; vol. II, p. 331; vol. I, p. 31.

[44] Mrs. Austen, chapters xix–xx, *passim.*—*J.*

[45] Mrs. Austen, p. 300.—*J.*

[46] *Ibid.,* p. 296.—*J.*

[47] *Ibid.,* p. 297.—*J.*

[48] Printed complete by Mrs. Austen, pp. 303–4.—*J.*

[49] J. F. Jameson, "The American Historical Review, *The American Historical Review,* vol. XXVI, no. 1, Oct., 1920, p. 5.

[50] *Ibid.,* p. 8.

[51] The article on the Loyalists referred to above.—*J.*—He also contributed "President Witherspoon in the American Revolution," to the July, 1896, number, pp. 671-9.

[52] Tyler MSS. James K. Hosmer to Moses Coit Tyler, March 24, 1896.

[53] Tyler MSS. Letter from Philip A. Bruce to Moses Coit Tyler, Jan. 21, 1896.

[54] Mrs. Austen, p. 288.—*J.*

[55] *Ibid.*—*J.*

[56] Tyler MSS. Diary for Dec., 1893–April, 1898.

[57] *Ibid.* and in Mrs. Austen, p. 288.—*J.*

[58] Mrs. Austen, p. 289.—*J.*

[59] *Ibid.,* p. 293.—*J.*

[60] Preface to the revised edition of *Patrick Henry.*

[61] Tyler MSS. Diary for Dec., 1893–April, 1898.

[62] Tyler MSS. Manuscript draught of the preface, pasted into the cover of the author's copy of *Glimpses of England.*

[63] *Ibid.*

[64] Tyler MSS. Letter from Moses Coit Tyler to D. H. Chamberlain, May 19, 1894; letter from John C. Calhoun to Moses Coit Tyler, May 26, 1894.

[65] Tyler MSS. Letter from Andrew D. White to Moses Coit Tyler, March 28, 1898.

[66] Tyler MSS. Noonings of Moses Coit Tyler, Oct., 1898–May, 1900.

[67] Mrs. Austen, pp. 315-7.—*J.*

[68] Mrs. Austen, p. 318.—*J.*

[69] Mrs. Austen, pp. 318-24.—*J.*

[70] Tyler MSS. Noonings of Moses Coit Tyler, Oct., 1898–May, 1900.

[71] See George Lincoln Burr's beautiful tribute to Tyler in *Annual Report of the American Historical Association for the Year, 1901,* vol. I, pp. 189-95.

[72] Tyler MSS, "John Randolph of Roanoke," p. 20.

[73] Mrs. Austen, p. 325.—*J.*

[74] Mrs. Austen, p. 324. The cause of death is given as a cystitis, the result of an enlarged prostate.—*J.*

INDEX

INDEX

351

INDEX